SCUBA DIVING

A TRAILSIDE GUIDE
BY
KAREN BERGER

Illustrations by Frank and Ron Hildebrand

A TRAILSIDE SERIES GUIDE

W. W. NORTON & COMPANY

NEW YORK   LONDON

WARNING: SCUBA DIVING IS A DANGEROUS SPORT IN WHICH YOU MAY BE SERIOUSLY INJURED OR KILLED

Safety is a vital concern in all outdoor activities, but particularly in SCUBA diving. This book is not a substitute for professional training and sound judgment. Your diving safety depends on your training and your commonsense judgment as you acquire skills and begin open-water diving.

SCUBA diving is a technical sport in which training and certification are REQUIRED. You cannot rent or buy gear or fill up a tank or go on a dive through a dive center without a valid C-card (certification card). Also, if you have not dived in longer than six months, you should take a refresher course before diving again.

NEVER dive beyond your training and experience. If you make errors, serious injury or death could result. SCUBA skills can only be acquired from professional, certified instructors.

This book is intended to introduce you to SCUBA diving and give you a foundation on which to build your skills under a certified instructor. *Do not attempt to SCUBA dive after merely having read this book.*

Copyright © 2000 by Karen Berger
Original illustrations copyright © 2000 by W. W. Norton & Company, Inc.
All rights reserved
Printed in Hong Kong

First Edition

For information about permission to reproduce selections from this book, write to
Permissions, W.W. Norton & Company, Inc., 500 Fifth Avenue, New York, NY 10110

The text of this book is composed in Bodoni Book with the display set in Triplex
Page composition by Michele Newkirk Fairchild
Color separations and prepress by Bergman Graphics, Incorporated
Manufacturing by South China Printing Co. Ltd.
Illustrations by Frank and Ron Hildebrand

Book design by Bill Harvey

Library of Congress Cataloging-in-Publication Data

Berger, Karen, 1959 —
Scuba diving: a trailside guide / by Karen Berger.
p.   cm. — (A trailside series guide)
Includes bibliographical references and index.
GV838.672 2000   796.2'3'082—dc21   99-088409 CIP

ISBN 0-393-31944-X

W. W. Norton & Company, Inc., 500 Fifth Avenue, New York, N. Y. 10110
http://www.wwnorton.com
W. W. Norton & Company Ltd., 10 Coptic Street, London WC1A 1PU

C O N T E N T S

INTRODUCTION

Sanctuary. That is my definition of the underwater world. As a boy I would stare into the deep blue Atlantic Ocean waters from my grandfather's fishing boat. When we navigated into shallow waters, I could make out faint shapes and shadows of reefs below the waves. The array of colors mesmerized me. I yearned to dive beneath those waves and explore that unfamiliar yet inviting world.

Those early childhood dreams began to come true when I discovered SCUBA diving at the age of 12. I vividly recall my first reef dives, my first night dives, my first shark sighting. I had joined a tight-knit community of individuals seeking to explore and understand aquatic life. They, like me, wanted to defy their terrestrial existence and enter that serene underwater domain. SCUBA divers delve into territories that most people rarely conceive of, much less visit.

SCUBA diving is an escape. During meditation, some people visualize themselves entering other dimensions to escape the stress of everyday life. When diving, one leaves behind the telephones, beepers, radios, televisions, cars, and masses of people, and is consumed by a purely natural aquatic realm. I remember once focusing on a damselfish living under a coral stalk; for 30 minutes, I watched entranced as this two-inch fish scurried about, chasing fish away from his home. Each week, over several months, I returned to that coral stalk on the reef, anticipating visiting my new friend. Like a pet, this energetic damselfish developed a personality that I found delightful, even admirable.

SCUBA diving is sensual. To breathe underwater is one of the most fascinating and peculiar sensations imaginable. Breathing becomes a rhythmic melody of inhalations and exhalations. The cracks and pops of fish and crustaceans harmonize with the rhythmic chiming of the bubbles as you exhale. Soon, lungs act as bellows, controlling your buoyancy as you achieve weightlessness. And, as in your dreams, you are flying. Combine these otherworldly stimuli and you surrender completely to the sanctuary of the underwater world.

SCUBA diving is exotic. A myriad of environments awaits you, from turquoise waters alive with the most brilliant colors of the spectrum, to the darkest black during a night dive. To freely descend in limitless cobalt-blue water without seeing the bottom or anything around you is surreal. Out of the blue a dark shadow emerges, and momentary exhilaration, mixed with fear of the unknown, grips your attention. Finally, the apparition of a sunken wreck becomes distinguishable as you anticipate diving on an ancient ship.

Whether snorkeling, skin diving, free diving, or SCUBA diving, each brief encounter with the world underwater is an adventure. Few other sports give you such intimate encounters with the environment. Author Karen Berger captures the science, the art, and the magic of SCUBA diving in this Guide. Whether you are a novice or an advanced diver or a SCUBA professional, this Guide will become an invaluable reference. Exquisite photography and detailed illustrations provide clear understanding of multiple topics. Full of tips and techniques, Karen's matter-of-fact writing style makes you feel as if the Guide is your dive instructor and buddy.

To enjoy this underwater sanctuary you must have a passion for exploration and feel comfortable in water. You must also have a desire to learn and grow as a responsible diver. Getting trained and certified to dive is fun and rewarding. Once certified, maintaining your proficiency and re-sharpening your skills when necessary is equally rewarding. You have a duty to respect the buddy who trusts your judgment, and you have a duty to protect the fragile aquatic environment while you are visiting it.

A profound foreign world lies just off shore. Explore it. Embrace it. Dive it.

— Tec Clark
Director, YMCA SCUBA

THE
UNDERWATER
WORLD

I will never forget my first sight of a tropical reef. It was in East Africa in 1991, and I was on one of those glass-bottom boats with a group of tourists. My husband, Dan, and I were the only ones who accepted the boatman's invitation to grab a mask and snorkel and get in the water.

The boatman's next big challenge would be convincing us to come out.

We adjusted our gear and slid off the boat — no fancy backward rolls for these rank beginners. When we opened our eyes underwater and looked through the leaky, borrowed masks, we saw a whole new world.

Until that moment, I'd always thought of "natural" colors as browns and greens and beiges — the colors of my native landscape, the northeastern United States, which are punctuated by flowers and foliage but rarely dominated by them. Here "natural" colors included sunshine yellow and neon green and electric blue and fire-engine red, a palette of bright hues splashed across a shimmering turquoise canvas.

Then, there were the corals. I remembered learning — yet not comprehending — in high school science class that corals might look like plants, with structures that resemble leaves and branches and trunks and flowers, but that they are actually animals. Underwater, some

A nineteenth-century
diving bell along with two
air barrels, which supply
the bell through hoses.

of them looked
barely animate,
but others opened
and closed —
pulsing, pro-
cessing, and
pumping water
and nutrients.
As I watched,
I began to
understand how the
very essence of some-
thing can change when certain
universal rules are turned on
their heads. Water is 800 times
denser than air. Gravity is no longer
the absolute monarch. Given different rules, life adapts differently.

And let's not forget the fish.
Thousands of them shimmered in
silvery schools. Quick flashes of
bright color flickered in front of my
mask. The more I looked, the more
I saw. Some of the fish hid in coral
crevices; some lay on the sandy
bottom or camouflaged themselves
against a rock or a sponge. Others
swam in multihued schools, brazenly
flaunting their finery. I tried to count
the different kinds, but got lost in
the colors.

"Madam?" the boatman was
saying. "Madam? You must get back
on the boat now. Madam? We must go
back with the tide. Madam?"

After that introduction, it was

inevitable that
I would take
up SCUBA
diving. (I'm the
first to admit, my hob-
bies quickly turn into
addictions.) Once I saw
what was just under the
surface, I wanted to go
farther, to see more.
Instinctively, I knew that
the experience of being
fully underwater would
be more intense than
that of hovering on the
surface. Snorkelers fre-
quently come up out of the water
to adjust equipment or chat with
a friend, but divers are fully
immersed in the experience. Weight-
less, balanced, slow-moving, we
float through an ancestral aquatic
environment that is both alien and
strangely comfortable. It is like
being in a trance.

Welcome to the world of inner
space!

SCUBA: A BRIEF HISTORY

Because divers rely on inarguably
high-tech equipment to keep them
alive, it seems logical to think of
SCUBA diving — unlike cross-country
skiing, kayaking, or snowshoeing —
as a sport that belongs wholly to the
modern era. As it turns out, however,
people have been fascinated with
inner space for thousands of years.

The first divers were *breath-hold*

Wrecks are among the most popular sites for SCUBA divers. Here, a diver visits a U.S. B-17 bomber shot down off Guadalcanal during World War II.

divers (also called *skin divers*). In search of food, shells, and treasures like pearls, they reached depths of more than 30 to 40 feet — and sometimes more than 100 feet — with nothing more than the air they could hold in their lungs.

Then, sometime in the fourth century B.C., Alexander the Great put a bucket over his head and went underwater. The bucket limited both the swimmer's mobility and visibility, but it brought air underwater. For the first time, human beings were able to breathe beneath the sea — at least until the air in the bucket ran out.

Diving technology pretty much stalled at the bucket level for the next 2,000 years, until the late 1700s, when a hose was added to draw air from the surface into the bucket. In the early 1800s, the bucket (now shaped like a bell) was retired in favor of a diving helmet and a watertight suit. In the late 1800s and early 1900s, divers experimented with putting air under pressure in a cylinder. But it wasn't until 1943 that two Frenchmen created the first true SCUBA (self-contained underwater breathing apparatus) gear. The Aqualung combined the

A diving suit from the early days of the twentieth century; air is supplied from the surface.

use of compressed air in a cylinder with a regulator that delivered air to the diver on demand. One of its inventors was Jacques Cousteau.

Why this 2,000-year quest to gain access to the world below? Initially, SCUBA was for professionals. The oceans were both a military and a commercial resource; thus, divers were more likely to be building bridges, welding structures, installing plumbing, cleaning equipment, salvaging debris, or looking for oil than they were to be floating around looking at colorful fish. It was the United States Navy that developed the first set of U.S. *dive tables*, which have since been modified for recreational use.

Today, the vast majority of people who strap on a tank and go underwater are diving for recreation, not for work. But commercial and military divers continue to work on oil rigs, wrecks, and military installations. Training for such a career is highly specialized (many commercial divers start out in the navy, which uses divers in a host of military roles) and has very little in common with

recreational-dive training. For instance, commercial divers frequently descend to depths unheard of in recreational diving, using highly specialized equipment and mixed gases.

The other significant professional application for divers is in academic research, including oceanography, biology, ecology, geology, and a number of other -ologies whose purpose is to understand the world down under. Jobs for divers include observation and data collection, along with photography and filmmaking. As with commercial diving, many of these jobs require specialized training.

RECREATIONAL DIVING

Given SCUBA's commercial and military pedigree, it's no wonder that when people think of SCUBA, they often imagine some combination of Jacques Cousteau, Hollywood stuntmen, Navy Seals, and maybe a couple of deep-sea salvage divers who show up on the news now and again. Add to that a few tall tales about sharks, and a giant octopus or two. And then, of course, there's the bends, that mysterious illness that we've all heard about. When you combine diving's gonzo media image with the need for life-support equipment to ensure survival in an

The exotic beauty and diversity of life amidst tropical coral reefs gives them pride of place. This diver is framed by red and yellow soft corals in waters off Fiji, in the southern Pacific.

environment where humans don't belong, it's no wonder that most people feel just the slightest trepidation before their first dive.

Forget about movies, TV shows, and true-life rescue dramas. Forget about Navy Seals. Even, for the moment, forget about Jacques Cousteau — you don't need to be thinking about all of his technological innovations and extreme deep dives just yet. Most of all, forget

about the creatures of the deep (although we'll talk about them in Chapter 6). The truth is, recreational diving is a safe sport, *when undertaken responsibly*. SCUBA equipment is carefully engineered; much of it has fail-safe, backup, or can't-screw-it-up features. (In fact, equipment failure is one of the least common underwater problems.) The diver certification process also contributes to safety; much of SCUBA

training focuses on teaching divers
how to stay out of trouble.

Staying out of trouble means
learning what you need to know to
avoid such potential problems as
the bends (see Chapter 5), as well
as other diving-related illnesses
(see Chapter 6). It means understanding how your equipment
works, knowing the rules, and being
able to make the right decisions in
the unlikely event of an emergency.
Whether you're just thinking about
taking a diving class, whether
you're a newly certified diver who
needs to brush up on the basics, or
whether you're an experienced
recreational diver thinking of taking
up a new specialty or buying new
gear, you must understand the
basics of safe diving techniques,
equipment use and maintenance,
first aid, and dive planning. That's
what this book is about.

The bottom line: With proper
training and respect for the environment and equipment, almost anyone
who is healthy and a comfortable
swimmer can learn to dive.

Kinds of Diving

So, now that we've dispensed with
the daredevils, what picture pops
to mind when you think of diving?
Maybe it's an aquamarine sea with
a coral reef. Fair enough. Tropical
coral reefs are to SCUBA diving what
alpine peaks are to backpacking.
Reefs are the highlights, the places
where equipment manufacturers
strut their stuff, and photographers
shoot magazine covers. With their
warm temperatures, clear visibility,
colorful fish, and magnificent coral
formations, it's perfectly logical that
tropical waters would hold pride of
place on anyone's list of the world's
best dive sites.

But you don't have to go to the
tropics to dive. The types of recreational diving are as broad and
varied as the kinds of marine environments. And, as a quick visit to
any aquarium will show, those environments are varied indeed. As with
hiking, bicycling, kayaking, or rock
climbing, you can also find some
remarkable diving opportunities in
your own backyard.

Want proof?

● Puget Sound, Seattle: Locals
proudly claim that Jacques Cousteau
was a regular here.

● Lake Erie, Pennsylvania: Divers
can check out wrecks of sunken
ships that plied the Great Lakes 100
or more years ago.

Monterey, California: Enormous underwater forests of kelp support a rich and varied ecosystem. Expect a wide variety of marine life, from the tiny orange Garibaldi fish to the occasional curious sea lion.

Long Island, New York: The treacherous waters off Long Island have claimed a number of ships. These sunken wrecks make a great habitat for lobsters, so divers get two for one: wreck diving and lobstering all at the same time — if, that is, you have a permit.

Florida Springs, Florida: Northern and western Florida boast gigantic freshwater springs that feed a labyrinth of caves, caverns, and sinkholes boasting unique rock formations and fossils. To get the most from some of these surreal sites, you need special training in cavern or cave diving.

And that's not all. Even murky local waters can offer divers a rewarding experience. Some dive shops organize treasure hunts, which reinforce navigation skills and teach divers about search and recovery. Don't have a shipwreck in your land-locked hometown? Maybe not, but in some places, local dive clubs or shops make their own wrecks by sinking an old bus or a train car. The inland wreck might be contrived, but it offers some introductory wreck-diving experience and acts as a magnet to attract aquatic life. There's also ice diving, lake diving, night diving, and a whole host of other kinds of diving to

Wreck diving off Long Island. New York's busy sea lanes make these waters rich with sunken vessels.

explore. Chapter 8 discusses some of the most popular specialties and tells you how to get started.

CERTIFICATION

So, are you ready to go? There's one catch: You need a *certification card* (a C-card, in diver lingo) to rent equipment, go out on a dive, or even fill up an air tank. The C-card tells other divers and diving professionals that you know how to take care of yourself underwater.

There are six major organizations in the United States (and many more in other countries) that certify divers. Although the basic requirements of the courses are similar — all diving programs aim to teach new divers enough to enable them to dive competently and safely without supervision — there are differences in classroom time, teaching philosophy, and teacher training. It's even possible that two schools certified by the same agency will operate a little

HOW TO CHOOSE A DIVE SCHOOL

It's good idea to check out one or two shops, dive centers, or organizations before signing up for a class. Some questions to ask include:

- What certification will I receive?
- What are the prerequisites for the class?
- What will be expected of me before I can become certified?
- How many pool sessions and how many classroom sessions does the class require?
- Will I be provided class materials (workbook, logbook, dive tables, textbook), or will I have to purchase them?
- Where will the open-water dives take place? Are they included in the price of the course?
- Will I be provided equipment as part of the price of the course, or do I need to provide my own?
- How would you characterize your style of teaching SCUBA?
- How long have you been teaching?
- Do you have references from former students I can contact?

You can also collect a lot of information simply by observing the following:

- Does the instructor seem intent on teaching you to dive or selling you gear?
- Are all costs discussed up front or did the hidden costs appear only when you started to ask questions?
- If there is rental equipment, what condition is it in?
- What is the instructor's attitude: boastful? macho? too informal?
- Is the shop neat and professional?
- Does the instructor seem sensitive to any concerns or special needs you may have?

Fresh water also affords opportunities. Here a diver explores Jackie's Blue Hole, a grass mat pool in Espiritu Santo, Vanuatu, South Pacific.

differently from each other. SCUBA instructors run the gamut, from informal Gen-Xers to grizzled veterans to ex-military divers. It's worth checking out a few programs, schools, or shops in your area to find the one that suits your style. You may also find special classes; for instance, some schools have classes designed especially for women or for teenagers. (Note: You must be 12 years old or older to take a SCUBA course.)

Below is an alphabetical list of organizations that certify divers and train instructors.

IDEA (International Diving Educators Association) 904-744-5554
NAUI (National Association of Underwater Instructors) 800-553-6284
PADI (Professional Association of Diving Instructors) 800-214-7234
PDIC (Professional Diving Instructors Corporation, Int.) 570-342-9434
SSI (SCUBA Schools International) 800-892-2702; Note: SSI has merged with the NASDS (National Association of SCUBA Diving Schools)
YMCA National SCUBA Program 888-464-9622

The Course

Typically, a basic open-water certification course involves 16 to 24 hours of classroom instruction and pool work, followed by four or five open-water dives. During the pool sessions, you'll be introduced to basic SCUBA skills such as putting on and adjusting equipment, mask clearing, ascending and descending, and controlling buoyancy. During open-water sessions, you'll perform these skills under an instructor's supervision. The course might be spread over several weeks. Some agencies offer condensed sessions that take place over a couple of intensive weekends. Others offer advanced courses that go into more detail but require a greater time commitment. Some dive shops offer special learner's packages, which include travel and a course. You do your classroom and pool training near your home, and your open-water training at a vacation (read tropical) destination.

In addition, resort "fun" courses are aimed at vacationers who want to try SCUBA just once without making a commitment to a complete course. These introductory dives take place in calm, shallow water under close supervision. They're a great way to get a taste of the underwater world, and they can be a low-key, low-stress introduction for a non-diving spouse or travel partner. But to dive on your own — or even to go on a guided open-water dive — you need a C-card.

Is the classroom course difficult?
Much of the classroom instruction aims at teaching new divers how being underwater affects the human body. This includes some basic science. We're not talking nuclear physics, but you will learn about such essentials as air pressure, water pressure, and nitrogen and how they affect you during and after a dive. You'll also learn how to use dive tables to calculate how long you can dive and how long you must wait between dives in order to reduce the risk of getting the bends. Finally, the classroom sessions review the use and care of equipment. For a sampling of SCUBA science, turn to Appendix I. Here you'll find an explanation of the scientific principles you'll need to know to understand the how and why of SCUBA.

What about the physical demands?
Anybody in average physical condition can learn to dive — as long as they are comfortable in the water. Different agencies have different requirements, but they usually require a swim test. Before beginning a YMCA course, for example, students must demonstrate that they can swim 200 yards, tread water for ten minutes, and perform a 25-foot underwater swim without pushing off from the side of the pool. Before being certified, it is expected that their skills will have improved so that they can swim 300 yards, tread water for 15 minutes, and perform a 50-foot underwater swim without a push-off. Other agencies have similar requirements.

What about the bends?
Most prospective divers have heard about *the bends*, or *decompression*

A pair of divers cross Ponderosa Cenote sinkhole in Puerto Aventuros, Mexico. The importance of the buddy system in SCUBA diving cannot be overemphasized.

sickness. The bends, discussed in Chapters 5 and 6, is the result of diving too deep for too long and/or coming up too fast. It can be a serious problem, but it is largely preventable. It's unusual for a sensible, conservative recreational diver to get the bends — but it is possible. During your classroom training, you'll learn how to use *dive tables* to figure out how long you can dive at various depths to minimize your chances of getting the bends. On dives of less than 30 to 40 feet, you can simply come to the surface without any problem, as long as you ascend at a safe rate.

Although no tables can entirely eliminate the possibility of getting *bent,* following the guidelines in the tables, paying attention to your depth and time while underwater, and diving conservatively can greatly reduce the risk.

What medical conditions prevent people from diving?
You'll be asked to sign a medical questionnaire and fill out information pertaining to your medical history. If you have certain medical conditions (for example, heart problems, asthma, recurrent ear infections, or high blood pressure), you'll be asked to provide a doctor's statement that it's okay for you to dive. (So if you're going on a vacation and you plan to take up diving, check

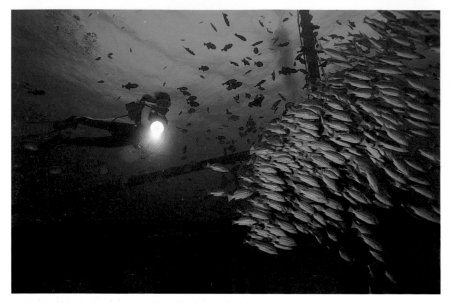

A school of bluestripe snappers glint off a diver's flashlight in the deep blue waters off Oahu, Hawaii. A World War II U.S. Navy oiler was deliberately sunk in 100 feet of water in 1989 to create habitat and a destination for divers.

locally with a dive shop or an instructor for a list of conditions requiring a doctor's okay.) In addition, pregnant women are advised not to dive, mostly because there has (understandably) been very little research on the subject. Most of what is known derives from the few cases of women who dived in the early stages of pregnancy, before they knew they were pregnant. Although doctors have not reported a pattern of problems resulting from such dives, evidence is insufficient to warrant a definitive statement.

Finally, people with a cold should refrain from diving because a cold makes it difficult or impossible to equalize the ears and sinuses (see Appendix I).

All that high-tech life-support equipment looks intimidating. What if I screw up?
It does look intimidating, but recreational SCUBA equipment is actually very simple once you know which part does what job. (That's one of the things you'll learn in the classroom, practice in the pool, and then apply in your open-water dives.) Modern SCUBA equipment is built with plenty of safeguards. Once you master the basic procedures, putting together and using the equipment becomes almost second nature.

Do I have to buy all that expensive equipment just to take the course?
No. Rental equipment is available, and many schools include it in the

price of the course. Most dive shops have a wide variety of sizes to fit people ranging from adolescents to large adults. However, if your body type varies substantially from the norm (especially if you're very overweight or extremely tall), you might find it difficult to find rental equipment that fits properly. Talk about this with your instructor before the course. Custom-made equipment can be tailored to people of all sizes and shapes, so don't let the fact that you don't have a "typical" body size keep you out of the water.

CONTINUING EDUCATION

SCUBA diving is a lot like driving a car. You start out driving under the supervision of an instructor. You review some written material, practice your skills, and after only a little while, you take a driving — or a diving — test. Then you get your spanking-new license — or your spanking-new C-card — and it's off to the races!

Whoa there a minute, cowboy! Slow down!

On the road, a new license doesn't mean that you're ready for the Los Angeles Freeway. And in the water, it doesn't mean that you're ready to dive a 100-foot-deep wreck. Indeed, diving instructors routinely stress that the way to learn is to build slowly, stay within the limits of your experience and instruction, and tackle new skills

under the supervision of a teacher. Most new divers stick with guided dives for a while. Dive masters or instructors who know the local waters are a great resource, not only because they can point out natural features you might not have noticed on your own, but also because they can pass on a few tips along the way.

The best way to keep your skills sharp is to use them often. Habits practiced become habits learned. Also, if you dive frequently, you'll stay up-to-date on changing equipment and technologies. Just because you don't live near a great dive site is no reason not to dive. Although your local swimming hole might not seem like much compared to the Great Barrier Reef, it's amazing how much fun you can have if you hook up with a couple of like-minded folks. Joining a diving club gets you talking and swapping stories with other enthusiasts.

Your C-card is (as of this writing) good for life, but to keep your skills up to par you should try to get a dive in at least every six months. If you can't (northern winters being one good reason to keep many of us out of the ocean), you'll want to take a quick refresher class before you start diving again. Or take a pool session.

Another thing to consider is where and under what conditions you got your C-card. Not only are some programs more thorough than others, but let's face it, a diver who took his training off the coast of Maine has got a little more experience in handling adverse conditions than a diver who learned the ropes in a rock quarry or a quiet lake. Some divers actually take their beginning courses in dry suits. If your experience hasn't prepared you for certain conditions, or you don't know how to use a necessary piece of gear, seek additional training.

Specialty and advanced courses are good ways to increase both your competence and your confidence. These classes are much more fun than basic open-water training because you spend more time actually diving (and less time talking about it!). Advanced courses will introduce you to night diving, deep diving, diving navigation, and a whole range of other specialty dives, from wrecks to caves (see Chapter 8). In certain cases — for example, cave diving on private property — dive-site operators or landowners may allow only certified specialists.

Whatever your diving interest, you can be assured of one thing: You'll never run out of things to learn. And you'll never run out of things to see.

S K I N   D I V I N G

Skin diving is the oldest, simplest, and — some would claim — purest form of diving. Without a lot of gear to carry around, elaborate plans to make, dive tables to learn, and restrictions on how long you can stay down at what depth, *skin diving* (also called *snorkeling*, *freediving*, or *breath-hold diving*) boils down to just you, the water, and the undersea world.

Snorkeling offers many advantages for both the beginning diver and the experienced diver.

● It's a stress-free, inexpensive introduction to SCUBA diving. You'll get a look at what there is to see as you hang out over an especially interesting piece of coral and watch nature's dramas unfold.

● The learning curve for snorkeling is gentle. There aren't a lot of skills to master, and if you are reasonably comfortable in the water, you probably won't find them difficult to learn.

● Snorkeling isn't gear-intensive, which makes for easier travel and less impact on your wallet. The arrangements and planning tend to be easier, too, because you don't have to rent gear, fill up tanks, and attend to all the logistics diving requires.

● It offers something for a non-diving spouse, family members, or a travel companion to enjoy when

A snorkeler's paradise: Seven Mile Beach, Grand Cayman Island, the Caribbean. Wear your snorkel on your left side; that's where it will need to be when you begin SCUBA diving.

you're SCUBA diving. (They might enjoy it so much, they'll take up diving, too.)

● There's more flexibility. At one of my favorite vacation spots, I can walk two minutes from the villa to the beach, jump in the water, and snorkel till I'm cold, tired, or the whitecaps come up. After taking a break, I can go back in the water as often as I like without worrying about decompression limits and dive tables.

● There's more individual freedom. It's *always* a good idea to have a buddy in the water, especially if you are breath-hold diving (see page 38). But if you're just hanging out on the surface, you can let your buddy concentrate on playing with his underwater camera while you swim off somewhere else to study the coral.

You don't need to stay within arm's reach of each other as you do in SCUBA. (Again, the exception is breath-hold diving.)

● Because water absorbs so much light, the brightest colors are found nearest the surface, where the vast majority of skin divers spend the vast majority of their time. (For the same reason, many divers prefer shallow dives to deep dives because the light and colors are better.)

● Snorkeling and free-diving teach valuable SCUBA skills. You will become more aware of how you breathe, and you will become more comfortable breathing through a mouthpiece.

True, there are a few things you can do while diving that are difficult (or impossible) to do while snorkeling.

Divers can follow fish up and down as well as back and forth without worrying about running out of air. They can explore a reef from top to bottom, slowly, and see different life forms that live in different

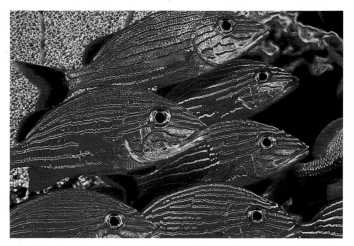

Some days the colors of tropical fish will look almost as electrifying as these outrageous oranges and pinks.

places. They are fully immersed in the underwater world for as long as their tanks or dive tables allow — which is a lot longer than a free-diver can hold his breath. Underwater photographers have more choices of angles when diving.

Nonetheless, you can't beat snorkeling for an introduction to SCUBA, and it's a fun experience on its own terms.

GEAR

The equipment list for snorkeling is gratifyingly short: Only a mask, snorkel, and fins are mandatory. A snorkeling vest, which can be inflated, is recommended and is sometimes required on dive boats. An exposure suit is recommended, although not always necessary. Weights help skin divers who want to go beneath the surface, especially

those who are positively buoyant, to descend and control their buoyancy (see "buoyancy" in the Appendices). If you use weights, however, be careful not to "over-weight" yourself; if you wear too many weights, it can be hard to swim back to the surface. Finally, a dive flag is sometimes required by law, even if you're just snorkeling.

Masks

Because your eyes can't focus without an air space in front of them, you need a mask. Goggles won't cut it. Although you can see perfectly well with goggles, you can't use them with a snorkel, because goggles don't cover your nose. If you try to use a snorkel and goggles together, you'll probably end up choking on the water you'll almost inevitably breathe in through your nose. Second, you can't dive more than a couple of feet below the surface with goggles

The first, most important thing to look for in a mask is the best fit for your face.

because of *squeeze.* When you dive below the surface, the pressure increases and compresses the air inside the goggles. That pulls the goggles closer to your skin until it feels as though they are "squeezing" around your eyes. *Mask squeeze* occurs, too, but with a mask, you can breathe out through your nose to add air into the mask and equalize the pressure; with goggles, you can't. (For more on this topic, see Appendix I, "The Science of SCUBA.")

The mask consists of the glass plate, a skirt that makes a seal between the mask and your face, and a strap that goes behind your head and holds the mask in place. The snorkel attaches to the strap via a *snorkel keeper.* The skirt and straps on most modern masks are made of silicone or plastics; older models may also be made of neoprene rubber.

Masks are available in a wide range of prices, from less than $20 to nearly $100. You don't need to spend a lot of money, but do buy a mask designed for SCUBA diving. Both snorkeling and SCUBA diving are very visual sports, and nothing is more frustrating than not being able to see properly. It's best to go to a dive shop rather than a general-goods discount mart in order to find a mask that meets the following criteria:

● Does it fit? You have to take it out of the box and try it on. A mask that fits has a good seal that keeps water out. A mask that doesn't fit will leak, and a leaking mask can seriously diminish your diving or snorkeling enjoyment. To determine whether a mask fits, move the strap out of the way and hold the mask up to your face. When you inhale, the mask should seal tightly to your face — without your pushing it into place. When you remove your hand, stop inhaling and hold your breath; the mask should stay firmly in place, even if you pull or tug on it. If the mask doesn't form a firm seal or if you have to push it to force it to form a seal, it doesn't fit.

● With a low-volume mask, the glass is as close to your eyes as possible. You can tell whether a mask is really low-volume by checking whether the pocket that covers the nose extends beyond the glass. If it does, it's a low-volume mask. Another

way to determine if the mask is high-
or low-volume is to imagine how
much water it would take to fill the
mask. High-volume masks can take
in more water than low-volume
masks. With low-volume masks,
there's less air in the artificial air
space (that is, the space enclosed
by the glass), which makes mask
squeeze less of a problem. A smaller
volume also makes it easier to clear
the mask when it floods.

Wraparound masks have clear
glass on the sides as well as the
front, which gives you peripheral
vision. In addition, some masks have
glass underneath (i.e., along your
cheekbones), so that you can look
down and see your torso. These features are more important for a
SCUBA diver than for a snorkeler,
because a diver needs to keep track
of lots of equipment, as well as his
buddy and other divers. Also, more
glass lets in more light, which is
important in low-light situations. But
a wraparound mask is helpful in
snorkeling, too, simply because you
get to see more. There is, however,
a downside: Wraparound masks tend
to be high-volume. They squeeze
more and it requires more air to
clear or equalize them.

Make sure your mask has a flexible nose pocket. All diving masks
cover your nose, but in order to
equalize you should be able to
touch your nose and squeeze it. You
can do this if you have a flexible
nose pocket.

Snorkeling among the fishes, Alligator Reef,
Florida Keys National Marine Sanctuary.

Tempered glass (or safety glass)
is more resistant to shattering and
scratching than regular glass, and if
it does break, it breaks into round
globules rather than long, thin
shards. Proper dive masks are made
of tempered glass. Don't even consider one that isn't. Look on the
faceplate or the packaging for an
indication that the glass is tempered;
it usually says "Tempered" or "T."

The non-glass part of a mask is
made of either neoprene rubber,
plastic, or silicone. Silicone — the
most common material in today's

An up-close view of corals and sea fans in shallow waters, Florida Keys National Marine Sanctuary. The Sanctuary protects the waters of the keys from Key Biscayne south and west to the Dry Tortugas, 90 miles beyond Key West.

masks — is more expensive but lasts as much as three or four times longer than old-fashioned rubber, doesn't rot, is hypoallergenic, and is more comfortable against your face. Masks made with clear silicone also let in more light. (Silicone can also be dyed.) Rubber masks deteriorate after repeated contact with oils, suntan lotions, chlorine, and heat. The most important factor, however, is comfort. Whichever type you choose, be sure that the seal is comfortable and doesn't chafe against your skin.

● Another comfort consideration is the *skirt* of the mask. That's the part

TECHNIQUE TIP

KEEP YOUR MASK DOWN

When your mask isn't in use, don't shove it up and wear it on your forehead, even if you're just treading water and waiting for the boat. A mask worn on the forehead can easily be knocked off by a wave and can end up sinking to the bottom. Also, because experienced divers make it a practice not to wear masks on their foreheads, wearing your mask this way may indicate to others that you are in distress.

that comes in direct contact with your face. Look for a double skirt (two layers of silicone along the part of the skirt that touches your face). It provides a second seal, which helps keep water out *and* provides a more comfortable fit.

● The *head strap* (also called a *mask strap*) should be

IF YOU WEAR EYEGLASSES

There's no need to squint underwater. Divers with less than perfect eyesight can correct their underwater vision in three ways:
① Most people find that they can dive while wearing soft contact lenses. It's best to check with your optometrist first. It is, however, possible to lose a contact lens when clearing a flooded mask. If you wear contacts when diving, be sure to close your eyes whenever your mask floods and you have to clear it.
② You can buy masks with preground lenses that closely approximate your prescription. Some optical masks have separate lenses for each eye, so even people whose vision is different

from one eye to the other can use preground lenses. In some states, masks with preground lenses are available only through an optometrist. In other states, they are sold directly in dive shops.
③ The most precise correction is to have lenses custom-made to your personal prescription by having an optometrist bond lenses to the inside of the mask. This is the most expensive option (although usually no more costly than a pair of glasses plus a mask), but it offers the advantage of precise visual correction. It also allows you to choose the most comfortable mask from among all available models, not just those that come with preground lenses. Many optometrists perform this service; if yours doesn't, ask for a reference at a local dive shop.

adjustable. Straps that are split in the back hold the mask in place better than do single straps.

● *Purge valves*, found on some masks, are one-way valves that help with mask clearing. Consider them optional — mask clearing soon becomes second nature (see page 37). PREPARING A MASK FOR USE Follow the directions that come with your mask. Usually, there will be an oily film on the glass that needs to be washed away; toothpaste will do the job.

You'll also need to prevent condensation each time you use the mask. Condensation occurs because of the difference in temperature between your breath and the water in which you are diving. When water vapor condenses into droplets, you might in short order feel like you're diving in a London fog. To prevent condensation, you can buy any one of a number of commercial preparations that you simply wipe on the inside of the dry mask just before diving, and then rinse. If you run out of commercial defogger, don't despair. You can always just spit on the mask and rub your saliva into the glass. Sounds unappealing, but it works. If your mask fogs up once you are in the water, try flooding it.

Snorkels

Think of the snorkel as an extension of your airway. Using it, you don't have to turn your head to breathe but can simply float, facedown, looking at the fish while "breathing" through the back of your head. In skin diving, the snorkel is your primary breathing apparatus. In SCUBA diving, divers use snorkels at the surface so they don't have to waste tank air.

Snorkels are simple pieces of equipment, consisting of a tube and a mouthpiece, and that's about it. Today's models are usually made of some combination of silicone and plastic. Some older or less expensive models use neoprene rubber. Here are some features to consider:

● How does it fit in your mouth? The mouthpiece should feel comfortable, with no chafing. You shouldn't have to clamp down your jaws to keep it in place. Some mouthpieces are offset at an angle so that both the mouthpiece and the snorkel barrel are in the optimum position. There are also swiveling mouthpieces that allow you to place the mouthpiece in the most comfortable position.

● Comfort in breathing is next. Pinch your nose and take a few deep breaths through your mouth. It should feel like you are breathing normally. If you have to work to breathe, you've got the wrong snorkel.

● There are several variations in snorkel height and width. A short, fat one is easier to breathe through. Most divers prefer a snorkel about 15 to 17 inches long (shorter than the snorkel you might remember using in your childhood), and a large-bore rather than a narrow-bore snorkel (translation: a fat snorkel rather than a skinny one). This combination seems to offer the best balance of easy breathing and easy clearing for most divers, although some smaller divers will find that slightly skinnier snorkels with smaller mouthpieces are easier and more comfortable to use.

This Dacor mask and snorkel features an adjustable, locking, quick-release snorkel keeper.

● The snorkel should fit comfortably around your face. Most modern snorkels are designed with curves that follow the lines of your face.

● A self-draining feature makes it easier to get rid of water that floods the snorkel, and some have valves that help prevent choppy surface water from getting into the snorkel barrel. These features aren't necessary — snorkel clearing is a simple skill. But if you'd like to let your snorkel help you with this task, get a self-draining model.

● Finally, there's color. It's amazing how easily a person can

SNORKEL KEEPERS

Snorkel keepers are little gizmos that attach your snorkel to your mask strap and keep it in position. All kinds of attachments and clips exist to do the job. The key requirement: It should go on and off with a minimum of fuss and bother, and once it's in place it should stay in place. Don't be tempted to just tuck the snorkel barrel under the mask strap. It won't hold the snorkel in the optimum position, and it will pull the mask out of alignment, which can cause it to leak. Take a few extra snorkel keepers in your repair kit, as they have a tendency to disappear.

seem to disappear in the ocean —
even when swimming right on the
surface. A snorkel with a bright tip
will help your buddy locate you.

Fins

Fins allow you to extend the impact
of your kicking motion and make real
headway underwater. Manufacturers
have spent hundreds of thousands
(literally) of dollars on product
research and design, and have come
up with some effective improvements.
But the basic fin pretty much takes
its shape from nature and isn't too
different from a sketch made by
Leonardo da Vinci 500 years ago.
Just like a frog's or a duck's webbed
feet, fins give your foot more surface
area. They extend the reach and
power of your leg muscles.

Fins come in a wide array of
designs and prices, but avoid the
discount-store variety. Cheap fins
made of flimsy materials can tear
after only a few uses, and they usually don't have features like channels
and ribs that help make each kick
more effective.

There are two basic kinds of
fins: *Adjustable-strap fins* and *full-
footed fins*. Most SCUBA divers use
adjustable-strap fins because they
can wear them with booties, which
provide both insulation and protection. Foot *insulation* is more important in colder water (less than 70°F)
than in tropical seas, but foot *protection* is essential if your dive
includes a beach entry where you'll
be walking through an obstacle
course of sea urchins and sharp,
skin-scraping coral rock. SCUBA
divers also gravitate to adjustable-
strap fins because most of the
"high-performance" models are

TECHNIQUE TIP

AVOID FIN BLISTERS

Seems like just about any kind of athletic footwear can lead to a big old
blister, and fins are no exception. A stray piece of sand between fin and
foot can turn into a nagging little sore that makes every kick cycle
painful. And diving cuts and scrapes take a long time to heal. Once
you've got that blister, there's not much you can do about it, so prevention
is a good strategy. Diving with booties and adjustable-strap fins can help
prevent blisters. But if you're diving in full-footed fins, and you're prone
to blisters, try wearing a thin pair of nylon socks. Let the fins rub *them*
instead of your skin, and spare yourself the annoyance blisters can cause.

Having trouble getting your fins on? Try wetting both your fins and
your feet before putting the fins on. It's a lot easier.

made in this style. High-performance fins have advanced ergonomic designs that channel water better and create more propulsion. This is important to SCUBA divers, because they are toting around a lot of heavy equipment and sometimes have to cope with strong currents. One disadvantage to adjustable-strap fins: The straps are easy to break, so be sure you have spares in your repair kit. Full-footed fins are often preferred by skin divers because they are more efficient for surface swimming. Additionally, many SCUBA divers choose high-performance full-footed fins for diving in tropical waters, especially when diving from a boat.

It doesn't matter which kind of fin you use if it doesn't fit properly. Fins that are too loose will wobble around and could even fall off. Tight fins are difficult to put on and can restrict circulation, which can lead to cramps. This is especially true for full-footed fins, because they aren't adjustable. If you are buying adjustable-strap fins, first buy the booties you plan to wear with them; then try on the fins over the booties.

Fins are made of several materials: rubber, polyurethane, graphite, and thermoplastics, either alone or in combination.

In a typical fin, the foot pocket is made of a flexible material like rubber; the blades are usually made of harder thermoplastics. Older all-rubber models are still on the market. These are less expensive, but they tend to be heavier than their plastic counterparts and less buoyant, which makes them easier to lose.

The size and stiffness of your fins determine how much propulsion they offer. Big, stiff fins give more propulsion than smaller, more flexible fins — but only if you are strong enough to use them! If you aren't, you'll end up working too hard and may develop painful leg cramps. Smaller divers, or divers with less developed leg muscles, are better off using more maneuverable fins.

Finally, for adjustable-strap fins, there's the strapping system. Here, the priority is

Most divers prefer adjustable-strap fins, which allow them to wear booties for warmth or protection from sea urchins and sharp coral rock.

Dive flags warn other boaters that you're diving. Limit your diving to within 50 feet of the flag.

ease of use. Older systems tended to require a little bit of elbow grease and a lot of tugging to affix properly. Today, swiveling fasteners and easy-to-operate buckles simplify donning a pair of fins and tightening them securely. If you want to see just how much of a difference a well-designed easy-to-operate strapping system can make, all you have to do is try putting on a couple of different kinds of fins while standing on one foot in the store. Now imagine standing on a bouncing boat while you're decked out in 30 pounds of SCUBA gear. Or trying to keep your balance while putting on your fins in heavy surf. Get the picture?

EQUIPMENT CARE

Basic equipment care for many pieces of snorkeling and SCUBA equipment is the same. For all equipment mentioned in this chapter:
● Give it a good rinse with fresh water.
● Allow it to dry, but don't let it dry in direct sunlight, which can break down some materials, especially neoprene rubber. (Be careful between dives, too, that you don't leave equipment baking in the sun.)
● Neoprene exposure suits should be hung up inside out on a non-wire hanger to dry.
● Store all equipment in a cool, dry place.
● Make sure that neoprene wet suits or neoprene rubber masks aren't touching other pieces of gear when you put them away (*especially* if they're damp). Over time, they can stick together — and then they tear when you pull them apart.
● Equipment such as masks and fins may warp if stored while being compressed, flattened, smushed, and the like, so be sure to give your gear plenty of room, and get it out of a tight travel bag as soon as possible after a trip.

Exposure Suits

Exposure suits are discussed in detail in Chapter 3, but two issues pertain especially to snorkelers.

First, in addition to thermal protection, exposure suits offer protection against sunburn. Because snorkelers spend most of their time at the surface where the sun's rays are strongest, there is a good argument for using an exposure suit while skin diving. A thin nylon or Lycra suit helps prevent sunburn and accidental encounters with lacerating coral. If you don't wear an exposure suit, at least wear a T-shirt.

Second, because snorkelers are unencumbered by the limitations of dive tables and air supply, they often stay in the water a lot longer than SCUBA divers. Even tropical water as warm as 85°F can chill a swimmer after a long immersion. So if you're serious about your snorkeling, you might want to consider a wet suit. For more on how temperature affects swimmers and divers, see Appendix I.

Snorkelers, who spend most of their time at the surface, should wear lightweight exposure suits for protection from sunburn.

Dive Flags and Floats

Dive flags tell boaters that you're in the area. In many states, the law requires dive flags for anyone using a breathing apparatus in navigable waters — and that can include snorkels. Be sure you know the local regulations.

If you are snorkeling from a boat, the dive flag can be flown from the boat. Boats may also fly a so-called *Alpha flag*, which indicates both that there are divers in the water and that the boat has restricted movement. Flags can also sit on an anchored buoy. But a dive flag does no good at all if you aren't near it, and local laws sometimes specify the acceptable distance you can roam from the flag. In general, you should be within about 50 feet of it. If you swim farther afield, you need to tow your flag with you, using a line affixed to a retracting device of some kind, for example, a reel.

Weights

Skin divers don't hang out only at the surface; they also dive down. The length of time free-divers can stay underwater can seem astonishing to divers who haven't learned the tricks of the trade. One of these is to use weights to get below the surface with a minimum of effort, saving your breath for looking around once you get to the bottom.

Weights are necessary because without them, most people float. Therefore, it takes quite a bit of effort to get below the surface, which uses up a lot of air. And once you do get down, your body's inclination is to pop up again. For skin diving, you'll generally use 1-pound weights made of lead, worn on a weight belt. Weights should be evenly distributed around your waist, not worn in the small of your back. You'll need to experiment a bit to figure out how many you need to use. The goal is to put on enough weight to help you descend but not so much that you can't easily come back up again. Correctly weighted divers are *positively buoyant* at the surface and need to use some effort to dive down to 10 or 15 feet, after which the pressure makes them slightly *negatively buoyant*. (For an explanation of these terms, see Appendix I.) Overweighted divers descend more easily, but this can cause a problem. Because they use less effort, they use less air and may be tempted to stay down longer. When their air supply runs out, they have to work to get back to the surface because of all those weights. The result: a possible blackout. So keep weights at a minimum.

Because weights may need to be ditched in an emergency, they should be worn on a quick-release belt with right-hand release. This means that the buckle is worn so that it can be released by one hand. The protocol of keeping the release on the right-hand side enables any diver to quickly release another diver's weights in an emergency without wasting precious seconds figuring out how the weight belt works (see Chapter 3).

TECHNIQUE TIP

KEEP SNORKELS TO YOUR LEFT

When diving, always wear your snorkel on your left side. The snorkel goes on the left to avoid getting it tangled up with the regulator hoses, which come in on the right. In snorkeling, it doesn't make much difference which side the snorkel is on. Always use a snorkel keeper to hold your snorkel in place. You may be tempted to just put the snorkel under the head band of your mask, but this pulls the mask out of alignment and distorts its fit. The result: a leaky mask.

Snorkeling Vest

On some dive boats you will be required to wear a vest. Snorkeling vests can be inflated as needed. The simplest versions are inflated by mouth, although some models can be inflated mechanically. Most divers find basic, less expensive models perfectly adequate.

TECHNIQUES
Mask Clearing

Sooner or later, most probably sooner, you're going to flood your mask.

Mask flooding can occur drop by drop, when little beads of water seep between the skirt of your mask and your skin. Or it can happen all at once, when, for example, your buddy's fin accidentally makes contact with your head.

Your first line of defense is prevention. Be sure your mask has a good seal. Also, when you put the mask in place, take care to pull all stray strands of hair back and away from your face. A seemingly innocuous strand of air acts as a channel; the hair breaks the seal between your mask and your face, and droplets of water seep in. Masks can flood for other reasons. A friend of mine floods hers whenever she smiles. (She has deep laugh lines, and the water seeps in through the creases in her skin.) Because she can't stop smiling underwater, she needs to clear her mask quite often.

To clear a mask *without* a purge valve:
1) Tilt your head back.
2) Firmly press on the mask in the area of your forehead.
3) Blow out through your nose. The air will force the water to exit from the bottom of the mask.

A variation on this method is to tilt your head to one side, press on the mask on its highest point (the side of the mask that is tilted up), and blow out. The air will force the water to exit the mask from the lowest point. This method allows you to maintain your streamlined swimming position while clearing the mask.

To clear a mask *with* a purge valve:
1) Hold the mask against your face and look down.
2) Exhale through your nose. The air will force the water to exit via the purge valve.

Snorkel Clearing

Snorkels take in water every time you dive beneath the surface. They can also take in water accidentally, especially in choppy seas. But all it usually takes to clear a snorkel is one big blast of air. Sometimes, however, you'll need a second blast to get out every last drop of water.

The *blast-clearing* method is used by snorkelers on the surface. Breath-hold divers coming up from below the surface use a different technique that employs simple

Blast-clearing, blowing water out of your snorkel with a big blast of air, should be followed by a second blast to remove every last drop.

physics to clear their snorkels without any effort at all. This technique is called *displacement clearing*. Here's how it works:

1) When the diver descends, the water fills the snorkel.

2) As the diver ascends, he is looking up toward the surface. Just before reaching the surface, the diver continuously breathes out a little air, which partially fills the snorkel.

3) The diver continues to hold his head back, exhaling slowly, looking up at the surface.

4) When the diver reaches the surface, his head is still tilted back. The air in the snorkel pushes out any remaining water.

5) The diver resumes his normal position (horizontal, looking down) and continues swimming.

However you clear a snorkel, control your impulse to take a big gasp of breath. Instead, your first breath should be a cautious one, with your tongue in place at the roof of your mouth to guard against any water that might still be lurking in the snorkel. If there's just a little water in the snorkel, you can breathe past it without inhaling it if you breathe slowly and carefully. Then it's a simple matter to give the snorkel one more blast and finish the job. Breathing

BREATH-HOLD DIVING SAFETY

● Never actually hyperventilate. The key is controlled hyperventilation for no more than three or four breaths. Exceeding this limit may cause you to literally hyperventilate.
● Take slow, deep breaths — not fast, rapid ones.
● Always free-dive with a buddy.
● Take turns with your buddy. One of you should stay at the surface and watch while the other dives.
● Rest between dives to let your body regain its equilibrium.
● If you feel anxious, winded, dizzy, or fatigued, stop!

The surface dive (left to right): From a typical swimming position (1), pull your body into a 90-degree jackknife position (2). Keeping your head down, thrust your legs into the vertical (3). As your feet re-enter the water, start kicking (4). That's all there is to it.

slowly and carefully past a little bit of water is the essence of airway control, a skill that is useful in SCUBA diving as well as snorkeling.

FREE-DIVING
Breathing

Free-divers can spend only as much time below the surface as they can hold their breath, but as you'll learn with experience, this is a lot more time than you might at first imagine.

The key to free-diving is *controlled hyperventilation*, a technique that relaxes the diver and delays the urge to breathe. Before diving, the diver takes three or four slow, deep, deliberate breaths and then immediately dives. That's all there is to it.

It's important to note that in this case, more is not better. In other words, do *not* assume that five or six or seven breaths are better than three or four breaths. Too much

hyperventilation will indeed delay your urge to breathe even longer, possibly so long that you become unconscious. On land, you'd simply lose consciousness and start breathing again. In the water, of course, you could easily drown.

Ups and Downs

Free-divers need to conserve their precious air by maximizing diving efficiency. The easiest way to descend is to perform a *surface dive*. A properly executed surface dive puts your body in a stream-lined position (headfirst, straight down), and it makes use of your powerful fins to propel your descent. This is by far the most efficient way for free-divers to get underwater.

To perform a surface dive, start by pulling your body into a 90-degree jackknife position with your head pointed down, and your hips up. Then, keeping your head down, thrust your feet up into a vertical

A snorkeler armed with a camera swims through a school of fish off the Florida Keys.

position. Start kicking as your feet go under the surface.

Another technique for descending is the feetfirst surface dive. This is useful in murky water with poor visibility and in kelp beds, where a headfirst dive might lead to entanglement or bumping into someone or something. It's a technique that is quite simple to perform, yet very difficult to accurately describe. Therefore, it's best explained and mastered during SCUBA training.

Begin ascending before you feel the urge to breathe. The proper position for ascending is also headfirst, looking up, and circling, with one hand above your head. This position allows you to see where you are going so that you don't inadvertently bump into another diver or an obstacle like a boat. This is a crucial technique for all divers — SCUBA and skin — to put into practice on every ascent, because it will help you avoid surface obstructions and potentially fatal accidents. Divers have died by ascending into the churning propellers of a boat overhead. Always look where you are ascending!

Air Pressure and Free-Divers

Just like SCUBA divers, free-divers will feel the effect of changing air pressure when they descend beneath the surface. Depending on how deep you go, you may feel an uncomfortable buildup of pressure in your ears (Appendix I explains why). To equalize, you will have to perform the so-called *Valsalva maneuver*, described on page 83. You might also feel mask squeeze, which can be eliminated by blowing out through your nose until the air pressure is equalized.

G E A R I N G   U P

When astronauts head into outer space, they depend on gear to keep them alive in an environment that doesn't support human life. Come to think of it, that's exactly what we divers do every time we don our buoyancy compensators (BCs) and tanks and head off to explore our undersea world. True, with practice and determination we might be able to free-dive to 30 or 40 feet or more below the surface. But without SCUBA gear, we'd never be able to hang out down there. Like astronauts, we need equipment to supply us with air and protect us from cold. We know that we are only visitors, but for the duration of

our visit our equipment does more than enable us to survive; it helps us feel as if we belong in the world of inner space.

SCUBA gear is life-support equipment, so it's no surprise that it's expensive. Getting yourself rigged up can easily cost a couple of thousand dollars — more, if you splurge on a top-of-the-line rig with all the bells and whistles. But there's no need to apply for a higher credit line or take a second job just yet. No one says you have to buy all that equipment all at once.

When you're first getting your feet (and everything else) wet, you'll probably spend some time using rental equipment. The quality of rental equipment varies vastly from shop to shop, making it one of the factors to check out before you sign on with a dive school. Using someone else's gear has big benefits for beginners. Most obvious: Your wallet is spared the immediate repercussions of your new hobby. More important: Trying different styles and models of equipment allows you to get a feel for how gear is supposed to, well, *feel*. For instance, you might notice that one regulator works so smoothly that you forget it's even there, whereas another makes you feel like you're sucking air through a cocktail straw. Good. Now you know firsthand the difference between a high-performance regulator and the bargain-basement version. Later, when you're ready to belly-up to the cash register and put your money on the table, you'll have a better idea of which qualities and features you're willing to pay for.

Three exposure suits, from left: 1) A Lycra body suit offers protection against sunburn and abrasions, but not cold. 2) A long-sleeve 3mm-thick neoprene shorty is appropriate for water temperatures in the 80s; it offers great flexibility and comfort. 3) A 5mm neoprene farmer Jane offers warmth in temperatures down to the mid-70s.

WHAT TO WEAR

Exposure suits can protect divers from jellyfish stings, accidental encounters with fire coral and sea urchins, cold temperatures, and blazing sunshine. But one suit does not suit all. There are suits for tropical waters and suits for ice diving, and everything in between.

Before you can even begin to consider which suit to buy, you'll need to know what kind of diving you're buying it for. A suit that keeps you toasty warm diving wrecks off Long Island could make you feel like you're inside a steam sauna when you're diving on a Caribbean reef. So question number one: In what conditions will you be diving? Once you know the answer, you can evaluate various suits based on warmth, fit, and comfort.

Body Suits

Many divers use wet suits in tropical waters, because even warm water can conduct heat away from your body. When the water temperature starts climbing into the high 80s, though, you'll probably be more comfortable in a body suit.

Body suits made of a thin layer of Lycra or nylon offer protection against abrasions and stings as well as sunburn, but they don't give any protection against cold. However, if you're planning a trip to a destination where the water temperature will reliably stay in the high 80s, a body suit might be just what you need. And — a big advantage — it takes up next to no space in your luggage.

Also available are body suits that are partly made with an insulating material such as fleece or a thin layer of neoprene, which covers the torso and insulates even when wet. These suits provide insulation around the body's core organs, where it is most needed.

Wet Suits

By far the most common exposure suits, wet suits can be used in water temperatures ranging from the low 50s to the high 80s.

As their name implies, wet suits do not keep you dry. Instead, they allow a small amount of water to leak in through the neck, ankle, and wrist openings. Your body heat warms this water, which then helps to insulate you because the cold water from outside can't circulate through the warm water that's already inside your suit and next to your skin.

Wet suits also keep you warm with a layer of insulation. Neoprene rubber is a closed-cell foam. Its insulating abilities are due to millions of tiny air bubbles, each enclosed in its own little cell. The closed-cell construction ensures that the material is non-absorbent; that is, water can't flow freely among the bubbles (as it can in, for instance, a sponge).

THICKNESS Wet suits come in different thicknesses, typically ranging from 3mm to 7mm. Three factors will influence your choice. First, the water temperature (see "Which Suit Suits You?," page 49). Second, the depth at which you will be diving, because on deeper dives the increased pressure will compress the air bubbles and reduce their insulating ability. And third, your own body's ability to tolerate cold. Your response to different temperatures is something you'll want to note in your logbook, so you can use information on how you felt on previous dives to plan for more comfortable dives in the future.

FIT For optimal performance, wet suits have to fit like a second skin. A well-fitting suit is snug and a little bit hard to put on — in fact, it should feel a little restrictive when you try it on in the store. The snug fit minimizes the amount of water between suit and skin, which means that your body uses less heat to warm the water near your skin. Neoprene is a flexible material; over time, it molds itself to your body's individual shape. Your own, well-fitting wet suit will keep you warmer than a rental suit because it minimizes the gaps and spaces between suit and skin. Most people can find a good fit in an off-the-rack suit, but divers whose body shape and size don't conform to standard sizes

A 7mm farmer Jane wet suit with long-sleeve jacket, hood, gloves, and booties for cold-water diving; it will keep you warm in waters as low as 50°F.

might prefer a custom-made suit. The surprising good news is that unless you have really unusual requirements, custom suits aren't that much more expensive than ready-made.

STYLE Dive suits also come in a bewildering array of styles. Here, too, water temperature is the most important consideration. One commonsense rule: The more of your body a wet suit covers, the colder the temperatures in which you can comfortably wear it. If you are planning on diving mostly in one environment, then a simple one-piece wet suit appropriate for that water temperature makes sense. If, on the other hand, you plan to dive in a variety of places, your wardrobe must be flexible enough to be functional in different conditions. As in other sports, like skiing and hiking, in which staying warm is a constant consideration, the principle of layering makes it possible to use different combinations of gear to combat a variety of conditions. In addition to full-length one-piece wet suits, there are wet-suit hoods, jackets, vests, and pants.

Shorties are designed for warm water. They cover the torso, leaving the arms and legs exposed.

FULL SCUBA GEAR

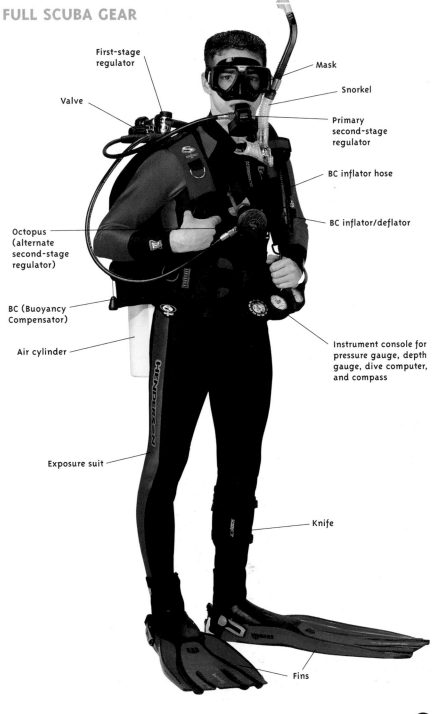

First-stage regulator

Mask

Valve

Snorkel

Primary second-stage regulator

BC inflator hose

BC inflator/deflator

Octopus (alternate second-stage regulator)

BC (Buoyancy Compensator)

Air cylinder

Instrument console for pressure gauge, depth gauge, dive computer, and compass

Exposure suit

Knife

Fins

One-piece wet suits come in a variety of different thicknesses. Thinner suits are used in moderate-to-warm water; thicker suits can be used in moderately cold water.

Two-piece wet suits consist of a jacket and pants (often "farmer John" or "farmer Jane" style overalls). This versatile style allows you to mix and match components, so you can better adjust to changing water temperatures.

Hoods protect the head area. Most body heat is lost through the head.

Vests increase the thermal insulation around the torso. Sometimes they come attached to a hood, which reduces the amount of water that can seep through around the neck.

DESIGN Finally, many wet suits have features designed to prolong the life of your wet suit, keep you cozy, or offer added convenience. The following list isn't exhaustive, but it will give you an idea of what to look for.

Reinforced stress points Wet suits get stretched and pulled a lot, and the first places to wear out are

GETTING DRESSED

If you've forgotten what it feels like to try to squeeze into a pair of really, really tight jeans, get ready for a trip down memory lane. Donning neoprene (especially a one-piece wet suit) can resemble trying to squeeze into a sausage casing. Just remember: It's *supposed* to be snug.

● Easy does it! It's better to wiggle and twist rather than yank and pull, which can stretch and ultimately tear the neoprene.

● First things first. Step into the suit and get it in place over your hips. Generally, if you win this battle, you've won the war.

● Once the suit is in place around your torso, put your arms in one at a time and work the

fabric into place, a little at a time.

● If the suit is defeating you in the store, try another style. A slightly different closure, zipper, or design can make a world of difference.

● The wet suit you own shouldn't require an hour of gymnastics just to put it on. But if you're trying to squeeze into a stubborn rental, a couple of tricks can help. Try wearing a body suit under the wet suit. (Neoprene goes over Lycra a whole lot more easily than it goes over skin.) Or smooth the way! Some divers get creative, using slithery substances like dish soap, KY jelly, or a mixture of hair conditioner and fresh water. Baby powder works, too. But avoid oils, because they can damage neoprene.

those that are subject to the most stress, like elbows, knees, and seat. Look for extra padding in these vulnerable areas. Also look for articulated knees, that is, knees that are designed to bend without overly stressing and stretching the fabric.

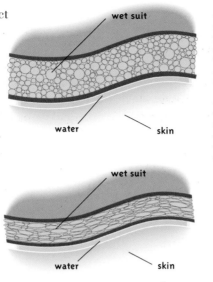

Closed-cell neoprene (above) insulates you from cold by trapping air in tiny pockets in the material, and also by allowing your body heat to warm a thin layer of water next to your skin. As you dive to greater depths (below), the increased pressure diminishes the neoprene's insulative properties substantially.

Pockets Your BC (see page 64) will have pockets, so there's no need to go overboard with pockets on your wet suit, which can stretch and tear and cause leakage over time. Nonetheless, many wet suits come with pockets installed on the arm or leg, which can be handy for storing knives and tools.

Spine pads These patches of neoprene fill in the gap that can develop between the indentation in the small of your back and your suit, where excess water often collects. You should also consider a suit with spine pads if you tend to be bothered by the pressure of the tank against your back.

Zippers No question: Zippers make it easier to get in and out of a wet suit. But they add to the cost and increase the possibility of leakage. You'll also want to consider whether the zipper goes in the front or the back. Front zips are much easier to take on and off; back zips sometimes lie closer to the skin and are not subject to as much stress (which can lead to leakage). If you do get a back zipper, be sure that it has a pull string (or that you can attach a pull string) so you can reach it. Finally, look for zippers mounted on the outside of the suit rather than the inside. Outside mounting helps prevent excess leakage by minimizing the channel that runs along the zipper.

Color Color is not just a fashion statement. Underwater — especially deep underwater — colors change. That sleek, all-black suit your partner is wearing can render her almost invisible 50 feet under, especially if the water is murky. Screaming-bright colors might not be your everyday style in "real" life, but underwater the rule is "see and be seen." Also, if you're diving with a group of people, you'll be able to more quickly pick out your

buddy from any angle — above, behind, or below — if she is wearing a distinctively colored suit.
QUALITY When exposure suits are under pressure, as they are when you dive, the air bubbles are squeezed and become smaller, decreasing the insulation. When you return to the surface, the bubbles return to their normal size. You may notice that with time and use, your wet suit becomes a little less resilient. High-quality wet suits have more air bubbles and better construction, so they tend to insulate better and last longer than cheaper models.

Dry Suits

No surprises here: Dry suits keep you warm by keeping you dry. Worn with the appropriate insulating undergarments, dry suits can keep you warm in temperatures from 50°F or so all the way down to near-freezing.
STYLES There are two basic dry suit styles:
1) *Neoprene suits* look much like wet suits, except they're a lot thicker. Like wet suits, they offer insulation, depending on how thick they are. Unlike wet suits, they are designed with watertight zippers, and neck and wrist seals, which keep water out. In very cold water, they can be worn over an additional layer of insulating undergarments.
2) *Coated fabric suits* rely on the "layering with a protective shell" principle. Underneath the dry suit, the diver wears layers of insulating

thermal garments. The outside layer, the dry suit, is the shell that keeps out the water and has no insulating ability of its own.

Both kinds of dry suits trap air, which is compressed as you descend underwater. The change in air volume affects your buoyancy, so dry suits — just like your ears and your mask — have to be equalized. You can add or vent air by use of special valves or with hoses that work like the low-pressure inflator of your BC. If you get your C-card diving in cold water, you'll probably learn dry-suit use in your training. If, however, you are certified in tropical water, you should seek instruction before diving with a dry suit. Air can collect in the arms and legs, turning you upside down when you least expect it, so you'll need to learn some new techniques. You'll also have to monitor and regulate the amount of air in your dry suit in order to control your buoyancy and, especially, your rate of ascent.
FEATURES Insulation and waterproofing are two big considerations. Look for the following features:
Zippers must be watertight. Most dry suits use a waterproof closure that was originally designed for astronauts to use in space suits! But no matter how watertight, a zipper is always a weak spot, so you want as few as possible, and you want them designed in such a way that they aren't under pressure every time you stretch and move. Unfortunately, this

often means that the zipper ends up on your back, making it impossible to take your dry suit on and off without a buddy to help you.

Seals around the wrists and neck are made of latex or neoprene. No matter which you choose, a little water will leak in. Latex tends to wear out faster but is easy to replace. Neoprene seals are longer lasting but more difficult to replace. Divers' argue about the relative comfort and

GEAR TALK

WHICH SUIT SUITS YOU?

With all the different exposure suits and accessories available, there are lots of ways to cope with cold. What you wear will also depend on your body's response to cold. Use the following chart as a departure point, and modify it according to your accessories, your body, and the depth of your dive.

TEMPERATURE	WHAT TO WEAR
HIGH 80s	A Lycra body suit, a shorty, or a dive jacket (the top of a two-piece suit)
80°–90°F	A shorty, a dive jacket, or a full-length, one-piece, 3mm wet suit
75°–85°F	A 3mm one-piece jumpsuit, or a two-piece wet suit
70°–80°F	A 5mm full-length wet suit, a two-piece wet suit, or a dry suit with lightweight insulating garments
50°–70°F	A 7mm full-length two-piece wet suit with gloves and hood, or a dry suit with insulating garments
BELOW 50°F	A dry suit with insulating garments, hood, gloves or mitts, and possibly a face mask

Confused yet? In addition to the water temperature, you'll also want to take into account the depth of your dive. Remember, there's much greater pressure on deeper dives, which will compress your insulating layers and make them less effective. Plan accordingly!

A neoprene hood is vital in water below 70°F; much of your body heat is lost through your scalp.

layers you use and how thick these layers are will depend on the water temperature and the type of dry suit you use.

EXTRAS In most cases, if you're wearing a dry suit, you will also be wearing a hood and booties. Hoods and booties (discussed below) are sometimes attached to some models of dry suits. These all-in-one designs give you less flexibility and may make the equipment more difficult to put on, but they also reduce leakage. When you try on the wet suit and its accessories, be sure to try on everything all together to be sure it fits comfortably and doesn't restrict motion. And try it on with your other equipment, too: Are you wearing so many layers that you need a larger BC? Are your booties and socks so thick that you need larger fins? The time to discover these problems is before you head out on a boat for a cold-weather dive.

seaworthiness of each, so there's no clear recommendation. It's probably best to choose your suit based on other factors, such as comfort and fit.

Undergarments used for dry-suit diving are a lot like the undergarments used for cold-water land sports like mountaineering and skiing. Made of fabrics such as polypropylene or fleece, these garments retain their insulating ability even when wet. (They shouldn't get wet when you're wearing a dry suit, but the fact that they can help keep you warm even if something goes wrong is important.) How many

Exposure Accessories

BOOTIES Booties protect feet against abrasions, blisters, and cold; they also provide traction on slippery

GEAR TALK

SUIT UP BOOTIES

If you are wearing booties and a full-length wet suit, put the suit on first and then the booties. Now, make sure to pull the pant legs out and over the tops of the booties. The booties will take in a lot less water.

boat surfaces. You'll be especially glad you have them when you find yourself walking out to a dive site over coral rock or in areas known to be occupied by sea urchins. And they are a requirement for diving in cold water.

Some booties pull on over your foot; others have side zips, which are especially useful if you have a high-volume foot or a high arch. Zippers make it much easier to put on the boots and take

them off, and they may prolong the life of the booties because they eliminate the need to yank and tug. The downside: Zippers can let in more water, which can be a problem in colder temperatures. Your choice should depend on fit and the kind of diving you expect to do.

GLOVES Like other protective clothing, diving gloves serve

BUDDY, CAN YOU SPARE A SNORKEL KEEPER?

A box filled with gizmos, thingamajigs, and whatchamacallits can help keep a dive from being scrapped just because your fin

strap snapped or your O-ring has a crack in it. You can buy a prepackaged kit or assemble your own in a tackle box or some other rugged container. Either way, here's what should be in your "Save-a-Dive" Repair Kit:

Dust caps	Mask strap	Matches	Miscellaneous
Wire ties	Snorkel keeper	Sunglasses	tools or a
Whistle	Insect repellent	Change	multipurpose
Sunscreen	Light sticks	Pencils	knife
Silicone grease	Mouthpiece	Cleaner	First aid
Fin straps	O-rings	(to erase dive	supplies (see
	Batteries	slates)	page 116)

two pur-
poses:
protection
from abra-
sions and
insulation
from cold.
Diving gloves
range from
lightweight non-
insulating gloves
(good for abrasion
protection) to neo-
prene gloves to heavy-
weight cold-water diving mitts.
HOODS By far the most body heat is
lost through your head. The old
saying has it, "If your feet are
cold, put on a hat," and
SCUBA diving is no
exception. In
water
below
70°F,
you'll
probably
need a hood.
Hoods are made of neo-
prene. There are three basic styles:
bibbed hoods (used with a wet suit;
the bib fits under the wet suit and
helps keep out water), non-bibbed

GEAR TALK

MAINTAINING YOUR WARDROBE

To prolong the life of your exposure gear, first read the manufacturer's
instructions for the care of your particular model. And follow these
guidelines:

- Rinse in fresh water.
- Dry inside out.
- Store in a cool, dry place.
- Do not hang on a metal hanger, which will leave rust stains.
- Hang loosely rather than fold. Folding in the same place time after
time creases and wears out the fabric, leaving a "cold spot." In addi-
tion, the fabric of a folded suit can stick to itself and be damaged when
it's pulled apart.
- Once in a while, lubricate zippers and fasteners with silicone.
- Give garments plenty of room so they air and dry properly. Some
coated fabrics can stick together if they are stored touching each other.
- Thick hangers are better than thin. They help the garment dry faster
and cause less creasing.
- Clean the garment with a commercial preparation, if the manufacturer recommends one.

(used with a dry suit, which already has a neck seal), and hooded vests (used with a wet suit in cold water). Hooded vests combine the functions of a hat and an extra layer of insulating clothing for the torso. They also help keep water out of the wet suit.

Fins let you efficiently push yourself through the water, even when laden with all that SCUBA gear. Without them, you'd be breathless in no time.

Fit is the most important consideration. The hood should be snug, but not tight, as a tight hood can restrict circulation.

SNORKELS, MASKS, AND FINS

We've already discussed these fundamentals in Chapter 2, "Skin Diving." SCUBA divers may additionally want to consider the following points:

Snorkels

Diving doesn't place any additional demands on snorkels (which you can use only at the surface), so the snorkel you used in skin diving is fine for SCUBA. Again, wear it on the left side so it doesn't interfere with your hoses.

Masks

A good, well-fitting mask that works for skin diving will be fine for SCUBA. Experienced divers look for certain features in a SCUBA mask, including VISABILITY Wraparound glass gives you better peripheral vision. Another good feature is a glass panel

TECHNIQUE TIP

MASK STRAP

Your mask strap can be worn either over or under the hood, but most divers prefer to wear it over the hood. This gives the hood a tighter seal, and lets you adjust your mask, if necessary.

below your nose that lets you see down to the controls on your BC. NOSE ACCESS In some masks, purge valves restrict access to your nose. A common complaint with purge-valve masks is that it's hard to reach and squeeze your nose (as you do when equalizing your ears) with just one hand. In SCUBA, you want to be able to equalize with one hand because you need the other hand free to operate your equipment.

Fins

SCUBA does make greater demands on your fins than does skin diving because with all that gear on, you are less streamlined. In addition to the issues discussed in Chapter 2, divers must consider propulsion when choosing fins for SCUBA. Swimming is one of the three major energy expenditures in diving. (The other two are breathing and staying warm.) To see how essential fins

are, all you have to do is try to swim in full SCUBA gear without them. Chances are you'll be panting and out of breath before you've managed to swim across the short end of a swimming pool — if, that is, you even make it that far!

Fin manufacturers are pouring money into fin design, which has led to a plethora of styles featuring different ways of channeling and moving water. Experienced divers agree that design does make a difference, so pay attention to various styles of fins when you are starting out and renting equipment, quiz experienced divers on what styles they prefer, and check out equipment reviews in diving magazines. The kind of diving you do will also make a difference. If you're an easygoing calm-water tropical diver, you have less need for high-powered fins than someone who drift-dives in the North Sea, for example.

WHAT'S MY FLIPPER DOING ON YOUR FOOT?

Sure, there are lots of styles and colors for SCUBA gear. But some makes and models are, shall we say, more ubiquitous than others. On a crowded, gear-cluttered dive boat, there may be another pair of flippers around that looks just like yours.

Waterproof marking paint can help you keep track of what belongs to whom. It's available in dive shops; simply apply it to a clean, dry surface and allow it to dry thoroughly. Write your first name, last name, or initials — anything that will differentiate your equipment.

HOW YOU BREATHE

Your SCUBA system — your self-contained underwater breathing apparatus — is the mainstay of your diving gear. It consists of five items:
1) A tank, which contains dry, compressed, filtered air.
2) A valve, which delivers that air to your regulator.
3) A regulator, which performs two functions: It regulates the pressure of the air so that you can breathe it, and it delivers the air to your mouth.
4) A submersible pressure gauge, which allows you to monitor how much air is in your tank.
5) A backpack system, which enables you to carry your equipment while you swim. The backpack will be discussed in the context of BCs, because the most popular models combine these two functions.

Tanks

MATERIALS SCUBA tanks are made of either steel or aluminum. Steel is

---

GEAR TALK

MAINTAINING YOUR TANKS AND VALVES

DAILY MAINTENANCE

- Rinse off your tank and valve with fresh water after each dive and let it dry.
- Don't overfill a tank. This can damage the valve, rupture the burst disk, lead to metal fatigue, and shorten the life of the tank. If you need more air, take a bigger tank.
- Tanks, like all SCUBA gear, should be kept out of direct sunlight whenever possible. If a full tank is overheated in direct sunlight (or in the trunk of a car), the air could expand so much that the burst disk is ruptured.
- When not under the direct control of a diver, tanks should be kept lying down so they don't get knocked over. This can damage gear and valves, not to mention toes. On boats, tanks should be secured by fasteners so they don't tip over.
- Never allow a tank to be completely empty. An empty tank is more likely to take in water, which is corrosive.
- If the tank is empty, be sure to close the valve to prevent any water in the regulator from backing up into the tank. Empty tanks should be visually inspected by a professional before they are refilled with air, to be sure that no damage has been done.

continued on page 56

continued from page 55

• Avoid overtightening tank valves when you turn them on and off.
• Store tanks upright in a cool, dry place with 100 to 300 pounds per square inch (psi) of air.
• If the tank has been stored for more than six months, refill it with fresh air before diving.

PROFESSIONAL MAINTENANCE

• Tanks and valves must be serviced by professionals. Don't try to fix a problem yourself.
• Tanks should always be filled with filtered, dry, compressed air — never oxygen. Always fill your tank at a reputable dive shop.
• Information about your SCUBA cylinder will be stamped into its neck. This includes the tank's maximum rated pressure. Never overfill your tank.
• Tanks must be visually inspected by a professional once a year for corrosion. By federal law, they must be *hydrostatically tested* (pressure-tested) once every five years. Before your dive center will fill your tank, you'll need to show your C-Card, and the person will check the tank's inspection stickers to be sure they are up-to-date.

tough and resistant to being scratched and dented, but it is more vulnerable to corrosion and rusting. Aluminum is softer but resists corrosion better. Aluminum tanks tend to be more buoyant than steel, so you'll need to wear more weights when using an alu-

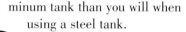

Tank markings show the tank material, serial number, working pressure in pounds per square inch, date of manufacture, dates of all pressure tests, and the manufacturer.

minum tank than you will when using a steel tank.

SHAPES Tanks can be short and fat, or long and skinny. This isn't a huge consideration, but if you have a choice, opt for a tank whose shape most closely matches your body shape. You'll be better balanced.

SIZE Tanks hold different amounts of air. Air is measured in cubic feet; that is, a 50-cubic-foot tank would contain as much compressed air as a container at sea level that has a volume of 50 cubic feet of non-compressed air. Most common are 50-cubic-foot aluminum tanks, 71.2-cubic-foot steel tanks, and 80-cubic-foot aluminum tanks. Divers who use a lot of air, or who go on deeper dives for which they need more air, choose larger-capacity tanks that let them stay down longer. Experienced, air-efficient divers might prefer smaller-capacity tanks because they are lighter (and hence more comfortable).

The first-stage regulator (above) fits onto the tank's valve (below) and is screwed in place. An O-ring in the valve creates a tight seal between the two.

BACKUPS Most commonly used on deep dives, backup air sources include special *pony bottles*, which are small, second tanks independent of your primary tanks. Double-tank systems are also used for dives that are especially long or deep.

Valves

Air moves through your tank and into your regulator through a valve that can be turned on and off. The regulator's so-called first stage is attached to the tank valve. Simple.

All tank valves have the following features:

O-RINGS These provide the seal between the valve and the

first stage. Check O-rings every time you use the tank. They should be free of debris and show no signs of wear and tear. Carry extras in your spare parts kit, where you keep extra thingamabobs like snorkel keepers, fin straps, and mask straps (see page 51 for what else should be in the kit). If your O-ring is shot, you can't dive.

BURST DISKS These safety features are designed to rupture if the pressure in the tank is dangerously high. If you overfill your

Tank valve, showing the on-off knob (left); the valve opening with O-ring (top); and the burst disk (right), a safety valve that allows excess air pressure to release, preventing the tank from exploding.

Left: the primary second-stage regulator, simply put, the gizmo through which you breathe. Right: the octopus, or alternate air source, on reserve for your buddy should she need it in an emergency.

second stage, which is attached to the mouth-piece. The second stage further reduces the pressure and delivers air to your mouth at the right pressure for breathing.

BREATHABILITY Ease of breathing is the most important consideration in choosing a regulator. Renting different kinds of equipment before you buy will show you firsthand the differences among regulators. One term to look for is "high-performance." This overused advertising description actually means something specific when it comes to regulators. It means that the regulator is designed to perform well under a variety of conditions, including cold water and deep dives. High-performance regulators are also designed to give you all the air you need, even if you are breathing hard. Some magazines, such as Rodale's *SCUBA Diving*, regularly test high-performance regulators. Before buying a reg, it's a good idea to get your hands on the latest evaluations. A dive shop will usually let you "test-dive" the model of regulator you are considering. This is the best way to find out whether a reg is right for you. Your test dive should be made under conditions similar to those in which you plan to use the regulator — especially if your diving preferences tend to deep or cold water.

tanks, or if a full tank gets very hot in the sun and the air expands, the burst disk ruptures and releases air. ON-OFF KNOB Air is turned on via a simple on-off knob. Don't overtighten the knob when turning off the air.

Regulators

The air in a tank is under pressure. For you to be able to breathe it, the pressure must be reduced. The *regulator* (if you want to sound cool, call it a reg) delivers air at a somewhat reduced pressure "on demand," that is, when you take a breath.

The regulator is a two-part contraption consisting of a *first stage* and a *second stage*. The first stage attaches to the tank valve and partially reduces the pressure of the air as it comes out of the tank. The air then flows through a hose to the

COMFORT Your diving enjoyment will be compromised if you're constantly tugging on and biting at your mouthpiece to get it to sit right. A mouthpiece that feels awkward can sometimes be improved by changing the mouthpiece angle or the

hose length. When you try a regulator, set up your gear as you would for a dive — attached to a tank, over a BC — so you can see how

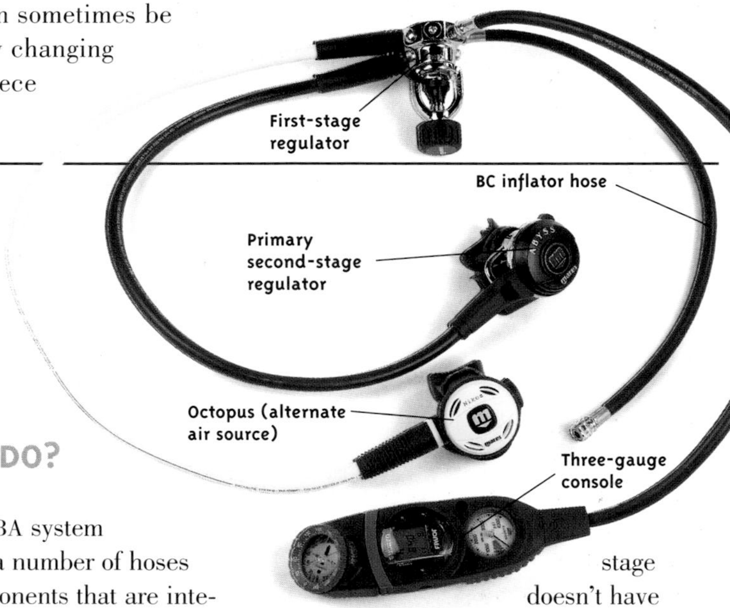

First-stage regulator

BC inflator hose

Primary second-stage regulator

Octopus (alternate air source)

Three-gauge console

WHAT DO ALL THOSE HOSES DO?

Your SCUBA system includes a number of hoses and components that are integral parts of your SCUBA system. These include your regulator and mouthpiece; an alternate air source, which allows your buddy to breathe from your air supply if she runs out of air or her regulator malfunctions; a submersible pressure gauge, which tells you how much air you have in your tank (see page 61–62); and a low-pressure inflator, which connects to the BC and allows you to add air from your tank to the BC (see page 64–66).

Hoses attach to ports that are built into the first stage. If the first

stage doesn't have enough ports, you can connect a port adapter to it. (It's the same idea as an adapter that lets you plug more than one appliance into an electrical outlet.) You'll use high-pressure ports for equipment like the submersible pressure gauge, which reads the pressure of your tank, and low-pressure ports for such equipment as the second-stage hoses, the low-pressure inflator, and the dry-suit inflator (if you use one). The initial setup and connections should be made by a professional when you buy your regulator.

everything sits and fits together. The dive shop pros can help you make adjustments if something's not quite perfect.

ALTERNATE AIR SOURCES The alternate air source serves the important function of providing a way for you or your buddy to breathe if there is a problem.

The most common alternate air source is a *backup second stage*, also called an *octopus*. Like the primary second stage, the backup is attached via a hose to the first stage. What this means in English is that you have two mouthpieces. Each of them gets air from the same place — your tank. Your primary air source is the one you breathe from. Your alternate air source is the spare, which your buddy can use in an emergency.

Most alternate air sources come with longer hoses, so that they can

GEAR TALK

MAINTAINING YOUR REGULATOR

Regulators should be serviced once a year. Discuss service when you buy the regulator to be sure that the shop will be able to get parts and perform necessary repairs. Between annual checkups there are several things you can do to prolong a regulator's life and reliability:

● Rinse your reg in fresh water after every use. If possible, rinse off the equipment when it is still attached to the tank and the air is still turned on. This will prevent water from entering the first stage, which can cause corrosion.

● Keep the dust cover in place to keep the regulator free of debris — of which there is plenty around, including particles of sand, mud, and various bits and pieces of organic matter. (The dust cover also keeps water out of the first stage. If you rinse the regulator separately from the tank, be sure the dust cover is on.)

● Two other habits can keep water out of the first stage. (1) Never press the purge button while you are rinsing the regulator. (But after rinsing, turn off the air and press the purge button or you won't be able to disassemble the unit.) And (2) rinse with gently running water, not a high-pressure hose, which can force water into the regulator.

● Be gentle with the hoses. No pulling, tying in knots, or packing too tightly.

● Check mouthpieces regularly to make sure that the bite tabs are in place and that there are no tears where they connect to the second stage.

comfortably be used by another diver. They are also distinguishable by their bright color, which helps a distressed diver more easily locate them. Alternate air sources are usually worn at the front right side of the BC, where they should be secured by a rip-away clip. Securing an alternate air source prevents it from dangling in the mud, and keeps it in one place so your buddy knows where it is. Your alternate air source should always be clearly visible.

Another type of alternate air source is integrated with the low-pressure inflator, which connects with and fills your BC with air. In this case, the mouthpiece and purge button are built into the low-pressure inflator. The air comes from your tank. If you use this kind of system, be sure your buddy knows where it is and how to operate it.

Alternate air sources can also be completely separate from and independent of your main tank. These redundant air systems range from pony bottles with their own regulators to very small spare bottles (also with their own regulators) that fit into a BC pocket and are designed to give you only enough spare air to ascend safely to the surface in an emergency. However, some divers feel that some of the very small bottles are not adequate for safe ascents from deep dives. You'll want to examine the capacity of your alternate air source carefully and consider the depth of your dive before using it.

Submersible Pressure Gauges

Early divers didn't have *submersible pressure gauges (SPGs)*. They estimated their air consumption and relied on a reserve valve (the so-called *J-valve*) to help them cope with running out of air. This style of diving could be compared to driving a car with a broken gas gauge, with a small spare can of gas in the trunk. J-valves are still sometimes found, but with reliable SPGs they are now redundant.

Today's SPGs tell divers precisely how much air they have left by monitoring the amount of air in the tank. The SPG connects to a high-pressure port on your first stage. Like a car's gas gauge, your SPG is a passive device.

Analog depth gauge

Pressure gauge

Temperature gauge

Analog air-pressure and depth gauges are a good deal less expensive than their digital cousins.

It works only if you use it. SPGs measure the amount of air in psi (pounds per square inch) or, if you are diving in Europe, in bars. Whichever system you're using, most SPGs have a shaded warning area; when the needle hits the red, it's time to come up.

TYPES SPGs can be simple analog devices or they can be integrated into a complex computerized digital system.

ATTACHMENTS The basic SPG rides on a console attached to a hose that is in turn attached to a port on your first stage. It can be attached via a clip to your BC to keep it close to hand and off the seafloor. This prevents it from banging into coral, silting up the bottom so no one else can see anything, or floating out of sight somewhere behind your left knee.

MAINTENANCE Simply rinse it and treat it gently. When you have your equipment inspected, be sure to bring your SPG in for a checkup, too. It's rare, but not unheard of, for an SPG to give an inaccurate reading (one reason, incidentally, that you should always plan to end your dive with a reserve of air left in your tank. But more on that in Chapter 7).

COURTESY As a courtesy to other divers and a safety mechanism for yourself, always turn the face of the SPG away from you or other people when you turn on the air in your tank. It's possible although rare, for the face of a defective SPG to blow out when the air is turned on.

Information Instruments

How much air you've got left isn't the only piece of information you need to know to plan and execute a safe dive. How long have you been down? At what depth are you? Which way do you have to swim to get back to the boat? What's the temperature?

Information devices can be analog or digital. Digital devices tend to be more accurate — and more expensive. Another consideration: Should you buy separate instruments (a watch, a compass, a thermometer, a depth gauge) or an integrated system? Integrated systems are much more practical, because everything is handy, all in one place. Whichever instruments or system you choose, it should be easy to operate (no tiny buttons that are hard to push with cold hands or gloves on), and the displays should be readable, even in low light.

Here's a rundown on the info you need and how to get it:

DEPTH GAUGE Depth gauges tell you how deep you are. You should check your depth gauge every few seconds when ascending and descending, and frequently during a dive. Remember, dangerous currents can sweep you up or down without your even being aware of it, so you need to pay constant attention to your depth. Note that on certain models the depth gauge must

Dive computer, temp/depth/time of dive/no decompression limit at any given depth

This three-gauge digital console includes a computer that senses your depth along with nitrogen's effect on your body at all times.

Compass

Pressure gauge

be calibrated if you dive at altitudes above 1,000 feet.

COMPASS Which way is the wreck you came to dive? Where's the boat? Which way is the current moving? Which way do you turn to get from the coral where the big eel hangs out to the place where the sea turtle can sometimes be found? If you surface into a thick fog, how do you know which way is shore? Compasses can be handheld, worn on the wrist, integrated into an analog console, or included in a dive computer.

TIMEPIECE How long have you been down? Knowing this information is critical, because you need to come up before you exceed the no-decompression limits. Dive watches should have a rating of 200 feet, which is deeper than recreational diving limits permit, so it provides

a margin of safety. Some dive watches are rated in meters or atmospheres (atms). Look for ratings of at least 60 meters or 7 atms. You can use special diving watches, which have stopwatches (or timers) to calculate bottom time and surface intervals. Or you can use appropriately rated multipurpose athletic watches. Be sure the wrist strap is big enough to fit over your wet suit.

THERMOMETER It's not essential to know the temperature on every dive, but it's a good piece of information to have for your logbook. This will help you keep track of how you feel under different conditions.

DIVE COMPUTER Computers can monitor all of the above. They can also be integrated into your submersible pressure gauge, which means that all essential information is together on one piece of equipment. Computers also count your dives, monitor your surface intervals, calculate your nitrogen levels, monitor your ascent rate, and tell you when and for how long to take a safety stop on your way to the surface.

Top: A jacket-style BC with integrated weight system has many pockets. Bottom: A back-buoyancy BC, the latest innovation keeps the air at your back for greater comfort.

FLOATING AND SINKING

In order to dive, you have to get below the surface and back up again. In between, you must control whether you are floating or sinking, and how fast.

Buoyancy Compensator

Otherwise known as a *buoyancy control device*, your *BC* (or *BCD*; both terms are used) is a device that lets you control your buoyancy by adding and subtracting air. The BC is used for adjusting buoyancy while you're diving, providing buoyancy while you're on the surface, and providing emergency flotation for a tired diver.

Note: It is not, however, a life jacket, and it does not meet Coast Guard regulations as a flotation device.

The BC's low-pressure inflator connects by means of a hose to a low-pressure port in your first stage. When you press the inflator button, air moves from the tank through the inflation hose and into the jacket itself. You can also inflate the BC manually (or, more accurately, orally) by blowing into the inflator. When you press the deflator button, air escapes via the deflation hose. If you overfill your BC, air will escape through an overpressure relief valve. This prevents the bladder from rupturing.

The most popular BC is a jacket-style model that looks

like a cross between a backpack (for carrying the tank) and an inflatable jacket (which controls buoyancy). Also popular are *back-buoyancy models*, also called *back-mount models*, which position both the tank and the buoyancy on your back. A third, less common option is to use a buoyancy control device that is separate from the backpack. These BCs look a little like snorkeling vests, although they have more features and controls.

BCs with built-in backpacks have straps that hold the tank in place, and a plastic bed to keep the tank in position (and keep it from banging into your back). The straps are easy to operate. Substituting an empty tank with a full one is simply a matter of releasing a couple of fasteners and popping the new tank into place.

Finally, you'll need to choose between BCs that are integrated with their weight systems and BCs that are independent of the weight belt.

JACKET-STYLE BCS At the front of the jacket you'll find shoulder straps, a waist belt, and adjustments. The jacket style distributes the air around you by means of a bladder inside the jacket. Jacket-style BCs usually have convenient pockets and clips in or on which to keep gear like slates, flashlights, and batteries.

BACK-BUOYANCY BCS Back-buoyancy models also come with

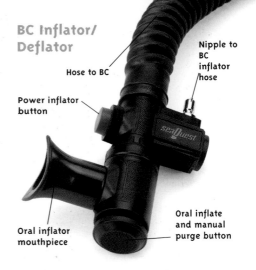

BC Inflator/ Deflator

Hose to BC

Nipple to BC inflator hose

Power inflator button

Oral inflator mouthpiece

Oral inflate and manual purge button

shoulder straps, waist belts, and adjustments to hold everything in place. These models keep the air at your back. Proponents say this helps put you in the best swimming position, and that it is less restrictive, especially when fully inflated. On the surface, the back-buoyancy BC will hold you higher in the water while you're swimming on your back, but when you are in a vertical position, it may also tend to force your face forward. Back-buoyancy BCs sometimes lack sufficient conveniently located pockets.

FIT Try on the BC over the bulkiest exposure suit you plan to use it with. Make preliminary adjustments to the shoulder and waist straps. Then try it on with a tank attached and refine the fit. Too tight, and your movement will be restricted; so, inflate the BC and see if it's comfortable when it's full of air. Too loose, and the BC may wiggle about and ride up, getting in your way and making it difficult to operate your equipment. Women, take note: As in other sports, "unisex sizes" really means "women should put up with men's sizes." Fortunately, some BCs are available in women's sizes, and these deserve a close look.

LIFT How much buoyancy do you need? Not too much, or you'll end up fighting excess drag. Not too little, or you'll have to fight to stay above the surface in choppy conditions. But how do you determine what's just right? Checking out some rental gear can help you determine how much lift, which is measured in pounds, you need. As a rule of thumb, your BC has the right lift when you can float on the surface with your head out of the water while wearing your normal weights, a full tank, and a half-inflated BC.

BUCKLES Make sure the buckles are conveniently located and easy to operate, even when you're wearing gloves.

TANK ATTACHMENTS Be sure the backpack is compatible with the size and shape tank you commonly use. Also check to be sure that the valve doesn't hit you in the back of the head when you attach the tank to the BC.

Weights

Weights are the next item of business. Most people equipped with a wet suit, a tank, and a BC are *positively buoyant* — that is, they float. To go down, they need to load up with lead weights.

There are two ways to carry the weight: on a weight belt, or on a BC that has a weight-integrated system.

WEIGHT BELTS Weights belts are the easiest choice. The basic weight belt is simply a webbed belt on which you string as many weights

---

GEAR TALK

MAINTAINING YOUR BC .

● Rinse in fresh water after every day of diving.

● Also rinse the inside, because salt water will sneak in and shorten your BC's life. Partially fill the BC with fresh water by pouring water through the inflator hose. Then fill the remainder with air. Finally, swish the water around and empty it out.

● Let the BC dry, but keep it out of direct sunlight.

● Try to avoid rough treatment that can tear or damage fabric.

● Avoid contact with petroleum-based products or solvents.

● Store BCs partially inflated.

● Have your BC checked and serviced once a year.

as you need. It is worn around the waist. You can add or subtract weights as needed. Pretty much any old weights will do, and you can rent them at a dive shop, which means you don't have to travel with an extra 10 to 20 pounds of lead in your luggage. Also available are neoprene weight belts. Weights used to be just hard chunks of lead, but the newest innovation on the weight-belt front are so-called *soft-shot weights*, which are vinyl pouches filled with lead pellets. These weights are more flexible, more comfortable, and don't strain the back; they are also less likely to break a piece of equipment or a

---

HOW MUCH WEIGHT DO I NEED?

How much weight you need depends on your natural buoyancy, which depends on a number of factors. A 5-foot, 7-inch woman who weighs 150 pounds will be more buoyant than a 5-foot, 9-inch man who weighs 140 pounds because muscle is denser (hence less buoyant) than fat.

But that's not all you have to think about. Other considerations include:

● Will you be diving in salt water or fresh water?

● What kind of exposure suit are you using?

● What kind of tank do you have, a buoyant aluminum tank or a less-buoyant steel tank?

At first your instructor will probably just take a guess at how many weights you'll need. At the beginning, it's better to be over-weighted than underweighted so you don't uncontrollably bob to the surface. But extra pounds are a chore to drag around, and they interfere with how streamlined you are. So use the following guidelines to get weighted properly:

❶ Before the dive, float on the surface with your BC almost empty. If you are properly weighted, you should be floating at about eye level, rising slightly each time you inhale, and sinking when you exhale.

❷ At the end of the dive, if you are weighted properly, you will be able to make a neutrally buoyant safety stop at 15 feet with 500 psi in your tank and an empty BC.

❸ Finally, if a few months have elapsed between dives, consider how many chocolate chip cookies you've had between then and now. If you've gained weight, you might need to add some lead.

For more on buoyancy control, see Chapter 4.

toe if they fall. Soft-shot weights can be used with BCs that have a weight-integrated system, or with independent weight belts designed to carry them. WEIGHT-INTEGRATED BCS These BCs have pockets or pouches for weights. These systems are more complicated than weight belts, but many divers find them more comfortable. Two caveats: Your BC's weight system may work only with certain shapes and sizes of weights, in which case you will have to travel with your weights. And the weight-release system can be difficult to find and operate. If you are using a weight-integrated system, be sure that both you and your buddy know how to operate the releases.

QUICK-RELEASE All weight systems have a quick-release feature. In an emergency you should be able to ditch your weights with one hand. Weight belts are held in place by a buckle that can be easily undone. The buckle is always worn so that

it opens on the right. Following this so-called right-hand release protocol means that in an emergency you'll know how to operate your belt — or any other diver's belt.

ACCESSORIES

In addition to the basic getup, a number of accessories can make your dive safer and more enjoyable.

Lights

WHY? Lights are required in some kinds of special diving situations, for example, night diving, cave diving, and wreck diving. They can also help you get a better view of something in a coral crevice or under a rock overhang. Lights can show you the true colors of whatever you're looking at, counteracting the light-filtering (and color-altering) effect of water at depth. Chemical light sticks can also help you out in poor visibility or low-light situations. Use them to signal a buddy or someone on the surface. WHAT TO LOOK FOR Lights must

PACKING AN EQUIPMENT BAG

Now that you've got all that gear, you'll have to carry it around with you. An equipment bag designed for SCUBA gear will be big enough to fit it all, and shaped so that you don't have to cram and jam to find room for your fins, not to mention all the rest of your stuff. Special equipment bags for traveling with SCUBA gear are also available. Before you jump to the conclusion that this is just one more unnecessary gizmo the marketeers have invented for you to spend money on, consider their function: protecting your life-support equipment from the tender ministrations of baggage handlers.

Here's the goal: to load your gear bag so that your gear is protected and can be taken out in pretty much the order you need it. The reason: On a crowded dive boat, you'll be the one who knows where all your stuff is.

● Rule number one:

No tanks or weights in the bag. Tanks and weights travel separately because they can break or damage delicate equipment. When carting equipment out to the boat, wear your weights on your hip or sling them over your shoulder.

● There's a way to pack so that soft gear protects fragile gear — and most everything comes out of the bag in order. Fins go at the bottom of the bag, followed by the mask and snorkel wrapped inside the BC, the regulator, the wet-suit bottom, and the wet-suit top. If you have a one-piece wet suit, wrap it around the mask.

● Use a mesh bag: It lets air in and smells out, which is exactly what you need with wet gear.

● SCUBA gear is heavy — wheeled bags are nice!

Dive knife with leg sheath and push-button release.

disentangling yourself from sea vegetation or fishing lines. You can also use them to pry something loose or to dig, making sure not to harm aquatic life. A knife can also be a useful attention-getting tool, because it makes a good strong thunk when you knock it on your tank.

WHAT TO LOOK FOR Look for a stainless steel knife. Some knives have both a cutting edge and a serrating edge. The knife should come with a sheath that can be conveniently worn on your leg, arm, or weight belt. Check local regulations. In some places, diving knives are prohibited; less frequently, they may be required or you may need a permit to carry them. Like other gear, knives will last longer if they are rinsed in fresh water after every use.

be especially designed for diving, which means that they are not only waterproof, but also usable at depth. O-ring seals keep out water; they should be checked frequently. Rinse out lights after use and take out the batteries before storing them to prevent corrosion. Lights should be worn with wrist straps so they are easily retrievable if you drop them. Some divers use a headlamp; others use a handheld light. At night or in a cave, you'll also need a backup in case the bulb burns out or the battery goes dead.

Knives

WHY? First things first: Diving knives are not defensive weapons; they are tools. Knives are useful for

Surface Float

WHY? Surface floats can be used to mark a dive site, for resting, or for temporarily storing equipment. WHAT TO LOOK FOR Surface floats can be small rafts, inner tubes, or other flotation devices. You can either anchor the float (in

The latest in diver convenience is the underwater diver propulsion unit, or "scooter" for short. It allows you to quickly cover ground to get to the best dive sites on less air.

which case you'll need a rope and anchor) or tow it behind you, using a retractable reel.

Slates and Tables

WHY? Hand signals are fine, but for precise communication you can't beat an underwater slate. You can use a slate to make notes regarding a planned dive, especially if it has a complicated dive profile. You can also use it to take notes or make sketches of something you saw that you want to look up.

You'll also want to take down your dive tables (available on waterproof slates) so you can calculate the corrective action to take if you accidentally exceed planned maximum depth and/or time (see Chapter 5).

WHAT TO LOOK FOR Make sure the pencil is tied on so it doesn't get lost, and check to be sure the slate fits easily in your BC pockets when not in use. (Some slates can be strapped onto your wrist or fit on instrument consoles. A new type of slate not only straps around your wrist but is also wrist shaped, so it stays out of your way.) Whichever you choose, don't let the slate dangle around — like any other loose piece of equipment, it will only get in your way and it could pose an entanglement hazard.

Note: You can buy underwater slates that have frequently-seen corals and fish pictured on them, letting you make an immediate, reliable ID.

Collecting Bag

WHY? If you're interested in bringing something up to the surface, you'll want a way to carry it. Having your hands full of shells can make it impossible to operate your equipment.

WHAT TO LOOK FOR Pretty much any collecting bag (also called a *goody bag*) sold in a dive shop will fit the bill. All you need to consider is how big you want it to be. A typical model will be made of mesh so it drains water, and will have some

TO RENT OR BUY?

Once you get hooked, diving involves plane tickets and gear. And let's face it: Air travel plus a ton of heavy stuff is a pretty rotten combination.

Not to mention the cost. You know that personal fit and comfort is important. You want the right gear. But do you have to buy all of it? And travel with it, too?

Relax. All SCUBA gear can be rented. You won't necessarily get the best stuff in the best condition, or the right fit, but you won't have to sit out a chance to dive simply because you didn't bring your gear.

EQUIPMENT	CONSIDERATIONS	TRAVEL INCONVENIENCE	EXPENSE	RENT OR BUY?
Mask	Fit is critical, but it's easy to rent one that fits at a shop.	Slight	$20–$150	Buy.
Snorkel	Easy to fit at a shop, but do you really want to rent one?	Slight	$17–$50	Buy.
Fins	Unless you have an unusual foot size, it's easy to find fins that fit at a shop. Won't necessarily be the most efficient model for you.	Medium	$30–$150	Buy.

sort of easy-to-operate closure to ensure that whatever you put in it doesn't fall out. Please follow minimum impact guidelines when deciding whether to bring something to the surface. This goes for living organisms as well as artifacts from a wreck. Be aware that a full collecting bag can act as an extra weight, in which case it should be, like all your weights, easy to get rid of in an emergency. Carry a heavy bag in one hand; don't tie it to your equipment.

Emergency Signaling Devices

WHY? Signaling devices should be part of your contingency plan for when things don't go exactly as planned. Currents can be stronger

EQUIPMENT	CONSIDERATIONS	TRAVEL INCONVENIENCE	EXPENSE	RENT OR BUY?
Regulator	Fit and comfort is critical. Performance is desirable.	Medium High	$150 – $500	Buy when you can afford the one you want.
Exposure Suit	Good fit minimizes water leakage and keeps you warmer. Neoprene will mold itself to your shape over time.	Medium	Varies according to type	Buy.
BC	Good fit is important for comfort. Easy to rent well-fitting BCs if you have a normal body size and shape.	Medium	$150–$500	Buy when you buy the regulator.
Weights	Unless you use a weight-integrated system, any old weights will usually do.	Very heavy	$1.70 a pound	Rent—and even if you do buy them, don't travel with them.
Tank	Fit not critical.	Bulky and heavy	$100–$400	Ditto.

than anticipated, and sometimes you don't come up where you planned to. Or your buddy might run out of air and need to surface away from the planned exit site. Or a fog could roll in while you're down below — and when you come up, you can't see the boat, and the boat crew can't see you. Or you might need to call for help — fast.

WHAT TO LOOK FOR A whistle blast carries much farther than a shout, and with less expenditure of energy. Your BC may come with a whistle; if not, get a good, solid, water-resistant police whistle. Flares, dye markers, flashlights, inflatable signal tubes (called *sausages*), and emergency strobes come in small sizes that fit in a pocket.

G E T T I N G
I N T O   T H E
W A T E R

Okay, it's finally time to put the gear together, put it on, and get wet! But first, there's just one more thing.

PRE-DIVE SAFETY CHECK

Most sports don't require anything as formal as a step-by-step safety check. In backpacking, for example, you tick off items on a gear list and pack your stuff. When you find out that you forgot something (say your pot holder), you try to make do (maybe by using an old sock to lift your pots from the fire). In bicycling, you give your bike regular maintenance and repairs and figure that it's ready to go when you are. But SCUBA diving is different: There's a lot of equipment, and this equipment supports life. You can't "make do" if you forget something. So diving, like flying a plane, requires a more systematic checkup. That's where your buddy comes in.

Chapter 7 discusses the buddy system in detail. For now, it's enough to know two things: Before the dive, you and your buddy will help each other ensure that all of your gear is ready to go. Once beneath the surface, you'll keep an eye on each other and let the dive master or instructor know if anything seems to be going wrong. Once you're certified, however, you and your buddy can dive on

SCUBA divers—their wet suits pulled down to their waists—relax as they are taken to their next dive site at Castaway Island Resort, Castaway Island, Fiji.

your own. This is when you become responsible for each other's safety, and sometimes, for each other's lives.

During the pre-dive safety check, you and your buddy will make sure you are familiar with each other's gear. (Where is the alternate second stage? What kind of weight system is he using and how does it release?) You'll also check that everything is in working order. (Air turned on? BCs and regs working?)

Different agencies teach students different procedures for remembering all the things you're supposed to review. PADI (The Professional Association of Diving Instructors) teaches students the somewhat strained

mnemonic "Begin With Review And Friend," to remind divers to check their BCs, weights, releases, and air supply, and to give a final okay when both divers are ready to go. The YMCA teaches a safety check that proceeds in orderly fashion from head to toe. You might want to concoct your own mnemonic, or keep a list, or develop a regular procedure. Regardless of how you remember, these are the things you need to remember:

BC Is it about three-quarters inflated? Are all the hoses connected? Does the BC inflate and deflate properly? Check the straps on your buddy's tank and have her check yours. Are they fastened tightly enough to hold the tank in place?

WEIGHTS Do you have the right number of weights on? Is your weight system affixed properly? If you're wearing a belt, is the quick-release buckle on the right side and easily accessible in an emergency?

RELEASES Are all your other releases securely buckled and adjusted? Give them a yank to make sure.

AIR Is the air on? Check the on-off knob of the air valve to make sure it's in the ON position. Then double-check by looking at the gauge to see if the needle indicates a full tank. If you breathe or depress the purge button and the needle drops, the air is only partially on. Open it fully.

Note: When turning on the air, holding the SPG away from you and anyone in the vicinity reduces the risk of injury in the unlikely event that the face blows off.

REGULATORS Are both the primary and the alternate air sources working? Press the purge button on each to be sure they are working and check the SPG at the same time. If the needle takes a dip when you purge the regulator, the air's not on. Breathe through each regulator in front of your buddy.

MASK Is it on properly, and is all your hair pulled back, away from the seal? Did you defog the mask?

SNORKEL Is it attached on the left side?

ACCESSORIES Watch, slate, knife, dive computer, compass, light: Did you remember the accessories you need and routinely use?

ENTRANCES

Splash, slide, or stride. There are several different ways to get into the water. Which one you choose will depend on the conditions and the dive site.

In general, the best entry is the most gentle entry — think transition, not collision. You want to use the entry that gets you into the water with the least possible jarring and jolting so that you minimize the chance of knocking your gear out of place or crashing into another diver. In all entries, your BC should be about three-quarters inflated — enough to keep you on the surface in choppy conditions, not so much that it will restrict your movement.

SHORE ENTRY In calm water, all you have to do is walk in until you're in water deep enough to swim in — about waist-high. Then put on your fins and swim out to your dive site. The only catch here is the surface underfoot. If it's rocky or infested with sea urchins, you'll prefer wearing booties to walking in bare feet.

ROUGH-WATER SHORE ENTRY Put on your fins while on shore and walk backward so you don't trip on them. (However, if the entry area is very rocky, don't put on your fins until you get beyond the rocks.) Also, breathe through your regulator so that if you are knocked down, you can continue

Giant stride entry, from top: Hold your mask and regulator in place, tuck your hoses and gauges between your sides and your arms, look forward—not down—and take a big step forward.

to breathe. Once you reach calmer water, you'll switch to your snorkel to save air on the swim out to the dive site. If waves are breaking, you'll want to pay attention to how and where they break so you can prepare for the impact by stopping, holding onto your mask and regulator, and leaning into the wave.

CONTROLLED SEATED ENTRY This entry is for deeper water. Sometimes called the *slither entry*, this method is simply a matter of sliding into the water. To practice, sit on the edge of a pool. Next, put both hands on the edge of the pool on one side or the other of your body. Now all you do is transfer your weight to your hands while turning so that you face the pool platform, and lower yourself into the water.

GIANT STRIDE This useful deep-water entry can get you into the water from a dock or a boat, even if the distance from the platform to the water is several feet. To perform this entry, put on your mask and regulator and hold them in place with your right hand. Tuck in your right elbow and hold it with your left hand; then tuck in that elbow, too. This position keeps your hoses, gauges, and alternate air source from flying all over the place when you hit the water. Stand as far out on the platform as you can — the front of your fins should be hanging over the edge of the boat or platform. Check the area to be sure it's clear of obstructions and other divers. Then, look forward, not down, and take a big step forward. When your feet hit the water, bring them together. The scissoring action will keep you closer to the surface.

BACKWARD ROLL The backward roll appears difficult — until you try it. After that, it might well become your favorite entry, especially if the sea is rough and the boat is rocking and the giant stride just takes too much balance and coordination. Simply sit on the side of the boat, with your bottom hanging over the water as far as possible. The arm position will be the same as for the giant stride: elbows tucked in, one hand holding your mask and reg in place. Don't worry about hurting your back when you fall in the water — the tank will absorb the shock and you won't even feel it. All you have to do is lean back and bring your feet up toward your head. Once you're in the water, let yourself roll around until you pop to the surface. Give the "okay" sign to the folks on the boat and move out of the entry area.

GROUP ENTRY When diving with a group, you might enter one diver at a time or all together. If you are entering one at a time, make sure that the diver before you has cleared the entry area before you take your turn. Once you're in the water, give the "surface okay" signal (see pages 142–143) and clear the area immediately. A simultaneous group entry should be performed on a count of three. If you pause and miss the

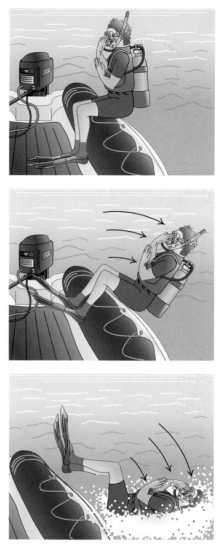

Backward roll entry, from top: Sit on the side of the boat; hold your mask and regulator in place, tucking hoses and gauges between your sides and arms; now lean back and bring your feet up toward your head; relax. When the sea is rough, it's the safest way to enter the water.

count, wait until everyone in the water has signaled that they're okay, then wait until they have moved out of the area before entering.

SURFACE SWIMMING

Once you're in the water, you may have to swim from your entry point to the dive site. Surface swimming in full SCUBA gear uses a lot of energy and, therefore, a lot of air. To avoid wasting the air in your tank, use your snorkel instead.

Coping with Surface Conditions

If you haven't done much previous open-water swimming, the first thing you'll notice is that the conditions are a lot different than they are in a pool. You might not be able to see very well because of high waves and surface chop. There could be a strong current that makes it hard to get where you are trying to go. You can do several things to conserve energy while swimming at the surface. First, keep your BC about 50 percent filled with air when swimming. This amount of air is

■

TROUBLE-SHOOTING

REGULATOR FREE FLOW

Sometimes when you hit the water hard (as you often do in the giant stride and the backward roll), you'll see a furious bubbling and hear a loud hissing. That noise is the sound of the air in your tank free-flowing out of one of your second stages. Usually the free flow will be coming from your alternate air source, which can get knocked out of place during a rough entry. Free flow can also occur if your regulator is knocked away from your mouth and ends up in an upside-down, mouthpiece-facing-up position.

There are two ways to stop the free flow:

❶ On the surface, turn the regulator so that the mouthpiece is facing down (that means bright side up) and place it in the water.

❷ Underwater, turn the regulator so it is in the correct position with the mouthpiece facing down.

When you are on the bottom it is extremely rare for regulators to free-flow — but it is possible. Additionally, regulators are designed so that if there is a breakdown, they will automatically default to a free flow. Free-flowing air rushes out so fast that you can't keep the regulator in your mouth. But it is possible for a diver to breathe from a stream of free-flowing air by taking the regulator out of her mouth, holding it near her lips, and breathing from the stream of fast-flowing air. (You may practice this in training.) Of course, you'll need to signal your buddy and ascend immediately.

enough to help keep you afloat, but it won't make your BC so cumbersome and restrictive that it impedes your mobility. Second, if you've got to swim somewhere, pace yourself by moving at a comfortable, sustainable rate. Third, assume a streamlined position, keeping your legs fairly straight and your fins underwater. Concentrate on making the downward kick the strong part of the kick cycle. And finally, look up every once in a while to check where you are.

If you get tired swimming on the surface, deflate your BC slightly so that you are swimming just beneath the surface. This reduces the weight of your tank.

Even an Olympic swimmer can have quite a time of trying to get anywhere while wearing full SCUBA gear. If you get tired, try deflating your BC and swimming just beneath the surface, rather than on top of it, with your snorkel just barely clearing the water's surface. This will reduce the weight of your tank.

Note: This technique is impossible to perform in any kind of choppy water because your snorkel will flood.

regulator. You don't even have to raise your head out of the water. Prepare for the change by taking a big breath of air. When you put the regulator in your mouth, make sure that it is in the correct upright position and breathe out a short, sharp breath. One blast is usually all it takes to get water out of a mouthpiece.

You can also clear the regulator by pushing the purge valve. Put the regulator into your mouth and block the mouthpiece with your tongue (so that you don't accidentally breathe in any stray water). Then push the purge button. The air from your tank will force any water in the regulator out through the exhaust valve.

The best position for descents is feetfirst, letting you pay attention to your depth and rate of descent.

If you use this method, breathe carefully so you don't swallow water.

Most divers, however, prefer swimming on their backs in choppy conditions. Basically, this means kicking on your back — your arms don't do any work. The advantage is that your BC holds you out of the water; also, most BCs are designed to keep you face up. End result: You go faster with less effort.

Snorkel-to-Regulator Exchange

Once you get to the dive site, you must switch from the snorkel to the

DESCENDING

First things first: Don't descend before you're ready. During your entry, you might have knocked a piece of gear out of place, or you might be fumbling to find your SPG, which is dangling somewhere behind your back. Stop, slow down, get yourself and your equipment reorganized (it usually takes just a few seconds to restore order). Do a final once-over check with your buddy to make sure everything is in place. Then signal that you're ready to go down. Check the time.

Note: *Bottom time* starts when you *begin* your descent, not when you reach the bottom, because you start taking on nitrogen as soon as you start going down.

Position

The best position for SCUBA descents is feetfirst. First of all, you have to be pretty much in a vertical position to let air out of your BC. (Air rises because it's lighter than water; this is also why you hold the BC inflator hose in an upright position when you want to let air out.) Second, a feetfirst descent lets you pay attention to the

EQUALIZING YOUR EARS

The Appendix describes several gas laws that affect how you feel and how your equipment works underwater. In brief, as you descend, pressure increases on the dead air spaces in your body, especially the ears and sinuses. It also increases in the dead air space in your mask. This is because the air is being compressed. To equalize the air space, you need to add more air to these areas.

The sign that you need to equalize your ears is unmistakable. There will be a feeling of building pressure, and if you don't equalize, pressure can very quickly turn to pain. The solution is a technique called the *Valsalva maneuver.*

To equalize, pinch your nose shut and try to gently try to exhale through it. The air you're trying to exhale will be blocked by your pinched nose, so it will end up in the dead air space in your ears, which equalizes the pressure. Swallowing also helps. Some people find that wiggling the jaw while swallowing is effective in stubborn

cases. You can even try all three techniques at once — a variation on rubbing your stomach while patting your head. Most divers continually equalize their ears as pressure changes during a dive. Sooner or later, it becomes second nature.

If you can't equalize, don't force it. Signal to your buddy and the dive master that you have a problem with your ears, rise up a couple of feet (until the pressure lessens), wait a few moments, then try again. Most people can equalize if they take it slowly enough. If you're on a group dive, the group may continue to descend at the normal pace. (This contingency should be covered in the dive briefing.) You and your buddy can keep track of the group by swimming above them or following the reference line, if there is one. Then you can descend at your own pace. If you can't equalize your ears, you'll have to abort the dive.

To equalize the air space in your mask, simply blow out through your nose.

things that need your attention: where you are, where your buddy is, whether your ears are equalizing properly, and how deep and how fast you are dropping.

How to Descend

To start sinking, exhale and slowly let air out of your BC by pushing the manual deflator button and holding the BC inflator hose up with your left hand. If you are weighted properly, you should start to sink. If you're not sinking, all the air is out of your BC, and you think you are properly weighted, try doing a surface dive to get underwater. Sometimes the problem is that there is a lot of air to compress, for instance, in a very buoyant wet suit. Often, just going a few feet below the surface will do the trick.

If you still can't get down, you might need more weight. You can't continue the dive if you don't have enough weight to descend — not only will you have difficulty sinking, but even if you do manage to get down, you might uncontrollably pop to the surface at the end of your dive, putting yourself at risk of decompression sickness. Nor should you grab an extra weight from the boat and go down clutching it in your hand. You need your hands to operate your equipment, and if you do drop the weight, you could, again, ascend too quickly.

If you start going down like a stone, you're too heavily weighted. If you are overweighted, you can continue the dive by adding some air to your BC so you can control the rate of descent. But remember to recalculate how many weights you really need before the next dive. Being overly weighted makes you work a lot harder than necessary because you have to carry the extra weight. You also have to deal

TROUBLE - SHOOTING

EQUALIZING

● Don't wait until your ears hurt. Start equalizing the moment you begin your descent. This prevents the painful buildup of pressure and keeps little problems from turning into big ones.

● Do not force it! Several slow, gentle attempts are better than one forced attempt, which can damage your ears.

● Never go deeper if you continue to experience pain. Stop or rise a little, wait until the pain stops, then try again.

● If you cannot equalize, you have to end the dive. (See page 83.)

with a BC that has more air in it (to compensate for the weight) and therefore is less stream-lined.

Rate

The rate of descent should be slow. Only a few feet below the surface, you will feel pressure building up in your ears. When you do, you must equalize them. To do that, you might need to slow or stop your descent. A slow descent also ensures that you won't ignominiously crash into the seafloor and stir up the sediment. Instead, as you near the bottom, slow your descent by adding little incre-ments of air to your BC: Your goal is neutral buoyancy.

A diver descends down an anchor line. Using a reference line for descents (and ascents) helps you pace yourself and provides a meeting point for you and your buddy.

Using a Reference Line

A reference line can help you mon-itor your pace during descents (and ascents, too). It can also act as a meeting point for you and your buddy if you become disoriented and lose track of each other.

BREATHING

The discovery that you really can breathe underwater initially seems miraculous. Soon enough, though, breathing underwater feels almost natural. But that's an illusion: There's nothing natural about all the equipment that lets you breathe. When breathing underwater, you'll need to think about and remember some key points.

Air Consumption

Low air consumption is a bit of a status thing among divers. While beginners are sucking air, the old pros seem to be able to stay down for another hour while the needle on their tank gauge moves nary a notch.

Air consumption is a function of how relaxed you are, how effi-ciently you move underwater, and your physiology. Men, for instance, often have bigger lungs than women and use considerably more air.

Same goes for big people. Some factors, like your lung size, you can't change. But over time you'll become more relaxed and efficient, and you will probably find that with experience you use less and less air.

It is important to be aware of how much air you have in your tank and how much air you tend to use. Formulas and some computers can help measure air-consumption rates, but there's no substitute for paying attention to your exertion, the currents, and your consumption during a dive. It's also important to check up on your buddy's air supply so that neither one of you will be surprised by an empty tank.

Air in your tank is measured in pounds per square inch (psi). (If you're diving abroad, you may use a metric-style gauge that measures pressure in *bars*. Don't worry: They're measuring the same thing, and in

THE PRIMARY RULE OF SCUBA DIVING

Breathe continuously and never hold your breath.

Review the gas laws in Appendix I. The compressed air you breathe at depth is denser than air at the surface. If you were to hold your breath and rise to the surface, the air in your lungs would expand. It could expand enough to cause serious lung damage. Lung overexpansion injuries are the most serious potential injuries in diving. Fortunately, they're almost completely preventable. All you have to do is continue breathing.

Some people tend to hold their breath for a few seconds when they are concentrating on something, or when they are scared or worried. Similarly, some beginning divers hold their breath, either because they are tense or because they haven't fully realized that, yes, you can indeed breathe down there. But these habits have to be broken — and quickly. Get into the habit of always breathing, even if the regulator is temporarily out of your mouth. For example, if the regulator has been knocked out of your mouth, be sure that you are exhaling while you are retrieving it. You should see a small, steady stream of bubbles coming out of your mouth.

A standard procedure that will keep you breathing: Always make an "ahhhh" sound whenever your regulator is out of your mouth. It is impossible to make this sound without exhaling — and exhaling will keep you from holding your breath.

"Never dive alone" is a cardinal rule of safe diving. You and your buddy will help each other with pre-dive safety checks; once below, you'll keep a constant eye on each other.

both cases, the low-on-air part of the gauge will be marked in red.) Regardless of the SPG you use, it's time to come up well before the needle gets to the red marker (500 psi or 50 bars). This amount of air is enough to get you slowly to the surface, take a safety stop, inflate your BC at the surface, and have air left over in case something goes wrong.

To be safe, always follow the thirds rule: use one third of your air

■

TECHNIQUE TIP
DEFLATING YOUR BC

Air is lighter than water, so air rises. Air cannot be released from your BC unless it can rise and pass through an outlet. If you find that you need to release air from your BC, get into a vertical position and hold up the inflator hose. This allows the air in the BC to rise and pass through the hose. You can also use the so-called *dump valve*, a backup feature that allows you to get rid of all the air in your BC at once. If you're using a rental BC, be sure you know how to operate the dump valve.

RETRIEVING YOUR REGULATOR

It's easy to lose a regulator. It can get knocked out of place by a careless buddy's fin, or if the hose gets entangled in kelp, or if you bump into someone on a night dive. If your regulator is dangling somewhere behind your hip, you might not see it. But there are two ways to find it and retrieve it, and they are so easy, you'll barely miss a breath. (Remember to breathe out, making the "ahhhh" sound, while performing this exercise.)

❶ The *arm-sweep method* is the easiest: Reach back with your right hand until you touch the bottom of your tank, then sweep your right arm forward until you feel the regulator hose. Slide your hand down the hose and put the regulator back in your mouth.

❷ The *reach method* involves reaching back over your shoulder to find the hose where it connects to the regulator's first stage, at the top of the tank. You might find it easier to reach the top of the tank with your right hand if you simultaneously push on the tank bottom with your left hand. Whichever method you use, when you put the reg back in your mouth,

it will be full of water. Now all you have to do is clear it by blowing one sharp breath into it — or by pushing the purge button.

Arm-sweep method   **Reach method**

for your descent and bottom time, one third for your ascent, and have one third to spare.

Learning to Breathe

So what can you do to breathe more efficiently?

Slow, deep breaths are more efficient than fast, shallow breaths. Each time you breathe, the first part of your breath takes in air that was left over from the last time you

The ideal position for swimming underwater is horizontal (above), using your legs for propulsion. Avoid using your arms and/or moving into an inefficient diagonal position (below).

splash guard (place your tongue against the roof of your mouth) and breathing especially deliberately and carefully. If you do inhale water, hold the regulator to your mouth and cough into it. You can also swallow a mouthful of seawater — a little won't hurt you, and swallowing water will reduce the chance of choking on it.

exhaled. This air is low on oxygen because it has already been used. But it stays around in your mouth, throat, and windpipe, as well as in artificial spaces like the regulator or snorkel. These are called *dead air spaces*. By breathing deeply, you'll take in more fresh air, which has more oxygen. So pay attention to your breathing, by inhaling deeply, slowly, and regularly as in yoga or meditation.

Airway Control

Good airway control is a habit that will prevent you from swallowing the occasional mouthful of seawater that sometimes sneaks into a regulator. Airway control consists of breathing slowly and deliberately. If you feel water in your regulator, or if you notice a slight gurgling as you breathe in, you can breathe past the water by using your tongue as a

MOVING UNDERWATER

Look at marine animals. It doesn't matter whether they are mammals, amphibians, reptiles, or fish: Animals that live in or spend part of their time in oceans, rivers, and lakes develop a streamlined shape that helps them get through the dense medium of water without having to work too hard. Copying them will make you a more efficient swimmer, which means you'll also become a more efficient breather.

The ideal streamlined position is horizontal. You want to minimize your resistance as you travel through the water; a streamlined swimmer has to push her way through less water than a swimmer who is not streamlined.

Unlike swimmers at the surface, who use both arms and legs to go from here to there, divers underwater primarily use their legs — their arms and hands being otherwise occupied with gauges and gadgets. The basic kick for a diver is similar to the "flutter" kick used in swimming at the surface. It differs in two ways: With fins on, the *kick cycle* (how long it takes to kick both legs) is much slower, and the SCUBA diver uses more of the whole leg to power her kicks, so the kick is bigger. Try to keep your legs fairly straight as you kick. One of the most common ways to waste energy is to bend your knees too much and kick in a motion that almost resembles bicycling.

Slow, deliberate movements are more efficient. Abrupt, jerky move- ments waste energy and can lead to overexertion. A common cause of overexertion is swimming against a strong current. If you start to feel fatigued, out of breath, or anxious, your first line of defense is to STOP and rest. If possible, hold onto something for support. And, of course, let your buddy know what's going on by means of hand signals or a slate.

BUOYANCY CONTROL

Buoyancy control is perhaps the most important skill divers develop. You can always spot the experi- enced diver in a group, and it's not because of his cool-looking wet suit. He's the one seemingly hov-

---

PRACTICING BUOYANCY CONTROL

This exercise will help you get the hang of how a lungful of air affects your buoyancy.

Once under- water, lie on the bottom. Then add a little air into your BC so that you are neutrally buoyant. Now breathe in deeply. You'll find that your torso floats upward while your fins stay in place. Exhale, and your torso will sink back down.

ering still in the water, floating in place with his arms leisurely crossed, while the rest of the group is bouncing up and down like a bunch of rubber balls.

Buoyancy control is simple to define but more difficult to achieve. Ideally, you should perform your dive in a neutrally buoyant state, and then be slightly positively buoyant when you ascend at the end of your dive. But that takes practice.

Buoyancy control looks elegant, but it's good for more than bragging rights. It keeps you from crashing into things. It helps you use less air because you use less energy trying to compensate for your lack of control. It avoids stirring up the bottom (which interferes with everyone's visibility) or accidentally brushing against a fire coral or stonefish. And most important, with good buoyancy control, you won't bob to the surface like a cork — which not only marks you as a beginner, but also puts you at risk for decompression sickness.

There are a couple of ways to control buoyancy:

BC CONTROLS A buoyancy compensator lets you control buoyancy by adding and subtracting small amounts of air. The more air you add, the more you float. Let air out, and the opposite happens: You sink. Note that a very small amount of air — no more than a puff or two of breath — can make a big difference in your buoyancy. Finally, notice that there is

a slight time lag between when you put air in your BC and when you start to rise (and the reverse is also true). So add and subtract air in small increments, slowly.

YOUR LUNGS You'll notice that your instructor rarely touches his BC controls. What gives? Your instructor is using the air in his lungs to control buoyancy. The more (or less) air in your lungs, the more positively (or negatively) buoyant you are. The exercise opposite will give you a feel for how air in your lungs affects your buoyancy.

PAY ATTENTION! Finally, buoyancy control requires that you pay attention. During your dive, your buoyancy will change. As you go deeper, your wet suit will compress and become less buoyant. Toward the end of the dive, your tank will be emptier, hence more buoyant. You might rise suddenly during the dive — for instance, by swimming up and over a coral head — and the change of pressure will make you more buoyant. By paying close attention to your buoyancy and making tiny, constant adjustments in your breathing, you can come close to the ideal dive: neutrally buoyant throughout, and slightly positively buoyant at the end.

ASCENDING

On a normal dive (no emergencies, no problems) it's time to ascend if one of two things happens: You've reached the time limit you planned for the

As you ascend, be especially aware of the water directly above you, keeping a sharp eye out for other divers and boat traffic on the surface.

boats. Rotate slowly as you ascend to be sure you see everything around and above you. Remember, this is important: It will keep you from crashing into kelp, other divers, and the moving propellers of a boat.

Rate of Ascent

The maximum recommended rate of ascent is *no more than* 30 feet per minute, and preferably less. Only practice will give you a sense of what the correct pace feels like. For an idea, try walking the length of a typical lap swimming pool (75 feet) at the rate of one-half of 1 foot per second. That means that it will take you 2 minutes and 30 seconds to walk from one end to the other. You may well feel like that short period of time was an eternity! Remember that feeling of slow movement when you are ascending.

Of course, you can't depend only on your memory of what the right rate feels like. You've got a depth gauge and a watch, so check them every couple of seconds as you are

dive, or you're low on air. In the first case, the dive leader will signal "out of time" to the other divers. Once everyone has acknowledged the signal, the leader will give the "let's go up" sign, and the group will proceed together slowly to the surface, taking a safety stop if necessary or recommended by the dive leader.

Once the signal has been given to ascend, check your watch so you can time your ascent rate.

Position

The position for an ascent is a vertical standing position, the same as for skin divers. Look up and reach up with one hand. This keeps you from bumping into other divers and (at the surface) ascending. You can also use a reference line to help control and monitor your ascent. Some computers have an ascent rate alarm that goes off if you ascend too quickly.

Controlling Your Ascent

The best way to start your ascent is to empty your BC a little. Sounds counterintuitive, right? After all, you want to go up, and more air in your BC will get you there.

The problem with this logic is that it doesn't take into account the fact that the pressure drops as you rise, so the air in your BC expands. Plus, your tank is emptier than it was at the start of your dive, so it's more buoyant, too. All of this means that as you rise you become more buoyant than you might expect. So yes, you want to go up, but not too fast. That puts you at risk for decompression sickness. So be cautious at the start of your ascent. It's better to have to kick a little to work your way to the surface than to lose control and surface too quickly.

A reference line can help you control your ascent, and it can also help keep you in place during a safety stop. Remember to recheck your buoyancy when you take a safety stop, and keep an eye on your gauges. Again, you are more buoyant during the safety stop than you were at the beginning of your ascent because the air in your BC has expanded and your tank might

GROUND RULES FOR SAFE DIVING

There's a lot to know in SCUBA diving, and the learning never ends. The following ground rules are good ones to keep in mind, no matter where you dive, or under what conditions.

● Always check your equipment and keep it in good repair.

● Do a pre-dive safety check before *every* dive.

● Never dive alone.

● Follow the SCUBA planning motto: "Plan your dive and dive your plan."

● Don't dive beyond your experience or with gear you haven't been trained to use.

● When underwater, always breathe continuously and never hold your breath. If the regulator is out of your mouth, make the "ahhhh" sound.

● Don't exceed the depth to which you planned to dive, and start your ascent when you planned to do so.

● If your computer tells you to come up, listen to it.

● Be on the surface by the time your SPG reaches the red "low on air" marker.

be slightly more buoyant. You might want to get rid of a little more air from your BC — and keep your eye on those gauges.

OUT OF AIR!

If you check and maintain your equipment, if you keep track of your air consumption, and if you check in with your buddy, you should never find yourself out of air. But sometimes things go wrong: An SPG gives an inaccurate reading. You get immersed in watching a sea turtle. Your buddy spaces out. And all of a sudden you take a breath — and nothing happens!

If you run out of air, the most important thing to do is stay calm. There are a number of things you can do to get to the surface safely. You'll practice these skills before being certified. Even if you never have to use them, you'll feel more confident knowing that you can.

Alternate Air Source

Some divers, especially deep divers, carry their own alternate air source, a small extra tank with a regulator attached. If you have an alternate air source, using it is your first solution to an out-of-air problem. Some of today's units are so small, they fit into a BC jacket pocket. The air supply must be double-checked each time you dive. Needless to say, if it's time to tap into your alternate air source,

it's time to signal to your buddy and start an immediate ascent. Your buddy should accompany you.

Your Buddy's Alternate Second Stage

Also called *octopus breathing*, or *air-sharing*, this is your first solution if you aren't carrying an independent second air source of your own. Your buddy is carrying an alternate second stage, and if you followed basic procedures before starting your dive, you know exactly where it is. Communicate to him that you are out of air. He should offer you an air source. If for some reason you didn't get his attention, grab his alternate second stage and start breathing. (That will undoubtedly get his attention.) Once you are breathing, you and your buddy will ascend to the surface together.

Ascending with a buddy isn't much different than ascending by yourself. To ascend with your buddy 1) You should be face-to-face, holding onto each other's forearm in a Roman handshake (see illustration, page 95).
2) Maintain eye contact and start the ascent. Each of you controls his own buoyancy; the rate of ascent is controlled by the donor.
3) Be sure to regulate the rate of ascent. It should be no more than 30 feet per minute, and you should take a safety stop if it is required or recommended for the dive you have just done.

4) Be sure that one of you is looking up during the ascent, to check for any dangers or obstructions on the surface.

Note: A panicked buddy might grab the regulator out of your mouth because he knows that the regulator you are using is working. If this happens, let him have it, and calmly switch over to your alternate air source.

To ascend breathing from your buddy's alternate second-stage regulator, or octopus, hold onto each other, face-to-face; maintain eye contact; and regulate your rate of ascent.

Buddy Breathing on a Single Air Source

This is one of those skills you shouldn't ever have to use. Think about it: For this technique to be necessary, your buddy has to have run out of air, or his regulator and alternative air source have to be malfunctioning. In addition, your alternate second stage has to be malfunctioning. For all these things to happen at the same time requires either extraordinary negligence or extraordinary bad luck.

Still, this is *breathing* we're talking about. You can't live without it, and this is why buddy breathing on a single air source is an important skill to have — if only for the confidence you acquire when you learn the skills that can keep you out of trouble no matter what. Here's the procedure:

1) Your buddy can't help if he doesn't know what's going on, so give two clear signals: that you are out of air, and need to share air.

2) The donor buddy takes a deep breath and passes the recipient buddy his primary second stage.

3) The recipient takes two deep breaths and passes the second stage back to the donor, who takes two breaths and passes it back to the recipient. Both the donor and the recipient should keep their hands on the regulator, without blocking

the purge button. However, the second stage should be under the control of the donor because the recipient may be prone to panic.
4) Once you have the rhythm of breathing down, it's time to ascend. You can position yourselves side by side or face-to-face; some divers feel that the latter position has the advantage of increasing communication with their buddy. In either position, hold onto each other's tank straps or BCs. Signal the ascent. The donor buddy takes control of the rate of ascent, which should be no more than 30 feet per minute. If a safety stop is required or recommended, take it, but remember that you are consuming air at more than twice the normal rate. Not only are two people breathing on one air source, but they also are undoubtedly breathing harder than normal because of the additional stress of an emergency maneuver.
5) During the ascent, the buddy who is not breathing through the regulator MUST be exhaling slightly by making the "ahhhh" sound while he waits for his turn to take back the second stage.

This skill requires practice, but it's not as difficult as you might think. A great way to get the hang of it is for you and your buddy to kneel on the shallow end of a swimming pool and pass a snorkel back and forth. Once you master that skill, try swimming together using only one snorkel, then practice with SCUBA.

Controlled Emergency Swimming Ascent

If you are less than 30 or 40 feet deep and your buddy is nowhere to be found, you can as a last resort perform a *controlled emergency swimming ascent*. This is almost a normal ascent, but it's performed under abnormal circumstances. As in a normal ascent, assume a vertical position in the water, looking up, with one hand raised above your head. Do not use the BC (you can't add air from an empty tank). Instead, start kicking upward, turning in a circle as you rise. Don't forget the most important rule of SCUBA: Never hold your breath. So, while keeping the regulator in your mouth, breathe out a continuous, slow stream of small bubbles as you rise, and make the "ahhhh" sound. It is *critical* that you breathe out while rising, because this is the precise situation that is most likely to cause a lung overexpansion injury.

Even though you are exhaling, you will continue to have air in your lungs because the residual air left in your lungs will expand as you rise. Also, any residual air in your tank will expand, possibly enough to give you an extra lungful as you near the surface. Try to resist your natural urge to rush. You'll get to the surface soon enough, but if you get there slowly, you'll minimize any risk of decompression sickness and lung overexpansion injury.

EXITS

Like entries, exits come in two kinds: natural environments such as beaches and rocky shorelines, and man-made environments such as boats and docks.

Natural Environments

In smooth water, beach exits are simply a matter of swimming toward shore until you run out of water. Then you sit, remove your fins, stand up, and walk out. (The hardest part is standing up with all that SCUBA gear on.)

Obstructions such as rocky shorelines can complicate the picture, especially if you have to scramble on rocks or coral (wearing dive booties with good traction helps). Where the shoreline is rocky or treacherous, you'll want to have a carefully thought-out exit plan before your dive, especially if surf is present. Strong surf can make getting into and out of the water the most adventurous part of the whole dive!

If there is surf, watch the wave pattern. Waves usually break in groups, and then there is a lull, and then there is another group. You're looking for the lull. Once you've got the hang of the wave pattern, plan your exit to hit the lull. If you are walking out, turn so that your back faces the surf. Keep your regulator in your mouth so you can continue to breathe even if you get knocked around. If the conditions are choppy, keep your mask on, but put one hand on it to prevent it from getting knocked loose. In very strong surf, you might want to swim until there's no more water and then crawl the rest of the way to shore. If you remove your fins, keep a good grip on them, because a strong wave can steal them quickly.

Man-Made Environments

These include boats, platforms, docks, and ladders. Like shore exits, boat exits can be very simple or quite a challenge, depending on the conditions.

Often the boat will have a ladder or a current line. A current line trails from the boat and shows divers which way the water is moving relative to the boat. Divers can hang onto it to keep from being swept away from the boat. Usually, you'll remove your fins and then climb up, wearing all your gear. Hang onto the boat or the current line while removing your fins, especially if there is a current; without your fins, you'll have trouble getting back to the boat if you lose contact with it.

Smaller boats may not have a ladder; in this case, you'll need to take off your equipment in the water, hand it up, and then haul yourself onto the boat.

To take off your gear in the water, first partially inflate your BC. Then remove your weight belt and hand it up. Slide off your BC and tank. This is easiest if you take it off like a jacket, one shoulder at a time,

When exiting up a ladder, remove your fins in the water and hand them up. This crew member is helping lift some of the weight of the tank.

capsize. Someone already on board can go over to the other side to counterbalance your weight. Or, as you haul yourself up, reach across the center of the boat to keep your weight as low and as evenly distributed as possible, then roll over and drop in. This move never wins any points for grace, but it gets the job done.

You may need to use your fins to help you pull yourself up and onto a boat with no ladder. If the boat is especially high, this skill takes a little practice. Ask the dive master or boat owner for tips, because each boat is a little different. Some divers — especially some women — have less upper-body strength than this task seems to demand, but getting into a boat is usually a matter of a little technique plus some help from your fins.

In any kind of deep-water exit, stay out of the way of other exiting divers. If they fall off a ladder or drop some gear, you could be seriously hurt.

Finally, and importantly, if you are anchoring a boat and diving, and no one is staying on board, make sure you can get back in! Don't forget to let down the ladder, or any other device that's necessary for you to lift yourself into the boat.

although you can also unsnap the shoulder straps and the BC will simply drop away from you. Keep a hand on it so it doesn't float away from the boat. Then hand up your tank and BC to someone on the boat. Be sure you're positioning your equipment so they can easily grab the unit.

In a very small boat, such as a rowboat or a kayak, make sure that you are counterbalancing your weight when you get in so the boat doesn't

DIVE
TABLES

This chapter is concerned with one subject: using dive tables to minimize the risk of the bends.

Appendix I discusses the science behind nitrogen absorption and decompression sickness. In summary: As a diver descends, the surrounding pressure increases. As pressure increases, nitrogen is dissolved into a diver's body tissue, much as carbon dioxide is dissolved into a can of soda. The deeper and longer you dive, the more nitrogen you absorb.

When you ascend, the reverse happens. The pressure decreases and the nitrogen can no longer stay dissolved, so it comes out of solution in the form of gas bubbles, which then off-gas, or begin to leave your body. But if you have taken on too much nitrogen and you are ascending too fast, your body cannot get rid of it quickly enough. The excess nitrogen can neither be dissolved (because the pressure is too low) nor off-gassed (because the body can get rid of only a certain amount of nitrogen at any one time), so it turns into gas bubbles in your blood and tissue, like bubbles in an open soda can. This is what causes decompression sickness — the bends (for symptoms and treatment, see Chapter 6).

The first U.S. dive tables were developed for military use by the Navy. They form the basis for many

A diver checks out her dive tables during a "surface interval," a break between two dives.

taken just to add a safety margin to your ascent. You'll also learn about *emergency decompression stops*, which are used if you accidentally exceed the no-decompression limits (see pages 110–112).

DIFFERENT AGENCIES

The dive tables you use may not be the same as the dive tables your friend uses. That's because different agencies have developed their own tables and protocols. In each case, they have tried to do the same thing: to use the U.S. Navy's dive tables and/or scientific research to establish limits that maximize a diver's bottom time while minimizing the risk of contracting the bends. But some agencies are more conservative than others, and the different dive tables reflect varying degrees of conservatism.

tables commonly used by recreational divers today, with some important differences. Military and commercial divers often dive much deeper and for longer durations than do recreational divers, so the tables they use must account for their frequent susceptibility to decompression sickness. Because of this, they must undergo a process called *decompression* on the way up. *Decompression diving* is defined as any dive that requires the diver to stop during the ascent and wait for a certain amount of time to allow nitrogen to off-gas.

All recreational diving is no-decompression diving. (You will, however, learn about *safety stops*, which, as their name indicates, are stops

This book uses the YMCA's tables, which are conservative. If you find yourself diving with a buddy or a dive master who uses another agency's tables, you may well find that a proposed dive exceeds limits you have been taught. Additionally, computer-assisted dives will frequently give you different no-decompression limits than your tables. In such cases, you'll want to consider four things before doing the dive:
1) Is the dive within your general level of training and experience?
2) If your buddy is using tables that are different than yours — let's say you've been trained by the YMCA,

and your buddy uses PADI tables — don't take his word that the dive is "okay" to do. Work the tables yourself to confirm that the dive is within PADI's no-decompression limits.

3) If you are planning multiple dives, all dives for that day must be worked out on the same agency's tables. NEVER use two different tables during one day of diving! (See pages 105–110 for how to work out a plan for doing multiple dives in one day.)

4) Are there any factors, such as currents or cold water, that would make the dive more difficult and contribute to the possibility of decompression sickness? If there are, you might want to plan your dive more conservatively.

DIVE TABLES

A dive table is actually a set of three tables. Each table gives you different pieces of information:

Each recreational dive certifying agency uses its own dive tables. When planning multiple dives, never use two different dive tables.

● Table A estimates the maximum amount of time you can spend at a certain depth, and it tells you how much nitrogen your body has in it after a given dive.

● Table B tells you how much time must elapse on the surface before you can dive again.

● Table C tells you the depth and time limits for any subsequent repetitive dives.

In general, all dive tables work the same way, but if you are using new tables, be sure to check the instructions.

A few rules always apply:

● Count conservatively! Each dive should be calculated using the deepest depth; e.g., if your dive starts at 60 feet and stays there for only 5 minutes, then goes to 50 feet and stays there for 5 minutes, then goes to 30 feet and stays there for 15 minutes, the entire 25-minute dive is calculated as if you spend all of your time at 60 feet.

● If the table doesn't have the exact

YSCUBA™
Sport Diving Table

READ BEFORE PLANNING A DIVE

YMCA SCUBA Sport Diving Tables are designed to enhance diver safety and assist in dive planning. The Sport Diving Tables should be used only by persons properly trained in their use. YMCA SCUBA Sport Diving Tables provide a conservative safety margin to help avoid decompression sickness. Use of these Sport Diving Tables is not guaranteed to eliminate the possibility of decompression sickness. To gain the greatest conservative margin from these tables, divers must carefully plan their dives in accordance with the No Decompression Stop Limits and ascend no faster than 30 feet per minute with appropriate safety stops. Do not exceed the No Decompression Stop Limits. Do not dive deeper than 100 feet. Do not use this table for high altitude diving without calculating an adjustment for high altitude. Susceptibility to decompression sickness varies in accordance with a diver's physical wellness and readiness, environmental conditions, ascent rates, and many other situations or conditions.

© 1997, YMCA SCUBA PROGRAM   SDT971.2

STAY THERE

Table A — TOTAL BOTTOM TIME (TBT) IN MINUTES

No Decompression Stop Limits

DEPTH Meters	FEET															
4.5	15	▼	35	70	110	160	225	350							
6	20		25	50	75	100	135	180	240	325					
7.5	25		20	35	55	75	100	125	160	195	245	315			
9	30		15	30	45	60	75	95	120	145	170	205	250	310	
10.5	35	220	5	15	25	40	50	60	80	100	120	140	160	190	220
12	40	150	5	15	25	30	40	50	70	80	100	110	130	150	
15	50	80		10	15	25	30	40	50	60	70	80			
18	60	50		10	15	20	25	30	40	50					
21	70	40		5	10	15	20	30	35	40					
24	80	30		5	10	15	20	25	30						
27	90	20		5	10	12	15	20							
30	100	18		5	7	10	18								
33	110	13			5	10	13								
36	120	10			5	10									
39	130	5			5										

Repetitive Group designation → A B C D E F G H I J K L M

Repetitive dive depth in feet/meters.

Table C — RESIDUAL NITROGEN TIME (RNT) IN MINUTES

	40/12	50/15	60/18	70/21	80/24	90/27	100/30	110/33	120/36	130/39
A	7/143	6/74	5/45	4/36	4/26	3/17	3/15	3/10	3/7	3/2
B	17/133	13/67	11/39	9/31	8/22	7/13	7/11	6/7	6/4	6
C	25/125	21/59	17/33	15/25	13/17	11/9	10/8	10/3	9	8
D	37/113	29/51	24/26	20/20	18/12	16/4	14/4	13	12	11
E	49/101	38/42	30/20	26/14	23/7	20	18	16	15	13
F	61/89	47/33	36/14	31/9	28/2	25	22	20	18	16
G	73/77	56/24	44/6	37/3	32	29	26	24	21	19
H	87/63	66/14	52	43	38	33	30	27	25	22
I	101/49	76/4	61	50	43	38	34	31	28	25
J	116/34	87	70	57	48	43	38	34	32	28
K	138/12	99	79	64	54	47	43	38	35	31
L	161	111	88	72	61	53	48	42	39	35
M	187	124	97	80	68	58	52	47	43	38

Note: For repetitive dives less than 40 feet, use the values for 40 feet.

37 — Minutes of residual nitrogen (RNT) added to actual bottom time to compute TOTAL BOTTOM TIME.

113 — Calculated maximum ACTUAL BOTTOM TIME in minutes. If this number is exceeded, a decompression stop is required.

Table B — SURFACE INTERVAL TIME (SIT) IN HOURS AND MINUTES (hh:mm)

Maximum time for this interval. (top)
Minimum time for this interval. (bottom)

Start Group	A	B	C	D	E	F	G	H	I	J	K	L	M
A	12:00/0:10	12:00/3:21	12:00/4:50	12:00/5:49	12:00/6:35	12:00/7:06	12:00/7:36	12:00/8:00	12:00/8:22	12:00/8:51	12:00/8:59	12:00/9:13	12:00/9:29
B		3:20/0:10	4:49/1:40	5:48/2:39	6:34/3:25	7:05/3:58	7:35/4:26	7:59/4:50	8:21/5:13	8:50/5:41	8:58/5:49	9:12/6:03	9:28/6:19
C			1:39/0:10	2:38/1:10	3:24/1:58	3:57/2:29	4:25/2:59	4:49/3:21	5:12/3:44	5:40/4:03	5:48/4:20	6:02/4:36	6:18/4:50
D				1:09/0:10	1:57/0:55	2:28/1:30	2:58/2:00	3:20/2:24	3:43/2:45	4:02/3:05	4:19/3:22	4:35/3:37	4:49/3:53
E					0:54/0:10	1:29/0:46	1:59/1:16	2:23/1:42	2:44/2:03	3:04/2:21	3:21/2:39	3:36/2:54	3:52/3:09
F						0:45/0:10	1:15/0:41	1:41/1:07	2:02/1:30	2:20/1:48	2:38/2:04	2:53/2:20	3:08/2:35
G							0:40/0:10	1:06/0:37	1:29/1:00	1:47/1:20	2:03/1:36	2:19/1:50	2:34/2:06
H								0:36/0:10	0:59/0:34	1:19/0:55	1:35/1:12	1:49/1:26	2:05/1:40
I									0:33/0:10	0:54/0:32	1:11/0:50	1:25/1:05	1:39/1:19
J										0:31/0:10	0:49/0:29	1:04/0:46	1:18/1:00
K											0:28/0:10	0:45/0:27	0:59/0:43
L												0:26/0:10	0:42/0:25
M													0:25/0:10

NEW Repetitive GROUP

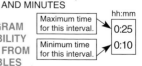

THE YMCA SCUBA PROGRAM ACCEPTS NO RESPONSIBILITY FOR ACCIDENTS ARISING FROM THE USE OF THESE TABLES

time or depth of your dive, use the *next greater* time or depth. In cold water or arduous conditions, count the dive as being deeper than it actually is when calculating bottom time. Adding 10 feet is a good rule of thumb to start with. In very arduous conditions, you might want to add more for an extra margin of safety.

● Don't push the limits. People differ in their susceptibility to decompression sickness. Even using the dive tables perfectly is not a guarantee that you won't get bent! Also, some people are more disposed to decompression sickness than others. Predisposing factors include fatigue, dehydration, exhaustion, cold, old age, illness, injuries, alcohol, and being overweight — but you could just have a bad day. If you avoid the maximum limits, you help compensate for any predisposing factors.

● Standard dive tables can be used only at elevations of less than 1,000 feet above sea level. If you are diving in a pond, river, or lake above sea level, you need to follow special procedures and calculate adjustments to compensate for differences in atmospheric pressure above sea level. (These calculations are beyond the scope of this book. If you plan to dive at altitudes above 1,000 feet, you should take a specialty course.)

● Dive your deepest dive first. This allows you to maximize your bottom

A dive table is actually a set of three tables, each of which gives you vital information.

time, because nitrogen accumulated during the first, deeper dive can be partially off-gassed during a less deep second dive.

● Ascents should be slow and controlled. The YMCA recommends that ascents never exceed 30 feet per minute; some other agencies limit the rate of ascent to 60 feet per minute.

● Novice open-water divers should limit dives to less than 60 feet. Divers with advanced training can dive to depths of 100 feet, and as they gain more experience and training, they can dive to the no-decompression limit of 130 feet. (Some agencies include dives of 140 feet on their tables as an absolute maximum emergency limit.)

● No matter what your training, limit repeat dives to 100 feet or shallower. (Because of the amount of nitrogen you absorb on deep dives, it is difficult to do more than one 100-foot dive in a day. If you try to do two 100-foot dives in a day, you'll have to stay up on the surface for a long interval between them, especially if you want the dives to last more than a few minutes.)

● Dive within your training and experience.

● Do not try to outsmart the tables. The tables are composed using complex models, and if you try to outsmart them to stay down longer, you could make a mistake. Remember, even divers using the tables correctly and conservatively have been known to get decompression sickness.

Table A
TOTAL BOTTOM TIME (TBT) IN MINUTES

Meters	FEET	No Decompression Stop Limits														
4.5	15	▼	35	70	110	160	225	350								
6	20		25	50	75	100	135	180	240	325					
7.5	25		20	35	55	75	100	125	160	195	245	315			
9	30		15	30	45	60	75	95	120	145	170	205	250	310	
10.5	35	220	5	15	25	40	50	60	80	100	120	140	160	190	220
12	40	150	5	15	25	30	40	50	70	80	100	110	130	150	
15	50	80		10	15	25	30	40	50	60	70	80			
18	60	50		10	15	20	25	30	40	50					
21	70	40		5	10	15	20	30	35	40					
24	80	30		5	10	15	20	25	30						
27	90	20		5	10	12	15	20							
30	100	18		5	7	10	18								
33	110	13				5	10	13							
36	120	10				5	10								
39	130	5				5									

HOW LONG CAN I DIVE?

The safest way to measure bottom time is to count it from the time you leave the surface until the time you return to the surface, rounded up to the next minute. Some agencies suggest that bottom time be calculated from the time you start descending (because that is when you start taking on nitrogen) to the second you start your return to the surface (because that is when you start off-gassing, or getting rid of nitrogen). This is fine if you go down, do your dive, and then come straight back up (at a safe rate of ascent, of course). However, most divers descend, stay deep for a while, then ascend a little and swim around some more. In these cases, the diver is still taking on nitrogen even though she could technically be said to be ascending. To simplify matters and be on the safe side of the equation, count your dive from surface to surface.

Single Dives
(TABLE A)

If you are doing just one dive, Table A (left) has all the information you need to calculate your limits.

Running down along the left side of Table A is a series of numbers representing the depth (in meters and feet) to which you will be diving. The numbers start at 15 feet and go down to 130 feet.

Starting at the row that indicates the depth of your dive, look along the row to the right until you reach the number next to a black box. That number represents minutes. If you dive only once, the time limit for any depth is the number next to the black box at the end of the row. Note: Shallower dives have numbers next to white boxes. The white boxes indicate that there is no decompression limit for these shallower dives. In other words, if you are diving at less than 30 feet, you can theoretically stay down as long as you like without getting decompression sickness.

So, looking at Table A, you can see that at a depth of 40 feet, you could actually stay down for 150 minutes (if your air lasted that long!). At 130 feet, you could stay down for only five minutes. These time intervals are called *no-decompression limits*.

Repetitive Groups and Multiple Dives

When diving more than once in a day, you must take into account how much nitrogen has accumulated in your body as a result of any previous dives. When you return to the surface, your body still has residual nitrogen in it. If you had dived for only 15 minutes at 35 feet, your body would have a lot less nitrogen in it than if you had

dived for 30 minutes at 60 feet. So, you not only have to calculate the depth and time limits of your new dive, but you also have to take into account the amount of nitrogen left in your body from the first dive.

Note: Any dive within 12 hours of a previous dive is considered a repetitive dive. Anytime you do repetitive diving, you need to factor in this residual nitrogen when calculating time and depth limits.

In the dive tables, the amount of accumulated nitrogen is expressed as a repetitive group, labeled from A through M. (These letters are the bold-faced capital letters just below Table A, page 106.) If you are in the A repetitive group, you have very little nitrogen in your body. If you are in the M repetitive group, you have much more nitrogen in your body and must wait much longer before it is safe to dive again.

To find your repetitive group, you need to know the depth and

SAFETY STOPS

A safety stop is nothing more than a three-minute break during your ascent to the surface, usually taken at a depth of 15 feet. (Sometimes, a dive computer will suggest taking a safety stop at a different depth.) These stops give

your body extra time to off-gas excess nitrogen. Safety stops are always recommended, especially if you are doing repetitive dives or diving deeper than 60 feet. They are required if you are diving to the no-decompression limits or if you are diving to a depth of 100 or more feet.

Table A
TOTAL BOTTOM TIME (TBT) IN MINUTES

Meters	FEET	No Decompression Stop Limits	A	B	C	D	E	F	G	H	I	J	K	L	M
4.5	15	▼	35	70	110	160	225	350							
6	20		25	50	75	100	135	180	240	325					
7.5	25		20	35	55	75	100	125	160	195	245	315			
9	30		15	30	45	60	75	95	120	145	170	205	250	310	
10.5	35	220	5	15	25	40	50	60	80	100	120	140	160	190	220
12	40	150	5	15	25	30	40	50	70	80	100	110	130	150	
15	50	80		10	15	25	30	40	50	60	70	80			
18	60	50		10	15	20	25	30	40	50					
21	70	40	5	10	15	20	30	35	40						
24	80	30	5	10	15	20	25	30							
27	90	20	5	10	12	15	20								
30	100	18	5	7	10	18									
33	110	13		5	10	13									
36	120	10		5	10										
39	130	5		5											

Repetitive Group designation

➤ A B C D E F G H I J K L M

time of your first dive. Let's say you did a 55-minute dive to 45 feet. Looking at Table A (above) the first thing you notice is that there is no box for 45 feet. So, following the standard rules, you use the next highest number — 50 feet. Similarly, as you go across the row, you won't find a box that contains 55 minutes, so you go to the next highest number: 60 minutes. Now, you simply drop down the column to find the bold-faced letter that indicates your repetitive group: in this case, H.

What do these letters mean?

A low repetitive group (A or B, for instance) means that you have a low amount of nitrogen left over. The result: Your next dive can be longer and/or deeper than if you were in a higher pressure group. If, however, you come up in a higher repetitive group (for instance, J), you have more residual nitrogen and your next dive will be more limited.

Surface Intervals (TABLE B)

One way to reduce the amount of residual nitrogen is to take a break on the surface between dives. When you do, your body begins to off-load all that extra nitrogen it has absorbed. If you have stayed within the limits of the dive tables, this off-loading happens naturally, with no ill effects. Even after a few minutes on the surface, you will be in a lower repetitive group than when you first surfaced. Being in that lower repetitive group will have an effect on how deep and how long your next dive can be.

To calculate your new repetitive group, simply find your original repetitive group beneath Table A, where you'll see rows of boxes containing two numbers. Looking down the column from your repetitive group, find the

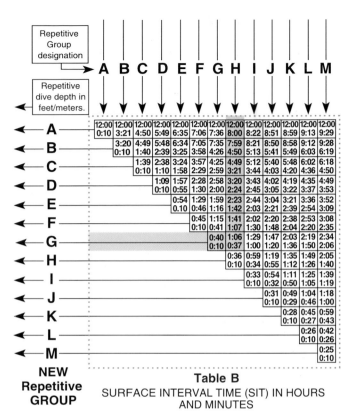

Repetitive Group designation →

Repetitive dive depth in feet/meters.

NEW Repetitive GROUP

Table B
SURFACE INTERVAL TIME (SIT) IN HOURS AND MINUTES

	A	B	C	D	E	F	G	H	I	J	K	L	M
A	12:00 0:10	12:00 3:21	12:00 4:50	12:00 5:49	12:00 6:35	12:00 7:06	12:00 7:36	12:00 8:00	12:00 8:22	12:00 8:51	12:00 8:59	12:00 9:13	12:00 9:29
B		3:20 0:10	4:49 1:40	5:48 2:39	6:34 3:25	7:05 3:58	7:35 4:26	7:59 4:50	8:21 5:13	8:50 5:41	8:58 5:49	9:12 6:03	9:28 6:19
C			1:39 0:10	2:38 1:10	3:24 1:58	3:57 2:29	4:25 2:59	4:49 3:21	5:12 3:44	5:40 4:03	5:48 4:20	6:02 4:36	6:18 4:50
D				1:09 0:10	1:57 0:55	2:28 1:30	2:58 2:00	3:20 2:24	3:43 2:45	4:02 3:05	4:19 3:22	4:35 3:37	4:49 3:53
E					0:54 0:10	1:29 0:46	1:59 1:16	2:23 1:42	2:44 2:03	3:04 2:21	3:21 2:39	3:36 2:54	3:52 3:09
F						0:45 0:10	1:15 0:41	1:41 1:07	2:02 1:30	2:20 1:48	2:38 2:04	2:53 2:20	3:08 2:35
G							0:40 0:10	1:06 0:37	1:29 1:00	1:47 1:20	2:03 1:36	2:19 1:50	2:34 2:06
H								0:36 0:10	0:59 0:34	1:19 0:55	1:35 1:12	1:49 1:26	2:05 1:40
I									0:33 0:10	0:54 0:32	1:11 0:50	1:25 1:05	1:39 1:19
J										0:31 0:10	0:49 0:29	1:04 0:46	1:18 1:00
K											0:28 0:10	0:45 0:27	0:59 0:43
L												0:26 0:10	0:42 0:26
M													0:25 0:10

range of numbers that includes the amount of time you will stay at the surface.

To continue our example, we are in repetitive group H; let's say we have been at the surface for 45 minutes. Starting at the letter H, we look down the column until we find the box where the range of time includes 45 minutes. In this case, that would be the box that includes the range from 37 to 1:06 (37 minutes to 1 hour and 6 minutes). From there, we simply look across to the left until we hit a letter. That is our new repetitive group (in this case, G).

Repetitive Dives: Residual Nitrogen Time (TABLE C)

Often you will know the depth of your next dive because you'll be planning to go to a specific reef. In this example, let's assume that the next dive we want to do is 40 feet deep. From our previous dive and surface interval, we know that we are in repetitive group G. Now we want to know how long we can dive at 40 feet.

In order to figure out how being in repetitive group G (or any other repetitive group) affects the length of

Table C
RESIDUAL NITROGEN TIME (RNT) IN MINUTES

Repetitive dive depth in feet/meters.

40 12	50 15	60 18	70 21	80 24	90 27	100 30	110 33	120 36	130 39	
7 143	6 74	5 45	4 36	4 26	3 17	3 15	3 10	3 7	3 2	A
17 133	13 67	11 39	9 31	8 22	7 13	7 11	6 7	6 4	6	B
25 125	21 59	17 33	15 25	13 17	11 9	10 8	10 3	9 1	8	C
37 113	29 51	24 26	20 20	18 12	16 4	14 4	13	12	11	D
49 101	38 42	30 20	26 14	23 7	20	18	16	15	13	E
61 89	47 33	36 14	31 9	28 2	25	22	20	18	16	F
73 77	56 24	44 6	37 3	32	29	26	24	21	19	G
87 63	66 14	52	43	38	33	30	27	25	22	H
101 49	76 4	61	50	43	38	34	31	28	25	I
116 34	87	70	57	48	43	38	34	32	28	J
138 12	99	79	64	54	47	43	38	35	31	K
161	111	88	72	61	53	48	42	39	35	L
187	124	97	80	68	58	52	47	43	38	M

Note: For repetitive dives less than 40 feet, use the values for 40 feet.

our next dive, we must convert the residual nitrogen to minutes. This is called *residual nitrogen time*.

To do this, go to Table C. Note that running along the top of Table C is a row with two numbers in it. These numbers indicate depths; the top number is in feet, and the bottom number is in meters. Starting at the letter G, your new repetitive group, move across the rows to the left until you reach the depth of your next planned dive (in this case, 40 feet). You'll see a box with two numbers in it.

The upper number in the box is the *residual nitrogen time* (73 minutes). The lower number in the box is the *adjusted no-decompression*

limit (77 minutes).

Okay, time out for a translation:

Residual nitrogen time is your repetitive group expressed as a number of minutes. Think of it as a handicap. These are the minutes you can't dive because of the nitrogen that is already in your system from your last dive. Remember the no-decompression limits you identified in Table A? When you did your first dive of the day, you could go to a certain depth for as long as the amount of time in the last box (the no-decompression limit). At 40 feet, that time would be 150 minutes.

But the handicap (residual nitrogen time) has to be factored in. Because of the nitrogen you took on during your first dive, you can't stay down to the no-decompression limit on your second dive. The upper number in the box on Table C is the amount of time you have to subtract from the old no-decompression limit to find the new (or adjusted) no-decompression limit. Instead of staying down for 150 minutes, you can stay down for only 150 minutes (the original no-decompression limit) minus 73 minutes (the residual nitrogen time). The answer:

77 minutes is the adjusted no-decompression limit.

Multiple Repetitive Dives

Of course you might not be planning to stay down for 77 minutes. What if you stay down for only 35 minutes? And what if you want to do a third dive? What repetitive group will you be in after your second dive (so that you can calculate all this stuff all over again for your third dive)?

To determine the repetitive group after this dive, you must add the nitrogen you were already carrying around from the first dive to the nitrogen you will absorb on the second dive.

This is simpler than it sounds. To find the new repetitive group, all you do is add the residual nitrogen time (73 minutes — it's your handicap, remember?) to the actual bottom time

(35 minutes). The sum (also called the *total bottom time*) is 108 minutes.

Now, you can go back to Table A and calculate the repetitive group for a dive to 40 feet for 108 minutes. Start at the 40-foot row and look across it until you find 108 (in this case, there is no box with 108, so you'll go up to 110.) Look down the column to find the repetitive group, and voilà! Your new repetitive group is (drumroll, please . . .) J.

Minimum Surface Intervals

If you've got a big boat in calm seas, or if you can detour over to a palm-fringed beach for lunch, or if there's a place to snorkel in the area, you might not care how long your surface interval lasts. But in some cases — say you're on a bouncing small boat in an open sea — you'd just as soon minimize the amount of time you're stuck on the surface.

DIVE PROFILES

Drawing dive profiles can be a good way to make sure that you've factored everything into your dive calculations.

Repetitive Dive Profiles

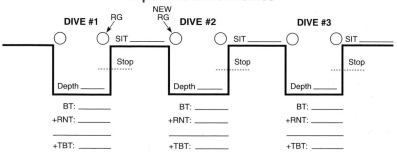

Conveniently, you can also work the tables to determine the minimum surface interval that is required between two dives.

To do this calculation, you need to know the times and depths of the dives you are planning. Let's say the first dive is to 65 feet for 36 minutes and the second is to 45 feet for 50 minutes. How long does the surface interval between these two dives have to be?

STEP 1 Find the repetitive group at the end of the first dive. This is simple. On Table A, start at 70 feet (there is no column for 65 feet), then look across until you reach 40 minutes (there's no box with 36 minutes in it, so we select the box with 40 minutes). Moving down, we find ourselves in repetitive group H.

STEP 2 The question we need to ask

■————————————————

RULES FOR MULTIPLE DIVES

● Limit repetitive dives to 100 feet or shallower.
● Do your deepest dive first.
● Always do a safety stop.
● When using Table C for repetitive dives, you'll notice that there is no column for dives shallower than 40 feet. All repetitive dives of 40 or fewer feet should be calculated using the 40-foot column.

regarding the second dive is not what repetitive group we will be in *after* the dive, but what is the highest repetitive group we can be in and still be permitted to do the dive? We start at Table C, at the depth of our second dive, which is 45 feet (we use 50 feet). We look down the column until we find a box where the bottom number (the adjusted no-decompression limit) contains the time of our dive, which is 50 minutes (so we use the box with 51 minutes). Looking across to the right, we find that the repetitive group in this case is D. So, in order to do this dive, we must use the data for repetitive group D.

STEP 3 Now we need to know how long it will take to get rid of enough nitrogen to move from repetitive group H to repetitive group D. For this we use Table B. We find Dive 1's repetitive group (H) on the top row of letters. We then find Dive 2's repetitive group (D) on the vertical column of letters. Now, we look right along the row and down the column until the two intersect. The box where they intersect contains a range of time, in this case, 3:20 to 2:24. Because you're looking for the *minimum* amount of time, the minimum surface interval, the lesser of the two times is the correct choice: 2 hours and 24 minutes.

DECOMPRESSION STOPS (TABLE D)

You may have heard of decompression stops. Professional divers use

Table D
Decompression Stops Table

Depth Feet Meters	Bottom Time (min.)	Time to First Stop	Decompression Stops (Min.) @20 Ft.	@10 Ft.	Total Ascent (Min:Sec)	Repetitive Group
40 **12.1**	200	1:00		7	8:20	N
	210	1:00		11	12:20	O
	230	1:00		15	16:20	O
	250	1:00		19	20:20	Z
50 **15.2**	100	1:20		5	6:40	M
	110	1:20		10	11:40	M
	120	1:20		21	22:40	N
	140	1:20		29	30:40	O
60 **18.2**	60	1:40		7	9:00	L
	80	1:40		14	16:00	M
	100	1:40		26	28:00	N
				39	41:00	O
70 **21.3**	50	2:00		14	16:20	L
	60	2:00		18	20:20	M
	70	2:00		23	25:20	N
	80	2:00		33	35:20	N
80 **24.3**	40	2:20		17	19:40	L
	50	2:20		23	25:40	M
	60	2:00	2	31	35:40	N
	70	2:00	7	39	48:40	N
90 **28.7**	25	2:40		7	10:00	J
	30	2:40		18	21:00	L
	40	2:40		25	28:00	M
	50	2:20	7	30	40:00	N
100 **30.4**	20	3:00		3	6:20	I
	25	3:00		15	18:20	K
	30	2:40	2	24	29:20	L
	40	2:40	9	28	40:20	N
110 **33.1**	20	3:20		7	10:40	J
	25	3:00	2	21	26:40	L
	30	3:00	8	26	37:40	M
	40	3:00	18	36	57:40	N
120 **36.5**	15	3:40		6	10:00	I
	20	3:40		14	18:00	J
	25	3:20	8	25	34:00	L
	30	3:20	15	31	50:00	N
130 **39.6**	10	4:00		4	8:20	H
	15	4:00		10	14:20	J
	20	3:40	3	18	25:20	M
	25	3:40	10	25	39:20	N

these stops when they have taken on too much nitrogen. They off-gas on the way up by taking a series of decompression stops. This is an extremely complicated and risky procedure, one that is never used in recreational diving. Note: All recreational diving is no-decompression diving. Staying within the recreational dive table limits means that you can always ascend to the surface without taking decompression stops.

However, in some rare instances (usually when you have made a mistake and exceeded the no-decompression limits) you may have to take an emergency decompression stop. Table D shows the procedures for figuring out at what depth and for how long these emergency stops should be taken. To safely ascend, you must follow the

∎

FLYING AFTER DIVING

As you rise above sea level, the pressure decreases. This causes any nitrogen left in your body to off-gas and can put you at risk for decompression sickness. The longer the surface interval between

diving and flying (and also, between diving and driving to a high altitude), the less the chance that you will develop decompression sickness.

A minimum of 12 hours is

continued on page 112

continued from page 111

recommended between diving and flying in a commercial plane or going in a non-pressurized plane or a car to an altitude of 8,000 feet. There are several factors, however, which can increase your susceptibility to the bends. Some dive computers allow divers to stay down longer and deeper than more conservative charts. So if you've been using a dive computer and diving to the maximum limits, you may have more nitrogen in your system than a diver who has been relying on charts. Also, if you have been diving for several days, doing many multiple dives, or if you have made an emergency decompression stop, you may also have more residual nitrogen in your system. If any of the factors described above apply to you, or if you are going to altitudes above 8,000 feet, you should wait at least 24 hours before flying.

table's directions regarding how slowly to come up.

To figure out the length and location of an emergency decompression stop, start at the left side of Table D with your maximum depth. Next to it, find the number that indicates your actual bottom time. The next column tells you how much time can elapse from the bottom to the first decompression stop. Let's say you did a dive to 80 feet, which has a no-decompression limit of 30 minutes (see Table A). You, however, stayed down for 40 minutes. The next columns tell you the time to the first stop and the depth of that stop. In this example, you have to take 2 minutes and 20 seconds to ascend from 80 feet to your decompression stop at 10 feet. Under the column labeled 10 feet, you'll find the length of time you need to stay there: in this case, 17 minutes. At the end of the dive, you will be in repetitive group L, as shown in the last column of Table D. Note: If you exceed the time limits and have to take an emergency decompression stop, you should refrain from diving for 12 hours, and refrain from flying for at least 24 hours. Also note: An emergency stop is not a fix-all solution. Putting yourself in this situation is putting yourself at serious risk for decompression sickness. This is an emergency procedure only; it should not be part of your dive plan.

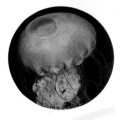

HEALTH
AND
SAFETY

I t was the day after I got my C-card, my first "real" dive. But if the truth be told, I didn't quite feel like a "real" diver — not yet. Come to think of it, I felt a lot like I did the day after I got my driver's license and my father handed me the car keys with a warning to "be careful." Fortunately, I was diving with the same instructor who had certified me, and he knew that the logbook I was carrying was filled with unsullied white pages.

"Here," he said as we were walking to the boat. "Why don't you read this on the way?"

I expected something on the ecology of a tropical reef, or perhaps a quick refresher-course article (you know, "Ten Things I Learned on My First Dive"). But instead Gary had given me a rather sobering accident-evaluation article. Someone who had logged more than 1,000 dives had somehow lost his weight belt on a deep dive and popped straight to the surface. In a split second, a perfectly normal dive turned into a near-disaster. The diver suffered a severe case of decompression sickness and almost died.

On the boat ride over to the dive site, Gary wanted to talk about the article: What had gone wrong? How could the weights have come off? Hadn't the diver and his buddy

could happen to me on this next dive. You've always got to be thinking, paying attention, asking yourself *what if?*"

SCUBA diving is a safe sport. But it's only safe if, as Gary so effectively pointed out, you remember to think, to pay attention, and to play by the rules.

As with most outdoor activities, the vast majority of SCUBA accidents don't

Although this moray eel looks mighty malevolent, the truth is that your mistakes, or your buddy's, are far more likely to put you in harm's way.

both checked them? And speaking of the buddy, where was *he* when trouble struck? Was he so far away that he couldn't help? And what, assuming the buddies had been together, should they have done? What first aid needed to be performed when the diver got out of the water?

"You can't ever think you've got so much experience that nothing can go wrong," Gary said. "It could happen to anyone — it

involve big-ticket dangers. The undramatic truth is that most accidents are fully preventable. Divers should be much more concerned with operator error than with snaggletoothed deep-sea monsters.

This chapter covers health-related diving problems. Some of them are more likely to be annoying nuisances than life-threatening dramas. Others are much more serious. Whether it's a minor snafu like a bout of seasickness or a major problem like the bends, knowing about the causes, symptoms, treatment, and, most important, prevention of these potential problems can help make your diving experience safer and more enjoyable.

A huge school of blackfin barracuda patrol a reef in the South Pacific. Large predatory fish rarely mistake divers for food.

BEFORE YOU DIVE

You can do several things before you even start your dive to help minimize potential problems:

● Keep in good physical shape. Although diving is often relaxing, it is a sport. As with any sport, the better your physical condition, the more easily you can meet the athletic demands. Additionally, being in good shape helps minimize your vulnerability to the problems divers can face, such as decompression sickness.

● Have a complete physical exam. This is commonsense advice for anyone, but it goes double for divers. Discuss diving with your doctor, and discuss any chronic medical problems (such as high blood pressure), or medications you use, in the context of diving.

● Avoid using alcohol, cigarettes, and drugs before diving. Alcohol can predispose divers to hypothermia and decompression sickness, as well as interfere with their judgment. Cigarettes are an obvious bad idea, because they interfere with how well your respiratory system works. Illegal drugs not only interfere with judgment, but they can also have unpredictable and dangerous repercussions when combined with SCUBA equipment and the effects of increased pressure underwater. You should discuss the use of any prescription drugs with your doctor before diving.

● Never dive when you have a cold. You won't be able to equalize. Antihistamines and cold medications can wear off during a dive, leaving sinuses and ears blocked and impossible to equalize.

DAN (DIVERS ALERT NETWORK) FIRST AID KIT FOR SCUBA DIVERS

MEDICAL INFORMATION/ REFERENCE
DAN Dive and Travel
Medicine Guide

WOUND CLEANING/ MANAGEMENT
20 cc irrigation syringe
providone iodine swabs/wipes
antiseptic towelettes
(wound closure strips (Steri-strips),
.25 inch x 1.5 inch
several butterfly closure strips
tincture of benzoin swabs
eye wash/normal saline,
4-oz. bottle
cortisone cream 1%
antibiotic ointment

DRESSING/BANDAGING
strip bandages (Band-Aid), 1 inch
or 1/2 inch x 3 inch
patch bandages, 2 inch x 3 inch
(Band-Aid)
fingertip and knuckle wound
strips (Band-Aid)
4 x 4 gauze pads
2 x 2 gauze pads
8 x 10 trauma dressing/pad
5 x 9 trauma dressing/pad
eye pad
eye patch

non-adherent sterile dressing
(Adaptic)
conforming gauze bandage (Kling,
Kurtex), 3 inch
ace wrap/bandage, 3 inch
stockinette bandages
adhesive tape, 1 inch
triangular bandage (cravat)

TOOLS/INSTRUMENTS/OTHER
EMT shears
hyperthermia thermometer
(96°F – 107°F)
splinter forceps (tweezers)
disposable razor
safety pins
accident report and pencil
cold compress
heat compress
infectious waste bag
latex gloves
antimicrobial wipes (for hand
cleaning)

DIVING FIRST AID

Taking a first aid and rescue course from one of the diving agencies listed on page 17 will increase your confidence in your own skills and make you more self-sufficient. If you've already taken a standard first-aid course, you'll note that many of the basics are the same, in particular, treating the "big three" life-threatening conditions: bleeding, stopped breathing, and stopped heartbeat. But SCUBA-oriented first aid courses are slightly different than their on-land equivalents in that they emphasize the skills most likely to be useful to divers. For instance, you'll be spending a lot more time on how to administer oxygen than on what to do if someone swallows drain cleaner.

Seasickness

Sometimes, trouble can start before you even have your gear on. If you dive for long enough in enough different places, sooner or later you'll end up being jolted and jarred as a small boat plows its way through rough seas. Some people turn their faces to the wind and enjoy every bump and bounce. Others turn green as spring grass and start promising themselves that they'll trade in their SCUBA gear for skiing equipment at the very next opportunity. Note: This promise tends to be forgotten as soon as they get into the water and start diving.

You probably already know if, and under what conditions, you're susceptible to seasickness. Some people are perfectly comfortable when the boat is slowly rocking back and forth but feel ill in a roiling sea; others handle whitecaps just fine but become queasy when the action slows down. I find that I rarely get seasick, except when I've got to concentrate on gearing up, keeping my balance, checking my buddy, and listening to instructions while the boat is bucking underfoot like a pent-up bronco.

If you know that you're prone to seasickness, it's a good idea to take preventative medicine. Check with your doctor for a recommendation. Avoiding greasy foods also helps. Make sure you keep yourself adequately hydrated, because dehydration can cause nausea — which only compounds the problem of being seasick.

If seasickness does strike, you might be tempted to curl up in a little ball at the bottom of the boat, but that's the worst thing you can do. As long as the boat is moving, it's best to stay outside in the fresh air. Some people find that looking toward a point on the horizon (a stable point in your rollicking world) helps. Getting out of the boat and into the water offers almost immediate relief, so if the boat is stopped and it's okay with the dive master or the boat captain, by all means, jump in sooner rather than later. (Just be sure to move out of the way if other divers are entering and exiting the water.)

An oxygen unit is a vital piece of first-aid gear for divers. It is used to treat decompression sickness, among many other ailments.

Sunburn

Another pesky but largely preventable problem is sunburn, especially if you're a pale-complected Northerner taking a winter ◼

vacation in tropical seas. A bout of sunburn can be acutely painful (making it almost impossible to don a wet suit); it can also have dangerous long-term implications like skin cancer.

Because so much of the sun's rays are absorbed by water, sunburn is more of a problem on the surface, on the boat, or on land than it is

OXYGEN

One of the most important pieces of first aid gear on a dive boat is the oxygen unit. Oxygen is the first line of treatment for suspected cases of decompression sickness (see pages 124–126). It's also used to treat air contamination (page 123), lung overexpansion injuries (page 126), and some injuries caused by venomous marine life. Some of this venom can cause respiratory distress (see pages 132–134). In fact, oxygen is so important that there are special classes to train divers in how to administer it for first aid. If you'll be spending a lot of time in the water, this class is well worth taking.

Think of an oxygen cylinder as you would a fire extinguisher. Most of us have fire extinguishers at home — and all of us should — but how many of us know exactly how to operate them without a quick look at the instructions? Even though a fire extinguisher is designed to be almost idiot-proof, doesn't it make sense to check out how it operates before you actually need to use it? The same is true in diving: In an emergency situation (picture a bouncy ocean, people yelling and arguing, and a very sick diver), you'll be very glad you don't have to add "learn to operate new equipment" to your list of things to do.

underwater. If you wear an exposure suit while snorkeling, you don't have to worry about sunburn as much while you're in the water. Just be sure to put sunscreen on your uncovered skin: hands, neck, etc. But on the boat, or if you're swimming without an exposure suit, you need to take precautions:

● Choose a waterproof sunscreen with a sun protection factor (SPF) of more than 15.

● Put sunscreen on at least one-half hour prior to exposure. It works better if it has time to be absorbed into your skin.

● Reapply sunscreen frequently: Even waterproof sunscreen will come off after several dives, some sweating, and toweling off.

● Men who are bald or have very thin hair might want to pay attention to their heads, either by using sunscreen or wearing a bathing cap.

● Take long-sleeved, light-colored clothing on board with you, or cover up with a towel.

● Take responsibility for your buddy while on board as well as underwater. She can't see if her back is turning lobster-colored, but you can.

● Sunglasses with ultraviolet (UV) protection help prevent sunburn of the retinas, a painful condition that causes temporary blindness. They also make you a lot more comfortable.

● A wide-brimmed hat keeps the sun off your head and out of your eyes, and helps protect your head and neck.

Hyperthermia and Dehydration

Hyperthermia and dehydration are additional problems that can be associated with diving. In Florida's freshwater springs, for example, the water temperature is 72°F year-round, which makes a wet suit pretty much mandatory. But the air temperature can easily be in the 90s. The result: Divers who don't pay attention to their body temperature frequently overheat. *Hyperthermia* (which can lead to heat stroke) is a condition in which your body's heat-regulating mechanisms can no longer keep your temperature stable.

Dehydration contributes not only to hyperthermia, but, interestingly enough, to hypothermia (see pages 120–122), as well, along with a host of other problems ranging from nausea to the bends. It occurs when you lose more water through sweating and respiration than you take in. Divers are especially at risk for dehydration, because after being in the water for a dive, they often don't perceive themselves to be thirsty.

Fortunately, both hyperthermia and dehydration are easily prevented. On the boat, wear a hat, and if there's any shade, spend some time in it. Drink often — don't wait until you're thirsty. (A water bottle or two should be part of your standard equipment.) In hot weather, refrain from putting on your wet suit until you're ready to get geared up for the dive. Spending an hour or so on a boat under a broiling sun with a wet suit on is a sure way to overheat. Before donning your wet suit, make sure all your gear is organized so you'll be able to get to what you need without a lot of unnecessary rummaging around. After you're geared up, try to avoid excessive activity, and stay in the shade (if there is any).

Sometimes (for instance on a small, crowded boat, especially if the water is rough), you might have to don your wet suit before you get on the boat, or keep your wet suit on between dives. In such cases, try wearing your wet suit half on. If you're wearing a one-piece suit, put on the bottom part but leave your arms and upper torso free. If you're using a two-piece suit, wear the bottoms only. You won't heat up nearly as fast, and when it's time to dive you can easily finish suiting up without a lot of complex choreography.

Heat Exhaustion and Heat Stroke

Symptoms of *heat exhaustion* include lightheadedness, nausea, headache, clammy skin, and a rapid pulse. If you find that the heat saps your energy, resting, drinking, and cooling off will help. If you're just feeling a little piqued, take advantage of your surroundings and jump in the water. A quick dip will bring your temperature down and your energy up. If you're symptoms are more severe — say you're dizzy and nauseous — it's best to cool off

slowly so as not to shock your circulatory system. Dip some towels in water and cool off and splash yourself, then ease in for a swim.

Given that, as a diver, you are surrounded by water, you'd have to be truly oblivious to your condition to let it progress into *heat stroke*. Much more serious than heat exhaustion, heat stroke, which can be fatal, is characterized by a high temperature and dry, not sweaty, skin. The victim's temperature needs to be brought down immediately. Pour water over him, put him in the shade, or cover him with wet towels.

Hypothermia

Hypothermia is a condition in which the body loses more heat than it can generate. Although we're more likely to think of hypothermia in conjunction with such activities as climbing frigid alpine mountaintops or ice diving in the North Sea, the surprising truth is that hypothermia can strike even in relatively warm tropical waters. And it can happen surprisingly fast because of the quick rate at which water conducts heat away from the body.

There's nothing you can do about the temperature of the sea, but there's plenty you can do to avoid hypothermia. Your first line of defense is the right wet suit (or dry suit) for the conditions. Coupled with insulating layers, an exposure suit can even keep you warm in water that's only a few degrees away from turning into ice.

Your logbooks can also help you make a decision about your exposure suit, if you've been thorough enough to include such data as water temperature and bottom time. Make a habit of noting what kind of suit you were wearing and how you felt (especially if there was a problem). You'll be able to refer to that information on future dives when you're trying to decide what kind of wet suit you should wear.

Once you're in the water, your best defense against hypothermia is to listen to what your body tells you. A pervasive feeling of cold and shivering are your body's normal responses to cold — and a message that it's time to come up.

Out of the water, wrap yourself in towels and warm clothing. It might seem like overkill to bring sweaters on board a boat in sunny tropical seas, but the combination of wind and water can be extremely chilling, especially at night. You might find that a light sweater or a windbreaker tucked into your gear bag can make the difference between a pleasant ride and a miserable ride back from the dive site. If you don't have warm clothes, keep your wet suit on. It may seem counterintuitive, but even a wet wet suit provides insulation because it doesn't let the wind wick water and heat away from your skin.

Hypothermia can occur in warm tropical waters, but the chances of a life-threatening condition are magnified in colder water, especially if the air is also cold. Symptoms of hypothermia include uncontrolled, spasmodic shivering; clenching muscles and contorting in an effort to keep warm; a pale face; low blood pressure and pulse; and errors of judgment. *Severe hypothermia* is characterized by sluggishness, slurred speech (above the water, of course), and poor motor coordination. Other symptoms (and evidence that the situation has become life-threatening) can include irrational, erratic behavior, sudden wild bursts of energy, the inability to focus or respond to questions, and violent reactions to suggestions or offers of help. In the final stages, the victim may suffer vision impairment and slip into unconsciousness.

There's no great mystery about treating hypothermia: Stop the heat loss! Uncontrollable shivering is a sure sign that it's time to get out of the water. Cold-water divers should always have plenty of warm, dry clothes. (Protect them from an accidental dousing by storing them in some sort of sack. Waterproof stuff sacks sold in backpacking stores are perfect for keeping water away from your warm clothes — but garbage bags work, too.) Dry off and change as quickly as possible. If you're on a boat, try to stay out of the wind (not always an easy task, but a wind-breaking jacket will help). Finally, have a thermos of hot drinks on hand.

A hot drink is one of the best ways to warm up someone who is borderline hypothermic (but avoid caffeinated drinks, which are diuretics). Snacks help, too.

Overexertion

Overexertion can occur if you are trying to maintain a higher level of activity than you are used to. Examples include swimming against a strong current, towing someone, or swimming long distances on the surface. (Swimming with full SCUBA gear is much more tiring than swimming laps in a pool — especially in choppy water.)

One symptom of overexertion is labored breathing, which may be accompanied by feelings of weakness, suffocation, anxiety, or panic.

Stopping overexertion is easy: Stop doing what's making you tired! Remember, in SCUBA the key is to pace yourself. Sudden, swift decisions and quick actions are likely to do more harm than good. So if you find yourself overexerting and feeling panicky, STOP. If there is something to hold onto, hold onto it for a minute. Make eye contact with your buddy. Take a minute to breathe, to rest, and to think — and then act.

Overexertion and panic can also lead to *hyperventilation*, especially if you find yourself breathing shallow, fast breaths. This can be dangerous because hyperventilating interferes with your reflex to breathe and can lead to unconsciousness (see pages 38–39). Again, the key is to stop and slow down, and to force yourself to breathe calmly, deeply, and slowly.

Cramps

Cramps are caused by uncontrollable muscle contractions, which in turn can be caused by overwork, impaired

---

DIVERS ALERT NETWORK

The Divers Alert Network is an organization that focuses on diver safety. It provides help in diving emergencies, publishes a magazine on medical research and safe diving practices, fields medical questions from members, helps maintain a worldwide network of hyperbaric facilities (where decompression sickness is treated), gives seminars, and offers diving insurance. This last benefit is especially important, because many ordinary medical insurance policies do not include diving-related injuries or treatment in a hyperbaric chamber, which can run to many thousands of dollars. For help in diving emergencies, call the 24-hour hotline at (919) 684-4326. For membership information, call (919) 684-2948.

circulation, or cold. In diving, they most commonly occur in the feet and legs, and are often caused by fins that are too stiff or too large. They can also occur as a "stitch" in the abdominal area, usually from overexertion.

You can prevent (or lower the chances of getting) foot cramps by proper fin selection. If you've had a problem before, talk to your instructor or to the pros in your dive shop about which fins might be best for you. Fitness helps, too: It might be worth exercising your leg muscles by swimming laps (with fins) in a local pool. Getting a correct fit (so that your circulation isn't impaired) and choosing an exposure suit that keeps you warm enough will also help.

If you get cramps in your side from overexertion, slow down or stop what you're doing and breathe in especially deeply.

Contaminated Air

If you have your tank routinely inspected by a qualified technician and you fill your tank only at reputable dive shops, contaminated air shouldn't be a problem. But consider any foul taste or smell in your air supply as a warning sign, and ascend immediately. Bad air doesn't always taste or smell bad, however. For example, carbon monoxide is odorless and tasteless, so you need to be aware of the symptoms of air contamination. Headaches, nausea, and dizziness are common symptoms of bad air (although they could also

be caused by breathing exhaust fumes while aboard a boat). Bright red nails and lips are strong indications that the problem is bad air. Don't ignore any of these symptoms; if you persist in diving, they could lead to unconsciousness.

If you suspect contaminated air, abort your dive and have the air in your tank tested afterward. Oxygen should be administered as first aid, and once you're back on shore you should seek medical attention.

Squeezes and Blocks

Boyle's Law (see Appendix I) states that if you put an amount of gas in a flexible container (let's say a balloon), and you then put that container under pressure (say, 30 feet below the surface of the sea), the container will shrink (the volume will decrease) and the density of the air inside it will increase. When you take the container back to the surface, the pressure will be reduced. As a result, the density of the air inside will decrease and the volume will increase.

How does this seemingly arcane physical law affect divers? It controls the density and volume of air in our equipment, in our lungs, and in so-called "dead air spaces," such as the space between our eyes and our mask. It is the cause of so-called barotraumas — injuries due to pressure. SQUEEZES The most obvious and immediate effect of Boyle's law is the pressure and pain a diver starts to feel as soon as she drops a few feet below the surface. Squeezes can occur wherever there is an air space: the sinuses, ears, the space between your face and your mask. They are caused by an imbalance in pressure: Air is compressed as the diver descends and the pressure increases. To stop the squeeze, the diver must equalize the pressure by adding air. To stop mask squeeze, a diver breathes out through her nose into the mask, adding air and equalizing the pressure. To stop squeezes in the ears and sinuses, the diver performs the so-called Valsalva maneuver (see page 83) by holding her nose and blowing gently. This forces air through the nasal passages into the air spaces, and equalizes the pressure.

Rarely, an air space between a filling and a tooth will be subject to a squeeze. There's nothing you can do about this underwater. Prevention via regular dental care is the only solution.

BLOCKS Similarly, when a diver ascends, it is possible for air that is trapped in the sinuses, ears, or intestines to expand and cause pain. This occurs more rarely than a squeeze, because usually, the air simply finds a way out. However, if air is prevented from escaping, a reverse block might occur. For example, if a diver has been using medication for a cold and it wears off, the sinuses could become blocked and prevent air from escaping. (For this reason, do not dive with a cold or when using cold medication. Also avoid anything that could create a block, such as ear plugs or a too-tight hood.) Reverse blocks can also occur in the intestines, especially if you've been eating gassy foods before a dive. Reverse blocks are more easily prevented than cured: About the only thing you can do is descend a little, wait a moment for the air to find its way out, and then ascend slowly.

The "Bends"

The causes of *decompression sickness*, otherwise known as the *bends* or *DCS*, are discussed in Appendix I.

TECHNIQUE TIP

RELIEVING A CRAMP

To relieve a foot or leg cramp, first stretch the affected muscle, then massage it. You can do this yourself, or your buddy can help you. Simply grasp the tip of your fin and pull it slowly toward you.

Avoiding decompression sickness is the whole point of the dive tables, which are covered in Chapter 5. But DCS is a sneaky illness: Although you can minimize the chances of getting it by diving conservatively and always staying within the limits of the dive tables, you can't eliminate the possibility completely.

Note: Even if you do absolutely every single thing right, double-check your tables, and use your computer, it is possible, although unlikely, to get bent! Every diver must be able to identify the symptoms of decompression sickness.

Physicians still don't understand why some divers get DCS, whereas others exposed to the same conditions don't. Certain factors can predispose divers to decompression sickness. These include age, being overweight, having injuries or an illness that interferes with the circulatory system, diving in very cold water, engaging in heavy exercise while diving, using alcohol, smoking, being dehydrated, flying after diving, or driving to high altitudes after diving.

Decompression sickness can be hard to diagnose because its symptoms are so wide-ranging. This is because nitrogen can be absorbed anywhere in the body; so, bubbles can form anywhere in the body, too. How they affect you depends on where they develop and how big they are. Pain (especially in the joints and muscles of the arms and legs) is the most common symptom of decom-

pression sickness. Other symptoms include fatigue, weakness, dizziness or lightheadedness, numbness, nausea, tingling, shock, paralysis, and unconsciousness. Obviously, many of these symptoms are also associated with other illnesses. But divers should always consider the possibility of DCS if these symptoms are present after a dive.

Most DCS symptoms happen shortly after a dive, often within a half hour, and usually within two hours. But sometimes symptoms occur as long as 12 hours after a dive, and in rare cases even longer. Symptoms can vary dramatically from individual to individual. Often, in extremely serious cases, symptoms such as paralysis or unconsciousness occur very suddenly, immediately after a dive. In other cases, symptoms such as fatigue, dizziness, nausea, and joint pain tend to come on gradually and persist, sometimes intermittently.

In many sports, it seems human nature to ignore minor-seeming symptoms. We tell ourselves that it'll go away, that we've got jet lag, that we're just not used to the activity, that everything is fine. People who engage in outdoor activities tend to be healthy, and many of us exercise regularly and are used to pushing ourselves a bit and ignoring minor discomfort. SCUBA is no exception: The Divers Alert Network (DAN) reports that up to 15 percent of divers who are treated for decompression sickness ignored symptoms and continued to dive anyway, making their condition much worse and risking their lives. If you suspect decompression sickness, it's time to call it quits for the day, even if you had planned several repetitive dives.

It's also time to seek medical assistance. Decompression sickness must be treated in a recompression chamber, which are found in some hospitals, especially near popular dive sites. You should know where the nearest recompression chamber is.

Warning: Some divers take risks because they know that, if the worst should happen, treatment is available. But treatment in a recompression chamber is a long, uncomfortable, multithousand-dollar ordeal that can involve lying in an enclosed chamber in temperatures that may be well over 100°F for many hours. And treatment is not always successful. A common myth is that resubmerging, then decompressing underwater (by coming up very slowly and taking frequent decompression stops), is a treatment for decompression sickness. This myth is grounded in old navy diving procedures; for recreational divers, it is dead wrong. Recreational diving is synonymous with no-decompression diving. Although emergency decompression stops (see page 110) may occasionally be used to try to *prevent* decompression sickness if a diver has accidentally stayed down too long, they are never used for *treat-*

ment. Treatment of decompression sickness takes many hours (longer than a diver's endurance and air supply), should be medically monitored, and may require medication. It cannot be done in the water.

First aid for decompression sickness includes treating for shock (see accompanying sidebar), administering CPR (if necessary), and administering oxygen.

Lung Overexpansion

Lung overexpansion injuries are among the most serious of all potential diving injuries, and may be fatal. They occur when a diver holds her breath and ascends. As the diver ascends, the pressure decreases and the air in the diver's lungs, following Boyle's law, expands. If the lungs expand too much, they can be seriously damaged, allowing air to enter the bloodstream. This can be life threatening. Fortunately, lung overexpansion injuries are easy to prevent if you follow one of diving's fundamental laws: Breathe slowly and continuously and never hold your breath. By breathing continuously, your lungs are constantly equalizing to the changing pressure.

First aid and treatment for lung overexpansion includes treating for shock, administering CPR, and administering oxygen, and treatment in a recompression chamber.

Nitrogen Narcosis

Nitrogen narcosis is a problem that occurs on deep dives. (The causes are discussed in Appendix I.) Different people are affected differently, but below 100 feet most divers will experience some of the symptoms. These can include a feeling of inebriation, sudden anxiety, or overwhelming well-being. An apocryphal example of "narked" behavior is taking your regulator out of your mouth and offering it to a passing fish. Buddies diving to 100 feet or deeper should pay special attention to each other for signs of nitrogen narcosis, and if a diver seems anxious or panicked or is acting "strange," the buddy should signal that it's time to ascend a little. Getting narked doesn't mean you have to stop diving. It just means that you should ascend to a depth at which you feel normal (or "clear"). Remember, during your ascent, that deep-diving rules apply: Your ascent should be slow and controlled — no more than 30 feet per minute — and if you're at the end of your dive, you should take a safety stop.

Oxygen Toxicity

Appendix I discusses how oxygen becomes toxic in extremely high concentrations. It is extremely rare for recreational divers to encounter this problem if they dive within the standard no-decompression limits and use normal air. On deep dives, divers

TREATING FOR SHOCK

Shock is a general depression of the body's functions, and it can kill, even if the original injury (a broken leg, for example) was not itself severe enough to be fatal.

Always treat any injured victim for shock, whether or not he exhibits the symptoms: pale, cold, or clammy skin; a quick, weak heartbeat; fast, shallow respiration; and dilated pupils.

The victim should be kept quiet and comfortable, lying down with the feet elevated unless there has been a bleeding injury to the head or torso or a neck or back injury. If there is a head wound or if the victim is having trouble breathing, raise the victim's head unless there is also a neck injury. A victim who is vomiting or bleeding from the mouth should lie on his left side.

Loosen clothing and keep the victim's body temperature stabilized. Generally, this means keeping the victim warm, although in extremely hot weather you might need to shade the victim from the hot sun or apply damp cloths to his forehead. Give the victim small amounts of water or bouillon, unless he is unconscious.

using enriched air such as Nitrox are at risk for oxygen toxicity, because such air has more oxygen in it and can reach toxic levels at depths well within recreational-diving limits. *Central nervous system (CNS) toxicity* is rare in recreational diving. (Using regular air, you would have to dive to a depth of around 220 feet before being at predictable risk of CNS toxicity.) However, if you are using Nitrox, the risk is much greater at depths well within the recreational-dive limits. Preliminary symptoms can include the rapid and sudden onset of anxiety, confusion, nausea, dizziness, and altered vision, and can worsen into convulsions and seizures. Underwater, of course, these problems are life-threatening.

ASSISTING A DIVER

In standard first aid classes, performing first aid starts with knowing how to use the telephone. In diving, as on land, calling for help is the first step to take when dealing with many serious emergencies. But even with cell phones and radios, help may be many miles away. First aid and the ability to diagnose and manage problems are therefore critically important skills.

A cell phone is now a routine piece of equipment on many dive boats, as is a radio. On a guided dive, your dive leader will tell you where the first aid kit, oxygen, and communications equipment are.

The equipment should have directions for use, including phone numbers for local paramedics or police, radio frequencies for Coast Guard, contact information for the Divers Alert Network (see page 122), which serves divers in the United States and the Caribbean, and the phone number and location of the nearest recompression chamber. If you're diving outside the United States, be sure you know how the phones work. If you're diving alone, with just a buddy, you should bring along some sort of communications device — either a cell phone or a radio or both, along with a list of local numbers.

Distress Signals

Two of the most important signals in your dive sign-language vocabulary are "I need help" (waving your arms when on the surface; wiggling your hand when underwater) and "I'm okay" (raising one or both arms above your head to make a circle while on the surface; making the "okay" sign with your thumb and forefinger underwater.)

This means that when you first jump off a dive boat, or when you come up from a dive, you have to resist the instinct to wave at people on the boat to show that you're okay. Remember: In dive sign language, waving means "I need help." The "I'm okay" signal — one (or both) arms in the air in a semicircle (or a circle) over your head — is a position a panicked swimmer is unlikely to assume by accident.

Stress and Panic

It's normal to feel a little stress the first few times you dive or when facing new and unfamiliar situations. Stress can be caused if you feel concerned about conserving your air supply, or if you are worried about remembering everything (this worry diminishes as you get more familiar with diving and with your gear). Stress can be exacerbated by exertion and cold, by limited visibility, or by the sudden feeling of a physical threat — for instance, a strong current or a dangerous marine animal.

Panic occurs when sudden and impulsive fear, rather than deliberate and logical reasoning, dictates the action a person takes. The feeling is a combination of being out of control, frightened, and confused.

If you find yourself getting stressed out, slow down and take stock of your situation so you don't start to panic. If you're at the bottom, you could sit down for a minute. Or hold onto your buddy or even a piece of (non-venomous) coral. If you're being swept away by a current, you could take refuge in the quiet water on the lee side of a large rock or coral. Stop, breathe, think — then act.

A diver who can't control stress may become a panicked diver. A panicked diver is not thinking clearly; he's acting on impulse. He is easy to recognize because his move-

ASSISTING A TIRED DIVER

Moving a tired diver takes a lot of energy, especially if the waves are up. It's far better to calm your buddy down. Get him to breathe calmly and take a rest, after which he might be able to move under his own power. If not, here are two ways to help you get him from here to there.

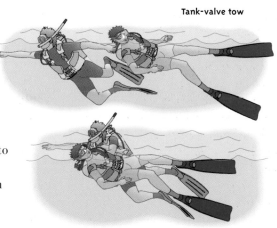

Tank-valve tow

Do-si-do or modified tired swimmer tow

ments will be jerky and uncontrolled. He might, for instance, struggle to hold his head out of the water (forgetting that he has a BC for that very purpose). When you get close to the panicked diver, you'll see that he is breathing rapidly and shallowly. A panicked person will often rip his regulator or snorkel out of his mouth, and throw his mask up on his forehead. (For this reason, and because masks worn on the forehead can easily be knocked off and lost, a person wearing a mask on the forehead can usually be identified either as someone in trouble or a beginner.) He may seem to have bad coordination or to be using bad judgment.

To assist a panicked diver, first help her establish positive buoyancy. But be wary about approaching too closely. Lifeguards learn early in their training that it is far safer to throw a flotation device to a panicked swimmer than it is to approach her directly, because a panicked person might lunge at you and try to use *you* as the flotation device!

In a diving situation, the emergency may happen some distance from a boat or a float. In that case, you'll have to approach the panicked diver directly. Stop about 8 or 10 feet away from her so that she doesn't try to climb on top of you. Keep your feet in front of you so if she lunges for you, you can propel yourself away with a couple of strong kicks.

Try talking to her, to calm her down. You can try instructing her to inflate her BC, or, if necessary, drop her weight belt. Or tell her you'll help her do it. There's no need to rush. The diver is unlikely to sink when she's in full gear. So proceed calmly, and try to talk her out of her panic.

Establishing buoyancy usually means just filling up the BC, although you can always get rid of the weight belt, too. If you have to assist the diver in these tasks, swim underwater to approach her. You should know the location and operation of her weight belt (remember: right-hand release) and the BC inflator. Once you've reestablished buoyancy, continue to try to calm the

COMMONSENSE SAFETY

- The best first aid is prevention.
- Have a first aid kit and an oxygen unit on board — and know how to use them.
- Take a rescue class, or classes

in basic first aid and CPR.
- Know the contact information for emergency evacuation, medical help, and the nearest hyperbaric chamber (a facility where decompression sickness is treated).

diver and help her reestablish control over her breathing. If necessary, you might have to assist her by towing her back to shore or the boat.

Under the Surface

Under the surface, problem prevention begins with keeping an eye on your buddy and frequently using dive signals to ask each other if everything is okay.

If, however, the worst happens, and your buddy becomes unconscious underwater, you will have to act quickly and decisively to save him. Don't try to mess with his regulator or try to get him breathing underwater. You must get him to the surface.

Here, especially in deeper dives, you're faced with a quandary. Do you get your buddy to the surface as quickly as possible, putting both of you at risk for decompression sickness? Or do you follow the ascent-rate guidelines, ascending at no more than 30 feet per minute, even though he will be unable to breathe during that time? Obviously, you can't take a safety stop while bringing an injured diver to the surface. But you should take the time to ascend slowly. Once you get to the surface, the victim will have a better chance if he's dealing with only one life-threatening emergency (drowning) and not two (drowning and the bends). And you'll be better able to help him if you haven't put your own life at risk or compromised

your safety by exposing yourself to decompression sickness or lung overexpansion injury.

To bring him to the surface, start by swimming horizontally, and then, once you have a little momentum, use it to start rising, adding a little air to your BC if necessary.

Rescue Breathing

As soon as you get the diver to the surface, check to see if he is breathing. If the dive boat is nearby, signal for help, but don't wait for it to arrive. If your buddy isn't breathing, you need to begin mouth-to-mouth resuscitation immediately. It can be performed in the water. (Note, however, that CPR cannot be performed in the water, because in order for chest compressions to work, a body must be supported by a firm surface.)

Start by establishing positive buoyancy. You'll need to fill the victim's BC with air and get rid of his weight belt and your own. How much you inflate your BC will depend on whether a fully inflated BC will prevent you from getting close to the victim to perform mouth-to-mouth resuscitation. Remove your mask and the victim's mask. You can hold onto them by sliding your arm through the straps to keep them handy.

Continue mouth-to-mouth resuscitation until breathing resumes or the boat arrives. Once you remove

A day octopus off Hawaii. As with most octopuses, the venom from its bite causes swelling and numbness in humans, but is not deadly.

the victim from the water, make sure his airway is open. Continue mouth-to-mouth resuscitation or administer CPR (if necessary, and if you are qualified to do so).

Once the victim resumes breathing, administer oxygen, treat him for shock, and try to protect him from excess heat or cold. You should take detailed notes of his condition (heart rate, respiration, color, and time; also note the names and con-tact information for any witnesses or bystanders) and get him medical help as soon as possible. In most cases of near-drowning, the victim inhales water, which can damage the lungs. A person who walks away from a near-drowning incident saying that he feels fine can suffer

fatal lung damage that manifests itself several hours later.

MARINE PLANTS AND ANIMALS

No question about it, the creatures of the deep occupy a mythic place in our imagination. Virtually every diver has at least had a passing thought about man-eating sharks and giant octopuses. But most encounters with marine life are benign, and the typical problems that do occur tend to be both mundane and preventable.

Nonetheless, there are potentially dangerous organisms down there. Marine plants and animals have evolved an astonishing array of defenses and feeding strategies, and some of them are dangerous to humans. A list of every single marine creature that could hurt us would be a long and frightening one. But despite the plethora of things that can hurt us, the fact is that very few of them actually *do*. Marine animals rarely attack humans. The great majority of problems occur when humans unknowingly or accidentally approach marine life, scaring it or irritating it. Sometimes, as in the case of fire coral, you don't have to irritate these organisms. Simply touching them is painful.

It's also possible, although rare, for large fish to mistakenly regard a diver as food. We most often think of sharks in this context, but other large and common species like barracuda and groupers occasionally inflict injuries, too.

There are two sure ways to avoid injuries from venomous plants and animals. First, avoid them (which obviously involves being able to identify them). And second, wear an exposure suit, even if it's just a body suit. If you simply can't resist the urge to touch, be sure you're wearing gloves. Or go diving with someone who knows the local marine life and can tell you which organisms are safe to touch, and (more important) which ones aren't.

Below is a partial list of organisms you'll want to be able to identify. Some of them are very common and cause only minor problems. A few are extremely rare but are included because of their potential for inflicting serious injury.

FIRST AID FOR STINGS

● Gently remove any part of the stingers left in the skin.
● Douse with vinegar.
● Use local anesthetic sprays or ointments to relieve pain.
● Prevent infection by irrigating and cleaning the wound, and cover it with a sterile dressing.
● Don't rub! If the wound itches, put on an antihistamine lotion such as hydrocortisone.

WARNING!

Stings, stabs, and bites from some marine organisms can be fatal to humans. A person who has been stung, bitten, or stabbed by an organism like a Portuguese man-of-war, a sea wasp, a stonefish, or a cone shell (among others) may suffer heart or respiratory failure. Here's how you can help:

● Ensure that the airway is open and check for breathing and pulse.
● Perform CPR if necessary.
● Administer oxygen.
● Treat for shock.
● If possible and while wearing gloves, remove any remaining sticker, spine, beak, or tentacle. Note: Removal may need to be done by a doctor.
● Control bleeding if necessary.
● If the injury is not bleeding profusely, immerse it in hot water for up to 30 minutes.
● Wash and irrigate the injury to dilute or remove the venom.
● Remove any clothing and jewelry (such as rings, necklaces, and bracelets) that might be constrictive if there is swelling.
● Immobilize the affected area.
● Keep notes on the victim's condition.
● Seek medical attention.

Stingers

Stingers — scientifically known as Cnidarians — use stinging capsules (called *nematocysts*) to find prey or to defend themselves from predators. Of some 10,000 species, at least 100 have the potential to harm humans. Symptoms of a sting might include burning pain and a red, inflamed area. Some of the stings can be extremely serious, and in rare cases they can be fatal.

FIRE CORALS are extremely common tropical species found attached to reefs, rocks, and wrecks. This organism looks like a coral, but technically it is a hydroid related to the Portuguese man-of-war (another dangerous organism). Stings from fire coral are among the most common venom-related diving injuries.

SEA ANEMONES These beautiful, soft-looking tubular colonies almost invite the inquisitive hand to touch

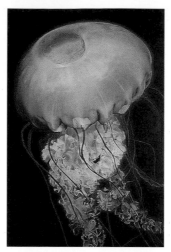

A trio of common stingers, from top: two jellyfish and a stinging fire coral. Of some 10,000 species of fire corals, sea anemones, and jellyfish, at least 100 can be harmful to humans.

them, but some varieties are poisonous to humans. The venom of a sea anemone plays an important role in the ecology of a coral reef: Some species of fish have developed resistance to the venom of certain anemones and live inside them, protected from potential predators by their venomous hosts.

JELLYFISH These creatures are more mobile than corals and anemones, and therefore a little harder to avoid. Not all are harmful to humans, but a few species pose the risk of serious injury. Portuguese man-of-war, commonly identified as jellyfish, are technically more closely related to hydroids and fire coral.

Regardless, the Portuguese man-of-war is mobile, like a jellyfish, and extremely venomous. This traveling colony of venom floats on the surface aided by a purple air sack. The stings can be very serious, causing a searing

sensation.
SEA WASPS
(technically
jellyfish),
found in the
Indo-Pacific,
are another
dangerous
species. Their
stings contain
a potentially
deadly venom.
Although most
sea wasp
stings are
minor, contact
with especially
large tentacles
can cause
almost imme-
diate spasms,
paralysis, and
cardiac arrest.
Relatives of
the sea wasp
include the
box jellyfish,
some species
of which
inhabit the Caribbean.

Clockwise from top: An orange (1) and a purple (2) crown-of-thorns sea star. This creature devours living coral, and can cause a painful sting. A crowned sea urchin (3), a giant red sea urchin (4), a long-spine sea urchin (5), and a fire urchin (6). Painful injuries from their spines is common among divers. Avoid contact with the delicate-looking stinging hydroid (7); it can inflict a painful sting.

Stabbers

Some venomous marine life forms
don't sting but can nonetheless
administer a nasty dose of venom.
SEA URCHINS These "underwater
cacti" are easy to recognize. Most of
them look like pin cushions. The
"pins" can vary in size from less than
an inch long to more than a foot in

length. Their spines break easily and
become embedded into skin. Sea
urchin injuries are among the most
common diver injuries. The spines
are difficult, sometimes impossible, to
extract without causing infection, and
should be removed only by a medical
professional. Eventually, they break
down in and are absorbed by the
body; not, however, without causing
significant discomfort, especially if

From top: The tasseled scorpionfish, spotted scorpionfish, and stonefish are venomous camouflage experts, native primarily to tropical waters.

cally on top of them and not even know it — and therein lies the problem. Stingrays attack when disturbed or frightened. A stingray flings its barbed tail forward, which inflicts a laceration and in some cases injects venom.

STONEFISH AND SCORPIONFISH These camouflage experts are native primarily to tropical waters. Their spines straighten when they are agitated, and inject a venom that can cause extreme pain, significant swelling, and potential cardiac or respiratory problems.

CONE SHELLS These are common, beautiful snails found in the Pacific. They often catch the eye of children and collectors. A cone shells injects venom through a harpoon-like structure on its proboscis. The venom can be fatal.

Biters

Biting animals can injure divers by injecting venom or by causing traumatic bleeding.

OCTOPUS Any problem you have with an octopus is likely to be of your own making. Some divers like to pick them up and "play" with them, an activity that is undoubtedly more enjoyable for the diver than for the octopus. If the octopus runs out of patience, it might bite. An octopus's beak is strong enough to break shellfish open, and it can inject venom, too. If you are nonetheless inclined to play with an octopus, one species to definitely stay clear of is the blue-ringed octopus

(as is common) the injury is on the bottom of the foot. Aloe is said to provide relief. Dive booties and a careful eye will spare you from an encounter of the prickly kind.

STINGRAYS These bottom dwellers like to lie on the ocean floor looking like a spot of sand. Their camouflage is so effective that you can be practi-

(found in the Indo-Pacific and common near Australia). Note that toxins from an octopus bite work slowly, starting with numbness that spreads, and can be followed by paralysis, respiratory failure, and death. EELS look fierce, no doubt about it. They pump their jaws in a movement we identify as threatening. Actually, all they are doing is breathing: That's how they move water through their gills. Generally, eels are not aggressive — except if you happen to carelessly stick your hand in a hole that they are occupying. When eels bite, they tend to clamp down, hard, and they can be difficult to dislodge. SHARKS comprise some 350 species, and they live in all marine environments. Only a few shark species are harmful to humans, however, among them the great white (up to 30 feet), the white-tip oceanic (up to 11 feet), the tiger (11 to 15 feet), the mako (up to 12 feet), the hammerhead (17 or more feet), and the blue (12 or more feet). Sharks detect prey by smell and vibration, and they attack to feed or to defend a territory. A shark that takes too much interest in a diver, behaves aggressively, or arches its back may be defending his territory. Your best response is to calmly and slowly retreat from the area. Stay underwater — sharks are attracted to movement, which is more evident when you are on the surface. Stay with your buddy, because two of you together present a bigger target. If you are attacked,

From top: the lionfish forages at night in the tropical waters of the Indo-Pacific. The highly venomous banded sea snake's bite can cause paralysis, while the olive sea snake's bite is less harmful.

fight back. Sharks sometimes brush against potential prey, and an aggressive response from you — smacking it in the head or punching it in the nose — might make it rethink its interest in you.

Any biting attacks from large fish can result in severe blood loss.

Top: a green moray eel. Bottom: a leopard moray eel. For all that eels look fierce, they are not especially aggressive.

Entanglement

Divers occasionally get themselves tangled up in plants like kelp and seaweed, or in fishing lines and nets, or even in submerged tree branches, especially if they get careless and let their hoses dangle all over the place. Although your first instinct might be to flail away at whatever is holding

onto you, thrashing about can actually get you more knotted up. It's best to stop, assess the situation, and then methodically untangle yourself or cut yourself out. This is one reason why divers should carry knives, even if they don't plan to use them. Make eye contact with your buddy so she knows what's going on and can help if necessary. If you've really got yourself caught, you might have to take your gear off (while keeping your regulator in your mouth, of course), disentangle it, then put your gear back on.

Lacerations

Live corals can inflict stings; but dead corals are dangerous, too. They can inflict lacerations. You'll sometimes have to walk across beds of fossilized coral to get to a dive site. Dive booties will protect your feet, but you must also be careful about being tossed into a hunk of coral by a renegade wave. Similarly, you'll find barnacles attached to rocks, docks, and other stationary objects, and they can give you a nasty scratch if you're not careful. If you have to climb on coral or on barnacle-covered rock to get to a dive site, wear booties and, if necessary, gloves. And move gently, because both corals and barnacles are crusty and sharp enough to tear an expensive wet suit — not to mention your skin.

Treatment for lacerations includes stopping bleeding if necessary, then washing out the area and covering it with an antibiotic and a bandage.

DIVE
SMART

O kay, you've got your C-card. You're ready to go. But before you take that giant stride into the water, you need to take care of a few things up here on land.

Remember the diver's adage: "Plan your dive, and dive your plan."

This chapter discusses choosing a buddy, choosing a dive site, evaluating local conditions, and a host of other planning issues. By covering all the bases while you're still above the water, you are ensuring that once you go below the water, you'll have the experience you came for: a safe and successful dive.

THE BUDDY SYSTEM

Hearing the term *buddy system* probably reminds you of summer camp, with whistle-blowing counselors making you tread water while they took what seemed like forever to count heads. The idea back at summer camp was that if you got in over your head, so to speak, your buddy could yell for help — if, that is, she actually stuck by your side and knew where you were.

In SCUBA diving, the idea isn't too different, except that you're using life-support equipment. Your buddy may not only have to call for help, but she may also have to provide it herself.

If something should go wrong underwater, you won't want to face it alone.

student from a diving class. Diving repeatedly with the same buddy allows you to develop a shared rhythm. You'll get a sense of how your buddy dives, and you might even find yourself anticipating what she's going to do next. You'll come up with your own way of communicating. Perhaps most important, after you've shared many hours of bottom time with the same person, you'll notice immediately if something starts to go awry.

What if you don't know any other divers? Try a local dive club, or dive shop, or go on guided group dives, where you'll be assigned a buddy if you show up solo. Sometimes that person will be a complete stranger. You'll want to tactfully find out a little about your new buddy's diving experience. Ask her where she got her C-card, and where else she has dived. This doesn't have to be an inquisition; light jabber about favorite dive sites can tell you a lot about someone's style. Trade stories. And listen. Mostly, you want to get a feel for your new buddy's attitude toward diving. Is your buddy a gonzo

The buddy system is a mainstay of SCUBA diving. It ensures that if something goes wrong underwater, you won't have to handle it alone.

The buddy system begins when you first start talking about a dive, and continues through the planning, the preparation, and the dive itself. Your buddy will help you (and you will help her) don equipment. She'll double-check your gear during the pre-dive safety check. Underwater, both of you will monitor depth, dive time, and air supply, so you'll be less likely to make careless mistakes and stay down too long. You'll keep track of each other's gear, noting any suspicious bubbles (they might indicate leakage in a hose or a valve), dangling hoses, or loosened straps. Above all, you'll communicate.

Often, your buddy will be a family member, a friend, or a fellow

type ("down as deep as I can get for as long as the air lasts") or a more cautious type ("I know the dive tables say it's okay, but let's come up early just to be safe")? And what's her idea of the buddy system? Does she expect you two to stay within arm's reach at all times, or does she think it's okay for her to wander off on her own?

One good place to find a dive buddy is at an advanced or specialty class. Divers who take these classes are demonstrating that they appreciate the value of learning about proper dive procedures and techniques. That's a quality you want in the person you will be relying on in an emergency.

Communicating with Your Buddy

Communicating with your buddy begins before you even hit the water. Talk about the kind of dive you want to have. Discuss your expectations: What do you want to get out of this dive? If you tell your buddy that you're fascinated by a certain kind of marine life, she'll understand why you're lagging behind. If you know that she's really serious about underwater photography, you can point out something you think will make a great picture.

But the most important reason to communicate clearly underwater is safety. Divers have their own sign language to communicate important concepts: "I'm out of air"; "I'm

having trouble with my ears"; "Follow me"; "Let's go up"; and so on. Many of the basic signals are standard throughout the diving world (see pages 142–143), but do review this basic information before you dive — especially with a new partner.

Signs can be used for more than just basic communication about your air supply and whether or not it's time to go up. There's no need to limit your vocabulary. Consider: If you happen to know sign language, you can have an entire conversation underwater! In fact, some divers have started looking at American sign-language books to increase their vocabularies. After all, why invent a whole new language when there's a perfectly good one available? Over time, you and your buddy will develop a vocabulary of signals to do everything, from checking each other's air supplies to pointing out interesting undersea life. Some divers take slates and markers down with them so they can communicate precisely.

You can also use sound to get someone's attention. Although it is difficult to tell which direction sound is coming from underwater, rapping on a tank with a knife makes a clearly audible sound that's bound to be noticed.

Finally, don't forget that you might need to communicate with the folks on the boat in an emergency. On the surface, whistles can be heard

Stop, hold it, stay there

Something is wrong

OK? OK.

Distress, help

OK? OK. (on surface or at distance)

OK? OK. (one hand occupied)

Danger

Go up, going up

Go down, going down

Low on air

Out of air

Buddy breathe or share air

from a long distance; they are much more effective than shouting (and require less energy). To communicate with divers, some boats are equipped with sound systems that emit an audible recall signal. The use of this signal should be covered in your pre-dive briefing.

Bottom Time and Your Buddy

If you and your buddy have been certified by different agencies, you could be carrying around different dive tables that give you different maximum bottom times. It's instructive to plan your dives using both tables, just to see how the answers compare. It's safest, of course, to use the most conservative tables to plan your dives.

If you are using a computer, you should *both* be using a computer — and you should *each* have one. Here's why: Computers make their calculations based on precise measurements of your exact depth and the amount of time you stay at it. When you move up or down, the computer takes that movement into account and calculates your nitrogen level accordingly. If you

 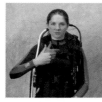  

Come here	Me, or watch me	Under, over, or around	Level off this depth

Go that way	Which direction?	Ears not clearing	I am cold

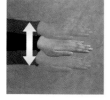 

Take it easy, slow down	Hold hands	Get with your buddy	You lead, I'll follow

dive several feet above your buddy, your computer will record different data than your buddy's computer. When one of them says "time to come up," the dive's over for both of you.

Air Consumption and Your Buddy

It's common for two people to consume air at radically different rates. Women tend to consume less air than men do because they have smaller lungs. Experienced divers consume less air because they are more relaxed and efficient.

Needless to say, it's important to come up well *before* you're out of air. Many divers are told to start their ascent when the needle hits the 500 psi mark, which is a good habit on shallower dives. On deeper dives, however, starting up when you have 500 psi left in your tank may not give you enough air to ascend slowly and take safety stops, especially if there are unforeseen circumstances or an out-of-air emergency. For this reason, many dive masters will want you back on the boat with 500 psi in the tank.

Cave diving, Rainbow River, Florida. Only certified cave divers led by experienced guides should explore underwater caves.

Whatever the protocol of the dive boat, it's your responsibility to monitor your air supply and consumption, and to come up well before you are at risk for an out-of-air situation. Don't be tempted to stay down "just a little longer." You need that extra air — just in case. (In case what? In case your SPG is for some reason inaccurate. In case your buddy's reg malfunctions or he runs out of air and needs to use some of yours. In case you surface in rough water far from the boat and want to swim to the boat below the surface, where it's easier, rather than on the surface in the chop. You get the picture.)

If it's just you and your buddy diving together, you both have to come up when one of you is low on air. But in a group situation, the partner who still has plenty of air left might be able to stay down longer. On a group dive, the dive leader should discuss procedures for this common contingency. Often the low-on-air diver will signal to her buddy and to the dive master that she is low on air and going up. In calm seas, an experienced diver can ascend alone by following the dive line and taking a safety stop while trailing above the other divers. Before you ascend alone, especially if you are ascending from a deep dive where a safety stop is required, you should be absolutely confident that you have the control to ascend at the recommended rate of no more than 30 feet per minute and the control to take a safety stop if required.

When one diver goes up and the other stays down, the "orphaned" buddy should either "triple up" with another dive pair, or become buddies with another orphan.

Note: If you are going up early, be sure that the dive master and your buddy have acknowledged that you're headed to the surface, or they will end up wasting the rest of their dive looking for you and surfacing unnecessarily.

Where'd She Go?

On dry land, I'm the independent sort. When I go hiking with my husband, I feel perfectly comfortable if we split up and there's a gap of a couple of miles between us. But underwater, we want each other right at arm's length. One of us doesn't go charging off in new and interesting directions without making sure the other is coming along, too.

Sometimes, if the visibility is poor, or at night, or if you're diving in a large group, you might temporarily lose sight of your buddy. In murky, low-light situations, one diver can look just like another. I learned this once when my husband and I were diving with a newlywed (and newly certified) couple on their honeymoon. All of a sudden, I felt someone's hand in mine — and it wasn't my husband's! The groom had gotten me mixed up with his bride.

Try to note something special about your buddy's equipment: the bright yellow fins, or the pink stripes on his wet suit. And, of course, frequently check up on where he is. Sometimes, if the visibility is especially poor and conditions are rough, divers use a *buddy line*, a short rope with hand loops at each end to keep buddies in physical contact with each other.

You should review the procedure for what to do if you and your buddy get separated. Look around for one minute, then go to the surface and regroup. If you are using a reference line with a buoy, it will be that much easier to find each other.

Solo Diving: A Warning

Your instructors will unanimously tell you that it's a bad idea, but once in a while, you're going to meet someone who tells you he dives solo. You might also hear rationalizations for it. Some people claim that diving solo makes you more aware and responsible, that it eliminates the liability of a "bad" buddy who pulls you into danger by risky behavior, that it encourages you to be more cautious, that it puts responsibility for your life in your own hands where it belongs. All of that may be true. No one knows exactly how many solo divers are out there, so statistics regarding accidents and solo divers are hard to interpret. But if you're reading this book for certification, review, or to learn about SCUBA, one thing is certain: Diving solo is far beyond your ability and experience. It's not something to even consider.

WHERE TO DIVE

Water covers more than 70 percent of the earth's surface, from the Arctic Ocean to a midwestern quarry, from the Great Lakes to the Great Salt Lake, from tropical reefs to continental shelves, from ponds to rivers to water-filled caves. The challenge isn't so much finding a place to dive, but choosing a place to dive.

But first things first.

Your open-water C-card is a license to dive, but do give some consideration to your actual experience. When you're starting out, look for conditions that are similar to (or easier than) those in which you were trained. You can't take the skills you learned in the lazy tropics and expect them to be adequate for a cold-water dive off the coast of Nova Scotia. You can, however, take a special dry-suit class that will familiarize you with the equipment and skills you need for rigorous conditions.

Dive Centers

Going on a few dives under the guidance of a professional is probably the best way to familiarize yourself with different conditions and equipment. A dive master who knows the local waters can introduce you to the conditions, recommend appropriate gear, give you a rundown of the ecology, and point out interesting things you can expect to see. You might also reap a financial benefit by sharing transportation costs on long boat rides out to a dive site. On the

---

KNOW BEFORE YOU GO: QUESTIONS TO DISCUSS WITH YOUR BUDDY

❶ How and where will you enter the water?
❷ What is your course and destination?
❸ Anything special down there that either of you will want to linger over?
❹ Are you using dive computers or tables?
❺ How long will you stay down?
❻ What is the maximum depth?
❼ At what air pressure will you stop the dive?
❽ What hand signals will you use?
❾ What will you do if you get separated?
❿ Where and how do you plan to exit the water?
⓫ What procedures will you follow if there is an out-of-air emergency?

downside, ask about the maximum number of divers the dive center will take at any one time. A group dive that involves 15 to 20 other people can resemble a three-ring circus, especially in limited visibility.

A typical guided dive will be led by a dive master. Occasionally, dives might be led by experienced open-water divers, not dive masters. *Be warned:* These leaders may know local conditions, but they do not have the dive master's advanced training in rescue, first aid, and emergency procedures.

Dive masters will usually plan the dive, using a dive table, wheel, or computer to calculate bottom times, depths, and surface intervals between dives. They'll also check tides and water conditions to ensure that you're diving a partic-ular site at the optimum time of day. Before the dive, a dive master will give you a brief orientation. This briefing should cover max-imum depth and bottom time; safety stops; entry and exit procedures; communication signals; contin-gency plans for low-on-air divers; the location of the first aid kit, oxygen unit, and nearest recom-pression chamber; emergency com-munications via radio or cell phones; local law; and rules of the boat. The dive master should also make sure that each diver is hooked up with a buddy and that divers have performed a pre-dive safety check. Finally, the briefing

Cold sea water is so rich with plankton and other life that it is cloudy, preventing sunlight from penetrating far. Dive lights (and full wet suits) are a necessity.

should give divers an idea of what kind of marine life they can expect to see.

If this information isn't covered in the briefing, you should ask. You should also perform your own bottom-time, pressure-group, and surface-interval calculations; and when you're underwater, make a point of frequently checking your computer, depth gauge, air supply, and timer. Remember: The ultimate responsibility for your safety belongs to you — not your buddy, and not the dive master.

Independent Diving

If you're diving in a familiar environment, you may well prefer independent diving. On a shore dive, for example, you don't have long rides out to the site, or boats to charter, or crews to hire. The water is usually shallower, and help is only a few swimming strokes away. If you feel comfortable with the conditions, you may well decide that you don't need the help of a dive master.

On independent dives, you take on much more responsibility than you do when you dive with a guide.

Note: *Independent dives* refer to non-guided dives, not solo dives. It's a ground-zero assumption that you *always* dive with a buddy.

You and your buddy will be responsible for calculating maximum depth and bottom time, surface intervals, and no-decompression limits for repetitive dives — and if you make a

■ _____

PLANNING MAJOR TRIPS

Although almost everyone can find a local place to dive, most serious divers end up logging a lot of frequent-flyer miles to and from dive destinations. After all, most of us don't live next door to a coral reef, or near an underwater graveyard of famous shipwrecks. Let's be honest: The local quarry might be a lot of fun, but it can't compare to a Caribbean reef. But before you pull out your credit card, buy your plane ticket, and lug 100 pounds of gear across the country (or even farther), there are a few issues to consider.

Beware: All magazine ads and brochures look pretty much the same. Turquoise water, clear skies, gorgeous reefs, and a gazillion fish. What a disappointment to land somewhere and find that the

pictures were taken before the reef succumbed to pollution, or that the beautiful boat in the brochure has been in dry dock for a year, waiting for parts, leaving you to bounce around on the H.M.S. Leaky Tub. You can get more objective opinions from your fellow divers, so ask around. Pros at a dive shop, a dive buddy, or your classmates might have some recommendations. Also check out diving guidebooks, which compare sites more objectively and give important seasonal information. Agents specializing in diving, and dive shops that offer trips, can also be good sources of information. They're looking for regular customers, so they're unlikely to steer you wrong.

● Does your destination offer enough activities for a non-diving partner?

mistake, there's no dive master to set you straight. You will also need to choose entry and exit points, determine the course of the dive, make the appropriate arrangements for gear and transportation, and develop a plan for emergencies.

CONDITIONS

The first step in dive planning is to acquire a thorough understanding of local conditions: how deep the dives are, what you can expect to see, water currents, and a host of other issues discussed below. If you're diving in a new locale, get input from local divers or sign up for a familiarization dive with a shop. You'll also need to check local laws and regulations. On private property, there may be fees or licenses, or the landowner may require special certifications. Other laws that can vary from place

---

● Does the diving available match your interests, training, and skill level?

● If not, is training available on site to qualify you to dive that deep-water wreck or the famous cave?

● Can you rent gear, and what brands are available?

● Are night dives available?

● Is there boat diving or shore diving or both? Are boat dives one-tank, two-tank, or three-tank dives?

● Will you dive independently with your buddy or with a dive master? Are both options available?

● Are there seasonal weather patterns (like monsoons, hurricanes, difficult currents, or times of predictable bad visibility) that explain those big discounts in September?

● How many different dive sites are there within a reasonable distance of your vacation's "home base"? You don't want to spend all your time on long boat rides to faraway sites. And you don't want to be stuck repeating the same dive over and over and over again.

● What about accommodations and food? Some dive sites are strictly no-frills above the surface of the sea — which may be fine for committed divers, not so fine for casual types. Don't rely on pictures from the Internet. With a good camera angle and a backdrop of pines and sea, even a shack can look enticing to a snowbound Northerner dreaming of a sunny escape. Be specific about your expectations when you book the trip.

The open ocean presents many faces, including somewhat choppy conditions (top) and large swells topped by white caps (below). Tides and currents—unseen beneath the waves—also must be factored into dive planning.

Lakes also experience these daily fluctuations of water level, caused by the gravitational pull of the moon. Tides vary according to the location and the phase of the moon. Local tide tables, often printed in the newspapers in seashore communities, tell you when high tide and low tide will occur, but to interpret whether and how tides affect conditions at a particular dive site, you'll need to speak with someone who has local knowledge about diving in the area.

Most obviously, tides affect water levels. For divers, this means that a dive that is 85 feet deep at low tide may be 100 feet deep at high tide. This variation will influence your maximum bottom time, pressure group, and the required surface interval. If in doubt, calculate the dive for high tide and double-check your depth gauge so you know how deep you actually went.

In addition to water levels, tides influence currents, especially during so-called spring tides. *Spring tides*, which occur during full and new moons, are extreme tides, with maximum variation between high tide and low tide. *Neap tides*, which occur between lunar cycles, cause less variation between high tide and low tide. Finally, *slack movement* is a period of slow or no water movement, usually occurring as the tides are changing and the tides and currents cancel each other out. Some sites can be dived only during slack-water periods.

to place include regulations concerning the use of certain gear, such as diving knives or dive flags, the collecting of marine animals, or the salvaging of souvenirs from wrecks (especially in national parks).

Water Movement

Tides rise and fall, currents surge and recede, eddies swirl, waves crest, surf crashes and pounds: Water is constantly in motion. How it moves — how fast, how strong, at what time of day — will affect your dive, perhaps more than any other single factor.

TIDES We think of tides as oceanic phenomena, but estuaries and large bodies of water such as the Great

CURRENTS Tides create currents; so do waves, wind, and the collision of hot and cold water. Smaller, more localized currents can also be caused by the shape of the shoreline and the direction and movement of water as it reaches the shore.

If possible, plan your dives to avoid predictable currents, such as those generated by the movement of daily tides. In some places, currents are so strong during certain parts of the tidal cycle that diving is impossible. In other locales, major seasonal shifts in wind and current patterns may make an entire area off-limits for a period of weeks or months. In such cases, checking locally will pay big dividends.

It is possible to swim against mild currents, but be aware that the average diver can't swim at much more than 1 knot per hour. So swimming against even a mild current uses much more energy and more air than diving in still water. You'll need to take this increased air consumption into account when you're planning your dive, and pay special attention to your SPG during the actual dive to make sure you have enough air to complete your planned route. If you have to dive against a current, plan to do so at the beginning of your dive, when you are fresh. Then, at the end of your dive, you can let the current carry you back to your dive boat.

Note: It is almost always easier to swim against a current beneath the surface than on the surface. This is because beneath the surface, currents tend to be weaker, there is no surface chop or wave action to fight, and as a diver you are more efficient and streamlined. If at the end of your dive you're having trouble with the current, drop down a little and swim beneath the surface. If you're still having trouble — and if (and only if) both your air supply and dive tables permit it — go even deeper. The closer you are to the bottom, the less current you'll have to fight.

With some currents, especially localized currents, it may be possible to avoid the problem altogether by swimming perpendicular to the current and thereby escaping it.

A strong current will simply take you with it, no matter which direction you think you're swimming in. If you are caught in a current that is stronger than you are, there's no sense in trying to fight it. All you'll do is use up all your air and exhaust yourself. If conditions permit, you might as well relax and enjoy a "drift dive." Spread out your arms, let your feet bend behind you, and fly along like Superman. In a really strong current, you'll be traveling so fast that you can't even slow down to examine something that interests you. The feeling of soaring through the sea is unbeatable.

But *drift diving* is not something you want to get into by accident. For one thing, a current of 2 to 3 knots could carry you quite a distance from your dive boat over

Waves
breaking on shore
create undertow. While undertow
feels like a powerful current pulling you out to
sea, it is only the backwash of the wave, and
soon harmlessly dissipates.

the course of a 40-minute dive. Where currents are strong and unpredictable, you'll want to have a backup drift-diving plan. This plan should not only involve the divers but it should also involve the folks on the boat, who will have to find the divers when they come up. Drift divers usually trail a surface float behind them so the boat can more easily track their movement. You should have a way to signal to the boat once you surface at the end of your dive, because water movement and surface chop can make it hard for people on a small boat to see a swimmer. (Tip: In an emergency, you can wave a fin to get attention. Just be sure you have a good grip on it, because the last thing you want to do is drop it!)

If you have not planned for a drift dive, and find yourself being carried away by the current, it's best to resurface and discuss the situation with the people on the boat.

WAVES, SURF, AND SURGE Waves are formed by wind transferring its energy to water. They can travel thousands of miles before they finally end up crashing on a distant shore. Waves break because as they reach the

shore, the bottom of the waves is delayed by friction with the seafloor while the top of the wave continues on, breaks, and then dribbles back to sea in an undertow. Undertows can feel very powerful, but they usually dissipate only a few yards from shore.

In open water, waves can be small ripples or choppy whitecaps that make you seasick, stir up sediment at the dive site, and rock your boat so much that gear assembly becomes a major challenge. Waves can also make surface swimming difficult and can obstruct visibility, as when people on a low boat are looking for surfacing divers.

Waves can also break on reefs and sandbars. In fact, often you'll be able to locate a reef because of the telltale chop of waves breaking against it. Sometimes, especially on shallow dives near shore, waves create a movement called *surge*, in which the water ebbs and flows quite strongly as it moves around or over a reef. Surge is potentially dangerous because it can be strong enough to knock you into a reef, which could injure both you and the coral.

Near shore, you'll also need to pay attention to *longshore currents*, which form when waves approach the shore at an angle. The resulting

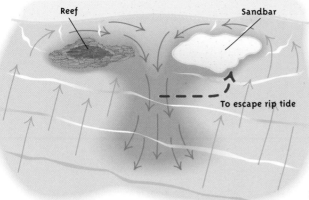

Reef

Sandbar

Rip currents, or rip tides, occur between reefs or sandbars, and can carry swimmers out to deep water quickly. To get out of their path, swim perpendicular to the current.

To escape rip tide

current moves down the shoreline and can carry you away from a planned exit point. If there are limited exit and entry points due to obstructions like coral rock and shallow reefs, being caught by a longshore current will create problems when it's time to exit the water. So if longshore currents are present, be sure to start your dive upcurrent from your planned exit point. It's also a good idea to have a backup exit point identified just in case you miss the first one.

Finally, there are *rip currents* (sometimes called *rip tides*). These are localized currents caused by water flowing around a narrow opening between such formations as reefs and sandbars. These currents are strong and can carry a swimmer out to deeper water quickly; however, they are very local — they won't take you all the way out to sea! Nonetheless, you'll want to get out of their path. The best way to do this is to swim perpendicular to the current.

Visibility

In the tropics it's not unusual to have visibility of 100 or more feet. You might hear some griping if the "vis" is less than 80 feet. But in the waters of my home turf, Long Island Sound, good visibility means that you can see the end of your arm; 20 feet of visibility would be reason to celebrate.

Visibility is more than an aesthetic issue; it's a safety issue. In murky waters, you must keep closer track of your buddy, your position, and your depth. You should also pay attention to your buoyancy so you don't crash into things like debris, a tree branch, or a bed of vegetation, that could hurt or entangle you.

A buddy line can help you and your buddy stay together even when you can't see each other. A reference line (see page 183) is helpful for orientation during descents and ascents. Keep track of your depth gauge to monitor your position. Without visual references, you may lose track of whether you are ascending or descending, and how fast.

SEA-FLOOR MORPHOLOGY

1) Shore
2) Beach
3) Sand
   underwater
4) Coral
5) Kelp
   (cold water)
6) Steep slope
7) Rocks
8) Wreck
9) Boat traffic

Visibility varies not only from place to place, but also from day to day. It can be affected by the weather (wind can stir up waves; runoff from rain might deposit silt and sediment), bottom composition, particles, pollution, and such phenomena as red tides (huge colonies of plankton).

Bottom Composition

What's down there, anyway? The bottom composition may be rock, vegetation, mud, pebbles, sand, silt, or coral. An experienced diver always approaches the bottom slowly, in full control of his buoyancy. Where there is a lot of silt or mud, crashing into the bottom can ruin everyone's visibility and brand you as the pariah of the diving day.

You don't even have to touch the bottom to stir things up. Merely flapping your fins too close to the seafloor can churn up a cloud of silt. In silty or muddy areas, concentrate on holding your legs up behind you so they don't drag on the bottom.

You'll also want to be careful in rocky or coral areas. Scratches and cuts from corals are painful and can take a long time to heal, and some marine life, like the common fire coral, is venomous (see Chapter 6). Coral is easily damaged by careless or out-of-control divers.

Finally, bottom composition may affect your entry and exit points, especially on shore dives, where patches of coral in shallow water can block the passage from shore to deeper water.

Temperature

Water temperature will determine what kind of exposure suit to wear (see Chapter 3). In addition, you'll need to consider the presence of so-called *thermoclines*, which are sudden abrupt changes in temperature of as much as 15°F to 20°F. Thermoclines occur when a mass of warm water and a mass of cold water meet, but don't mix due to their different densities. They can cause currents to form. Thermoclines can be found in any water, but they are especially common in freshwater lakes and quarries.

Resist the temptation to touch corals. Some, like fire coral, are venomous, while others, though harmless, are easily damaged by careless divers.

Weather

Don't ignore what's happening up at the surface! On windy days, the surface chop will be stronger and the visibility may be poor, so you might want to avoid a long, bumpy boat ride. Here's a surprise: Rainy days are sometimes fine for diving. (After all, you're going to get wet, right?) One of the few downsides is that clouds will filter out some light, making the colors less brilliant. Another is that if you are diving close to shore near the mouth of a river, rain-water runoff can affect the visibility. Lightning, however, is dangerous, especially if you are on a boat, or if you are swimming on the surface and your metal tank is sticking up, just inviting a strike from above. Take into account the temperature and also consider that on a moving boat, there will be a windchill factor. A windbreaker or rain jacket is always a good idea — as is sun protection. On cold-weather dives, of course, you'll want to bring plenty of warm layers and hot drinks.

Freshwater Considerations

You're less buoyant in fresh water than in salt water (for more on this, see Appendix I), so you'll need fewer weights (assuming that other considerations, like the thickness of your wet suit, remain the same). Freshwater diving can include river diving (which is like drift diving), cave and cavern diving, ice diving, and wreck diving (as in the Great Lakes). When diving in fresh water, you'll often encounter some combination of the following conditions: silty or muddy bottom composition, underwater vegetation, thermoclines, pleasure-craft traffic on the surface, and underwater obstacles below. For instance, if you are diving in a reservoir, you might find yourself navigating through what's left of the forest that was drowned when the reservoir was dammed. You may also need to consider how altitude affects your no-decompressions limit if the dive site is above sea level (see Chapter 5).

Obstacles and Hazards

Underwater hazards can include dams, wrecks, tree branches, fishing nets and line, garbage, broken glass, kelp forests, shallow coral beds or coral rocks that block passage from shore to the dive sites, and heavy boat traffic.

Hazards can also include marine life, from infestations of Portuguese man-of-war to encounters with larger creatures. Many of them respond defensively if provoked. Others — in extremely rare cases — may mistake a diver for a food source (see Chapter 6 for a discussion of the possible hazards of marine life). In the vast majority of cases, you can ensure your safety by being able to identify potential hazards, and then avoiding them.

With a respect for the environment in which you are diving, good buoyancy control, and thorough dive planning, you can greatly reduce the chance of unpleasant encounters with the denizens of inner space.

DIVING SMART

So let's say you've traveled to your dive destination. You've done a familiarization dive with a local pro. You've picked up information on tides and sites and conditions at the dive shop when you had your tanks filled. You've got a buddy. The waiter at your hotel says that his cousin has a boat; all you have to do is let him know when you want a ride to Paradise Reef.

What you do between now and the moment you get into the water will determine the safety and enjoyment of your dive.

STEP 1: Site Selection

Where will you dive?

What is the purpose of the dive (photography, lobstering, relaxation)?

What general logistics need to be addressed (transportation, time of dive, meeting place, responsibilities for bringing lunch, payment and extra costs such as tips)?

What is the character of the dive site and what conditions can you expect?

Are there alternate sites nearby that would be safer or easier, in case conditions are rough?

If multiple dives are planned, which site will you dive first? (Consider any conditions like tide and depth that may affect the feasibility and safety of the sequence of dives.)

Some encounters with underwater creatures are almost comical.

Are there any local regulations you must comply with (dive flags, use of knives, permits for lobstering)?

How will you spend your surface interval (traveling from one site to another, sunbathing on a sandbar, visiting a nearby beach, having lunch on the boat, snorkeling)?

STEP 2: Planning for Safety

Do you have the appropriate gear for the conditions and is it well maintained?

Does your rental gear fit, and do you know how to operate it?

Do you, your buddy, and any other divers have the training and experience for the conditions you expect to encounter and the equipment you will need to use?

Is the dive within the ability of the least-qualified diver in your group?

What will be the maximum depth and bottom times?

What will be the minimum surface interval between dives?

Who will be the dive leader?

If you are diving in an out-and-back pattern, how will you determine when to turn around: time, or air consumption?

Under what conditions might it be advisable to cancel this particular dive?

Do you have a first aid kit and an emergency plan that includes a way to call for help?

Do you have an emergency plan for what to do if you lose your buddy, become low on air or out of air, or exceed maximum allowable bottom time?

STEP 3: Day of the Dive

Review weather conditions.
Check your gear list.

Fill tanks and double-check the air pressure before leaving for the dive site.
Try on rented gear.
Make sure someone knows where you are going and when you are expected back. Agree on what they'll do if you don't show up as planned.

STEP 4: At the Dive Site
Make a final evaluation of the conditions and decide whether to do your planned dive, an alternate dive, or no dive at all.
Confirm the dive entry and exit points and procedures with other divers and boat personnel.

GEAR CHECK

Keeping a gear list handy is the best way to avoid forgetting things. Once you start going on dive trips, keep a note of the gear you used. Was the wet suit warm enough? Did you wish you had a hood and mitts? Also note any malfunctions so you can have them repaired before your next dive. A good time to get gear serviced is before a major trip.

FOR THE DIVE
Mask
Snorkel with snorkel keeper
Fins
Booties (if you use them)
Mitts and hood (if conditions warrant)
Appropriate wet suit
Weight belt and enough weights (more weights are needed in salt water than in fresh water)
BC
Regulator with octopus (alternate second stage), low-pressure inflator hose, and submersible pressure gauge; dry-suit inflator, if using a dry suit
Tanks (filled and checked)
Dive tables
Information system: compass, computer, timer, depth gauge
Other accessories, if used: knife, sheath, collection bag, dive float, dive flag
Specialty equipment: lights, cameras
Repair kit
First aid/Oxygen kit

FOR THE BOAT
C-Card and logbook
Hat
Sunscreen
Water and/or electrolyte replacement fluid
Windbreaker
Towels
Long-sleeved shirt for sun protection
Lunch and snacks
Seasickness medication

Review communication signals.
Confirm depth and time limits.
Confirm depth and duration of safety
stops.
Review emergency plan (out of air,
separation, exceeding depth
limits).
Do a final pre-dive safety check (see
page 75).

Suiting up for the dive. Go over your final pre-dive safety checklist with your buddy.

STEP 5: Diving Your Plan
Monitor your instruments
throughout the dive to be sure
you are not exceeding depth and
time limits.
Monitor your air supply — and your
buddy's air supply.
Take dive tables with you so you can
calculate any necessary emergency
decompression stops or modifica-
tions in your dive profile.
Plan to be on the surface with 500
psi left in your tank.

STEP 6: After the Dive
Make a note of any gear that was not
in top condition during the dive.
Suspicious bubbles, frayed straps,
and chewed mouthpieces must be
fixed before you forget about them.
Make any repairs you can make.
Have technical equipment serviced as soon as possible.
Replenish your first aid kit and your
repair kit.
If your dive was deeper or longer
than expected, recalculate your
pressure group, minimum surface
intervals, and no-decompression
limits for any subsequent dives.

Turn off the air valves in the tank and
secure equipment so it won't fall.
At the end of the day, rinse
equipment.
Log your dive.

THE LOGBOOK
A logbook can be nothing more than
a simple notebook in which you write
down the particulars of each dive. Or,
for a few dollars, you can buy a logbook at any dive shop. These logbooks have room for you to note the
dive site, the time of the dive, the
elapsed bottom time, the depth, the
temperature, the water conditions,
the time between dives, your air consumption, safety stops, and the

The bizarre shape of the hammerhead shark's head makes it unmistakable.

names of your buddy and/or the dive master or instructor.

There are as many reasons to keep a logbook as there are to keep a daily journal — and as many ways to do it. Your log can be as complete and organized or as random and/or patchy as you like, but the more complete and methodical it is, the more useful it will be.

First, there's the technical stuff. If you keep good records of things like dive times, depth, and air consumption, you can see how much you're improving over time. Keeping this kind of information puts your past experiences at your fingertips and lets you compare a dive you're planning to a dive you've already done. For example, say you've done a cold-water dive and you had to come up early because you were feeling chilled. You'd note how you felt in your logbook, along with the water temperature and the kind of exposure suit you were wearing. The next time you contemplate doing a similar dive, you can refresh your memory by looking at your logbook. Reviewing your experience will remind you to wear a warmer suit, or add a hood and mitts.

Another reason to keep a logbook is that an instructor or dive leader might want to take a look at it before letting you sign up for an advanced dive. If you're diving through a shop or a school, take the time to get your logbook stamped and signed, especially if you intend to continue your diving education. Some advanced courses require that you complete a specified number of dives, and official stamps help authenticate your records.

Finally, logbooks are a great way to relive your vacations. I like to keep a record of especially notable sightings of fish and other marine life — not that I need a logbook to remember the dozen dolphins that interrupted our dive-table calculations during a deep dive, or the reef shark I saw my very first time underwater, or the moray eel with a head as big as a watermelon (even allowing for underwater magnification). But over time, memories fade, and I find the logbook helps me remember the school of glass fish that made me feel I was swimming through liquid silver, or the octopus I saw on my first night

dive. One diver I know staples photos, postcards, and brochures from hotels and dive resorts into his logbook. He says that on a cold November day in London, he takes great pleasure in letting his book bring him back to the sunny seas of Zanzibar, Bali, and the Great Barrier Reef. Now that it's November in New York, I know exactly what he means!

LEAVE-NO-TRACE DIVING

Humans are visitors in the marine environment, and like visitors anywhere we have a responsibility to act in ways that cause the least disturbance to our hosts. In many places, coral reefs and other aquatic

BOAT PROTOCOL AND BOAT DIVING TIPS

● Listen to the boat crew.
● Show up on time.
● Ask permission before boarding.
● Help is always appreciated with muscle jobs like moving a beached boat into the water or lugging heavy equipment. Offer to help — but wait for instructions.
● Double-check your gear as it is loaded. Once you're en route, you can't replace something you forgot.
● Be sure your equipment is

marked so it doesn't get mixed up with someone else's.
● Keep your stuff where it's supposed to go, all together — not strewn around as if the boat were a teenager's bedroom. Loose gear can be lost, get broken, or trip someone.
● Pack gear in reverse order of how you'll put it on so you don't have to spread everything out to get your equipment on.
● Tie down tanks because waves can knock them around and damage them.

continued on page 162

continued from page 161

● Move carefully and deliberately. Ask your buddy for help with gear and help her in return.

● Know the rules of the boat, which may make some areas off-limits for wet suits and the like.

● Keep cool and hydrated. Be sure you have enough water and snacks. Keep water out of direct sunlight so it stays cool.

● If prone to seasickness, show up well rested and take any medicine suggested by your doctor. Avoid greasy foods. If you get seasick, stay in fresh air, and try to look at a fixed point on the horizon (see page 117).

● A container of water for rinsing off can make a long ride back to shore more comfortable. Use a water bag from a camping store.

● Take a hat and a windbreaker or a rain jacket — even in the warm, sunny tropics.

● Remember to bring plenty of sunscreen.

● Pay attention to crew instructions regarding communications, including signals and information about the boat's recall system.

● Never set weight belts or a mask on a bench or seat because they might fall and break something — either a piece of gear or somebody's toe.

environments are under ever-increasing pressure from tourism and development, not to mention local industry. A partial list of threats includes large resorts and their garbage and sewage; gasoline discharge from boats; litter; temperature and salinity changes due to effluence, pollution, and desalination; overharvesting of fish; and damage to reefs from careless anchoring of dive and snorkel boats. Even something so seemingly innocent as buying a beautiful seashell can have long-lasting negative effects, because it encourages overexploitation. The animals who are the rightful owners of those beautiful shells are part of the ecosystem. If shells are collected to near-extinction, the coral reefs can suffer irreversible damage.

There's not much the average diver can do about a desalination plant or overdevelopment — except, perhaps, to seek out remote sites. But divers can have an enormous effect, either positive or negative, in other ways. Here's a list of what you can do:

● Be responsible in your interactions with marine life, and encourage your dive leaders to be responsible, too. Feeding the fish to bring them closer to you might seem

The whale shark is an enormous, gentle, even friendly cousin to the more aggressive members of the tribe, of which there are 350 species worldwide.

innocuous, but over time it can disrupt the local balance of nature. Fish that are overfed by humans lose their fear of people, making them more likely to be killed by spear fishermen. They abandon or forget their natural feeding patterns, which disrupts the natural predator-prey relationships of the reef. And they become dependent on humans for food, which makes them vulnerable to starvation during the off-season, overly aggressive, and potentially dangerous to divers, whom they associate with food.

Even touching some corals can damage them. You can injure yourself, too, if you are cut by sharp coral or injected with venom by toxic marine animals. Never touch something you can't identify, and if you do touch something, be sure to leave it where you found it.

Don't hassle the locals! A diver who pokes and prods at a sleeping nurse shark to get a reaction deserves the reaction he gets. A diver who tries to hitch a ride on the back of a giant sea turtle might inadvertently cause the turtle to dive so deeply in its attempt to escape that it drowns.

Don't put your hands where you can't see them. Lots of crevices and cracks are occupied, and some of their tenants, like moray eels, have sharp teeth!

Avoid stepping on reefs. Your fins and booties might protect your feet from the reef, but what's to protect the reef from your feet? You can kill hundreds of years' worth of coral growth by standing on a reef.

● Practice good buoyancy control to avoid crashing into corals and silting up the bottom. Don't sit or stand on the bottom in silty areas, and keep your feet up so they don't drag on the bottom. Pay particular attention to your buoyancy when photographing something. Many beginning photographer-divers end up causing damage to corals because they are paying too much attention to their picture and not enough attention to their buoyancy and position.

● Keep your hoses and instruments attached close to your body so they don't drag on the bottom.

● Resist the urge to collect shells; they may be occupied. Similarly, when diving wrecks, leave the artifacts behind for the next diver to see.

● Remember: "Leave only bubbles, take only memories."

BEYOND
THE
BASICS

You've completed your training and you've done a few dives. Maybe you've even been on a diving vacation. Your C-card is no longer brand new, and the ink in your logbook looks blurry from seaspray.

What now?

Now you sharpen your skills and you explore.

You talk to other divers.

You check out your local diving shop, YMCA, college, or university to see what they've got going.

You subscribe to a diving magazine and you read articles about places you'd like to visit and things you'd like to see.

You join a dive club.

You already know there are a lot of choices — a whole new world to explore and to learn about. This chapter gives a brief introduction to five of the most popular diving specialties: navigation, underwater photography, night diving, deep diving, and wreck diving. It's a smorgasbord of new opportunities to explore and skills to learn.

Note: To get the most out of some of these specialties and to dive safely in challenging conditions requires special skills, equipment, and training. Advanced classes give you the chance to review the basics, sharpen your skills, learn new ones, and meet other divers. Have fun!

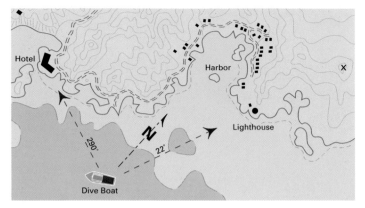

Triangulation with a compass: Triangulating, using two known points—in this case a hotel and a lighthouse—to find a third point, is most accurately done with the aid of a compass.

Taking a bearing: Point the directional arrow of your compass to the object whose bearing you want to know, in this case the lighthouse. Now rotate the compass dial so that the needle and the "N" indicator are aligned.

NAVIGATION

If it hasn't happened yet it will: You'll be out on a boat a mile or two from shore, surrounded by nothing but waves. And all of a sudden the captain will stop the boat and say, "Here's the reef." Sure enough, down you go, and what do you know? He's right. There's the reef right beneath you.

How did he do it?

And then there's your dive master. You follow her as you explore the reef, turning this way and that. At the end of the dive, you've got no more sense of direction than a kid who's been playing "Pin the Tail on the Donkey." You ascend to find that, miraculously, you're right back at the boat.

How did she do it?

Navigation begins with finding the dive site. It continues once you are underwater, swim from one place to the other, and find your way back to the boat or shore.

The diver who is comfortable with navigating has several advantages over the diver who isn't. First, there's the matter of finding the dive site. Divers who know how to navigate avoid long, tiring swims on the surface. They also avoid wasting air beneath the surface looking for a reef or a wreck that's "gotta be around here someplace." And during the dive itself, having solid navigation skills saves air because you're more relaxed when you know where you are. (Confused and disoriented divers use more air.) Finally, you're more likely to stick with your buddy if both of you are paying attention to where you are and where you're going.

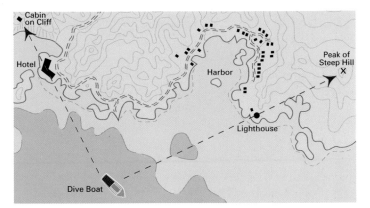

Triangulation without a compass: By locating two known points, the hotel and the lighthouse, and then lining them up with two other more distant fixed points, you can locate a dive site without the aid of a compass.

Finding the Site

In recent years, surface navigating has gotten a lot easier because of the Global Positioning System (GPS), which the U.S. Defense Department has made available to ordinary citizens. Once you know the coordinates of a dive site, a GPS unit can locate it within fifty feet or less, which is accurate enough for a reef and even accurate enough for a small wreck. But I have to admit most of the captains I've dived with haven't used GPS. They haven't needed to. Instead, they use landmarks from shore: lining up a lighthouse with an especially big grove of palms, or a hotel with a hut. To use landmarks to find a site, you might triangulate, which is a fancy expression for using two known points to find a third. Triangulating is most accurately done with the aid of a compass, although old salts can find a site without one. The more landmarks you use, the easier it is to find the site, with or without a compass.

Admittedly, this is a skill that takes time to master.

Underwater Navigation

Underwater navigation isn't just a matter of finding the site. It's also a matter of finding your way around the site. You have three tools at your disposal: natural features, navigational aids (such as a map, a compass, or a measuring line), and skills (such as your ability to measure the distance you are traveling without the use of aids).

NATURAL FEATURES A person navigating on land pays attention to the hill over there on the right, the clump of trees on the left, and the mountain in the distance. The SCUBA diver also pays attention to natural features but with one important difference. On land, you might well be able to see features for many miles around. In the water, your visibility is usually limited to 100 feet or less, and the natural features you will use as navigation aids will be smaller and closer. Underwater navigation is a matter of details. It's also a matter of paying attention.

Think about how it feels to be in any unfamiliar environment. The first time I was ever in a desert, for example, I thought I'd be able to find my way back to a certain place, no problem, because of the really big saguaro cactus that towered over my campsite. Imagine my surprise when at the end of my little walk, I finally got around to noticing that there were easily a hundred giant cacti in the area and they all looked alike. The same thing happens in the unfamiliar underwater environment, before you learn to differentiate between all the new things you are seeing. The most effective thing you can do is pay close attention. What makes this brain coral different from the other one? Look for prominent outcroppings, for an obvious coral head that juts above the rest, for an overhang under which a particularly large number of fish are hanging out (but remember: fish are mobile, and when you get back they could be gone). Note the clump of seagrass that grows in a certain place, or the composition of the bottom, which may be grass, sand, rock, mud, or coral. Learning your way around a reef is a matter of paying attention.

A number of other indicators are useful in finding your way around.

Which direction is the light coming from? During a typical dive of less than an hour, the sun doesn't move that much in the sky. Let's say the shadows are falling to your right and in front of you. That means that for the duration of your dive, whenever the shadows are falling to your right and in front of you, you're facing the same direction that you were facing at the beginning of your dive. If the shadows are to your left and behind you, you're moving in the opposite direction. Similarly, you can look up and note the position of the sun: Is it in front of you? Behind you? Early in the morning and late in the afternoon on a sunny day, the sun's position is especially helpful because all you have to do is look up and you know which direction is where.

Water movement, too, can help you find your way. Currents and surge patterns act as a reference against which you can orient yourself. Surge, for example, moves to and from the direction of shore (or shallow water). It is therefore a constant and predictable movement that can act as a reference for you as you progress through your dive.

Near shore, ridges of sand provide another excellent way to monitor your direction, because they always form parallel to the shoreline. Close to shore, you'll also have the slope of the bottom to help guide you. Obviously, if it's getting deeper you're on your way out to sea.

Finally, as you learn your way

around certain environments, you might notice patterns in marine life that give you a clue about your location. One obvious example is the sea fan, which always orients itself perpendicular to the prevailing currents.

NAVIGATIONAL AIDS Aids such as a compass, a map, and a measuring line are also used in underwater navigation, usually in conjunction with natural features. By far the most important aid is a compass, especially in low visibility, at night, or when your objective is beyond the range of visibility.

If you've never used a compass, try playing with one on dry land. Most compasses come with directions on how to use them. Read the directions and do a couple of exercises. (On page 166, you'll see how to take a bearing.) Learning to use a compass is a little like learning to tie your shoe-laces. It seems to be an impossible job until you learn it, and then you wonder what the fuss was about. It's best to spend the "impossible" part of the process on land.

An underwater compass works pretty much the same as a land compass, but there are a few differences. Usually, declination (the difference between magnetic north and true north, which confuses hikers, moun-

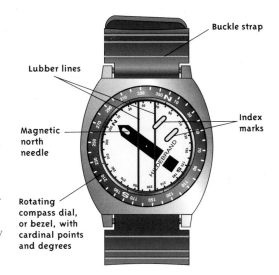

Buckle strap

Lubber lines

Index marks

Magnetic north needle

Rotating compass dial, or bezel, with cardinal points and degrees

taineers, and others trying to navigate on land) is not a concern in basic underwater navigation. Declination is important only if you are using a map and are navigating over considerable distances. It's not important when you're trying to find your way to a reef 300 feet from shore.

Another difference is the appearance of the compass, which might be so oversized that it looks like a child's toy. This feature makes it easier to read in low light and easier to handle with diving gloves. A compass may also be integrated into your instrument console, your timepiece, or your dive computer. Whatever compass you are using, be sure you can read it in dim light. An illuminated face is a definite plus.

The major difference between using a compass underwater and using

SIGHTING A COMPASS

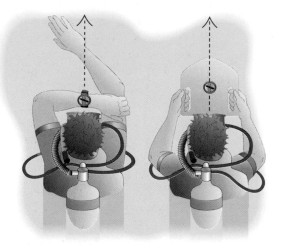

Two ways to hold your compass level: Wear the compass on your wrist and hold your arm perpendicular to your body so that the compass is always in the correct position, or carry a compass board on which to hold the compass straight.

dicular to your body so that the compass is always in the same correct position.

One important use of the compass is to help you find the dive site from the boat. When you're on the boat, you may know exactly which way the dive site is, either from triangulating, or because the captain tells you where it is, or because you can see telltale breakers rolling over the top of the reef. But once you descend, it's easy to lose your sense of direction. Take a bearing from the boat to the dive site. Set your compass. Once you're in the water, all you've got to do is follow that bearing.

it on land is that on land you can stand still. Underwater, you are never entirely still, and in currents or surge, you may be tossed around. One trick: If possible, kneel on the seafloor when you're working with your compass. Be careful about where you kneel, both to protect yourself (perhaps from a camouflaged stingray or a sea urchin) and to protect vulnerable marine life from you. Similarly, it's important to hold the compass in the same flat and level position each time you use it, because otherwise the needle can get stuck and send you in the wrong direction entirely. Two methods will help: First, you can use a compass board to hold the compass straight. Second, you can wear the compass on your wrist and hold your arm perpen-

To get back requires using a reciprocal bearing, which is simply the opposite bearing. If your original bearing was to the north, the reciprocal bearing is to the south. If the original bearing was to the northeast, the reciprocal bearing is to the southwest. Bearings are often expressed in degrees. The reciprocal bearing is always 180 degrees different from the original bearing. There are two ways to set a reciprocal bearing: One is to reset the compass for the new number. The other is to simply use the old bearing, but instead of lining up the north end of the compass needle (called a lubber line) with the north indicator (N) of the compass, line it up with the south indicator (S).

(The original bearing is 180 degrees from the bearing you need; the compass needle lined up to south is 180 degrees from north. The two "mistakes" cancel each other out, and the lubber line will point in the direction of travel.)

Two other aids are sometimes helpful for navigation. First, a map can help you find your way around by giving you a picture of, for instance, how a reef or a wreck is laid out. And second, a measuring line — simply a rope of a known length — is the most accurate way of measuring distance. SKILLS You don't have to have a measuring line to know how far you've gone. With a little practice, you can keep track of your distance using one of several methods.

Perhaps the most accurate way to measure distance (other than with a measuring line) is to count kick cycles. One kick cycle equals a complete up-and-down kick with one foot. The most basic way to use this technique is to count the number of cycles as you head somewhere; then turn around and count the same number of kick cycles on the way back. This is a good technique to use at the end of a dive, when you want to get as close to the boat as possible before surfacing. Say you descended and swam 20 kick cycles to a reef. At the end of your dive, you could swim 20 cycles back in the opposite direction (of course, you'll need to know the correct compass bearing to determine the correct direction) to return to your starting point. When you surface, you'll be right near the

---

T E C H N I Q U E   T I P

THE OUT-AND-BACK PATTERN

A simple out-and-back pattern is a basic navigational skill. Start at a point you'll recognize when you return to it. Now, choose a compass bearing and swim out a certain number of kick cycles, maybe 15 or 20. Your buddy should accompany you. Your job is to navigate; your buddy's job is to keep her eye on the depth gauge and other instruments. After 15 or 20 kicks, set the compass for the reciprocal bearing, turn, and try to return to your starting place. In clear water, of course, the exercise is easier, especially if natural features are nearby to help you stay on course. (And you might even be able to "cheat" on the return trip by spotting the starting point from some distance away.) To build your skills, practice in murky water and currents. Over time, you'll notice how much easier this exercise becomes, especially if you take advantage of natural features, which can help you maintain your sense of direction.

boat — eliminating the need for a tiring surface swim.

You can also use this technique for more precise navigation. Say you're diving a wreck, and the map tells you that part of the wreck lies 100 feet to the east of the main wreck. You would set your compass so that the lubber line is pointing east. Then, if you knew how many kick cycles it takes to swim 100 feet, you would also know exactly how far to swim, and in what direction, to get to the wreck. (And if you find yourself swimming 150 feet, you'll know that you've somehow missed it).

To determine the number of kick cycles required to swim a certain distance under normal circumstances, you'll need a measured line. You must take these measurements beneath the surface (you can't count kick cycles on the surface because you're more streamlined underwater and will kick more efficiently) using your typical SCUBA gear. If you significantly change your gear — especially your fins — your kick cycles will change. When counting kick cycles, concentrate on working and breathing at a normal rate. It's a natural human temptation to work harder when we're being measured, but that's not the point here. The point is to find out how many kicks are needed to swim a certain distance under normal conditions.

Timing is another way to measure distance, but only if you maintain a consistent rate of travel. A

FINDING YOUR WAY

● Navigating is always easier if you use a combination of natural observation, navigation techniques, and instruments.

● Pay attention to what's around you, which way you're going, and how far you've gone.

● Trust your compass. It's got a better sense of direction than you have.

● Don't wear your compass next to a watch or other instruments, because they can throw off your compass. Similarly, compasses can be inaccurate when used near shipwrecks.

● Notice currents and water movements and whether they are taking you off course.

● Stay as still as possible when working with your compass.

● Split up the work. If you're the navigator, your buddy should take responsibility for watching other instruments such as the depth gauge and timer. Note: It's easy to lose control of your depth if you're concentrating on your compass.

● Descending feetfirst helps you stay oriented.

third method is to measure the elapsed air in your tank. This technique is best used over longer distances; over short distances, it's not accurate. Note that any method of estimating distance becomes less accurate if you stop and start, detour from the route, or find yourself being pushed or pulled by currents.

A more accurate way to measure distance is the arm-span method, which can be used if you are swimming near the bottom and can touch it. (Don't try this if the bottom is live coral; you'll damage the coral and injure yourself.) Reach one arm forward and pull yourself along the bottom until that arm is back against your leg. Then move the other arm forward and pull yourself forward again. This is a slow way of traveling, but it's very accurate for measuring distance. It's especially useful when strong currents make other estimating methods little more than guesses. CURRENTS AND NAVIGATION Underwater navigation gets complicated when currents start pushing you off course. You might think you're heading in a northerly direction, and your lubber line might point in a northerly direction, but if the current is pushing you west, you'll end up somewhere to the northwest. And, as discussed earlier, measuring the distance you've traveled is also difficult in a current, unless you're using the arm-reach method.

To compensate for this, it's effective to combine the use of navigational aids and your measuring skills with careful observation of natural features. Say you want to swim in a northerly direction and the current is pushing you to the west. Set your compass for north, then look around for a prominent feature. Maybe there's a clump of rock 50 feet away to the north and a little to the east, and maybe there's a coral head just beyond that, a little to the northwest. Aim for a point between them. Even with a rambunctious current pushing you due west, you won't get thrown off course because you know what you're aiming for. When you get to that place, stop and take another bearing, look at the natural features ahead of you, and repeat the process.

UNDERWATER PHOTOGRAPHY

It's only natural that after spending time in the incomparable beauty of the undersea world, you might want to bring back a picture or two to show the folks back home.

The basics of underwater photography are not difficult to learn, but taking perfect close-ups of colorful fish surrounded by coral gardens in aquamarine seas is a challenge that takes some time to master. To get started, you might want to take a class. Courses are offered by many dive schools, by professional underwater photographers, and at some resorts.

Snapping a shot of "Christ of the Abyss," in the Florida Keys National Marine Sanctuary. Underwater photographers find unique challenges and rewards.

Photography Basics

The underwater photographer faces all the challenges of his landlubber counterpart — only more so. To see why, let's look at the fundamentals of picture taking: film, lens, light, and how they interact underwater.

FILM Any kind of film needs a certain amount of light for a picture to be properly exposed. Films that need more light are called slow films and are identified as having a lower film speed (also known as ASA). Slow films are usually preferred in well-lit conditions because they are less grainy (hence more clear) than faster films. But fast films — with speeds of 400 or more — offer a powerful advantage in low-light situations. They might be grainier, but you don't need as much light to take a picture. This is important in SCUBA, because there's less light underwater than at the surface.

A tip on film: Whichever kind you get, be sure you buy a roll with 36 exposures, not 24, since you can't change film in the middle of a dive.

Most modern cameras read the speed of the film automatically, but on older models you may have to set the film speed. If you don't, your pictures may be overexposed or underexposed.

LENS The amount of light that reaches the film is determined by the lens. Think of the lens as a drain in a sink. The amount of water you can pour through the drain depends on two things: the amount of time the drain is open (that's the shutter speed) and the size of the drain (that's the aperture). Note: Just to confuse you, a large lens opening is identified with a small aperture number, known as an F-stop or, simply, a stop. Small openings have large F-stop numbers. Go figure.

You can use various combinations of shutter speed and aperture to take a picture, as long as the combination lets through adequate light for the film speed you are using. Automatic point-and-shoot cameras and many quality 35-mm cameras (see pages 176–177) choose the shutter speed and aperture for you. This can be a big advantage for the beginning underwater photographer because there are fewer things to worry about. But advanced photographers often want to control the outcome of their picture taking by deciding the shutter speed/aperture combinations themselves. Also, automatic-exposure cameras have limits in unusual lighting; in some situations, like backlighting, an automatic camera will choose an incorrect exposure. Finally, better-quality camera lenses have more options — higher shutter speeds and bigger maximum apertures — than less expensive models, which gives you more flexibility in low light and with moving subjects.

SHUTTER SPEED With a high shutter speed, the lens is open for only a short time, making it possible for you to take pictures of fast-moving fish or other marine animals. In underwater photography, where both the subject and the photographer are often moving (even if the photographer is trying to stay still), a high shutter speed is often useful. But remember, there is limited light in underwater photography, so if you use a fast shutter speed, you will need a large aperture. Going back to our original example of plumbing: If the drain is open for only a short time (the shutter speed), it needs to have a wide opening (the aperture) to let the water (or light) through.

APERTURE Aperture also affects something called depth of field. Say you are focusing on a fish. Depth of field refers to how much of what is in front of the fish and how much of what is behind the fish will be in focus. Think of those ultraenlarged close-up insect pictures in National Geographic, where the mosquito's eyes are really clear but its back legs are fuzzy. That is an extreme example of a short depth of field, which is what you get with a wide-open aperture. (The wide-open aperture, remember, lets in a lot of light.) In summary: A wide-open aperture (a small F-stop) has less depth of field than a small aperture (a big F-stop).

The problem with shutter speeds and apertures is that they present a "wanting to have your cake and eat it too" dilemma: In many conditions, you'll want both a high shutter speed and a small aperture, and the only way you can get them both is to use a faster film or to get more light.

LIGHT UNDERWATER Underwater lighting has its own challenges. Not only is there less light underwater, but colors may be distorted as well. This is because of the way water filters light, especially on deeper dives. What looks to you like a yellow flipper on the surface might appear sort of grayish green on your picture. Finally, light catches on particles suspended in even the clearest water; this is what makes so many amateur underwater photographs look fuzzy and gray. Having enough light gives photographers much more control over film speed and aperture and, ultimately, photo quality. So serious underwater photographers bring lights down with them.

Equipment

How much equipment you use will be determined by your goals, skills, and budget. All kinds of underwater cameras are available, from simple point-and-shoot models to high-quality professional models. Which you buy will depend on your level of interest, your photographic skills, and, of course, your budget. CAMERAS Most good modern cameras have light meters and the ability to work automatically; that is, they choose the exposure settings for you. The camera might choose both the shutter speed and the aperture, or you might choose one (which one depends on the camera model) and the camera chooses the other. Better cameras also offer the photographer the option of manual override, which is important for creating a special effect or when working in unusual lighting (as you often do underwater). Some fully automatic point-and-shoot cameras have adjustments that let you change the exposure by one or two stops to compensate for problems like backlighting. Even if your camera doesn't offer this feature, you may be able to fool it into changing the exposure by "lying" to it about the film speed. Check to see if you can change the film-speed setting in the middle of a roll of film. If you want to expose a particular picture by one more stop, lower the film-speed setting. If you want less exposure, raise the film-speed setting.

There's another argument in favor of an advanced camera. SLR cameras (single-lens reflex cameras; these are the cameras we picture when we think of traditional quality 35-mm cameras) have a system of moving mirrors that enable the photographer to see exactly what the camera sees when she looks through the viewfinder. When you look through the viewfinder of a basic point-and-shoot camera, the picture you see is not the exact picture the camera takes. In scenic shots, it doesn't make much difference; the subject is so far away that the distortion is minimal. But in close-ups, which are popular dive shots, failing to compensate for this error can ruin a picture by chopping the head off a person or the tail off a fish, or entirely missing the subject of a photo. Some point-and-shoot cameras have markings to help you compensate for this problem (read the directions that came with your camera).

A king crab mugs for the camera. Shining enough light on the subject is one of the underwater photographer's chief aims, and means bringing along powerful strobe lights.

In general, you need to hold the camera higher than you would think, if you're holding the camera horizontally. For example, say you're taking a close-up picture of a person's head, and you want the head to fill the entire frame of the photo. With an SLR, you'd simply look through the viewfinder and take the picture. But through a so-called "sportsfinder," you have to frame the picture so that when you look through the viewfinder, the person's nose is at the bottom of the picture and a few empty inches of air are at the top. If this seems confusing and inconvenient — considering that you already have enough on your mind (you're underwater; in low light; monitoring depth gauges, timers, air supply, and buoyancy;

and that fish just won't stay still) — you're right. Serious underwater photographers use SLRs. If, however, you just want to play around and get some mementos of your trip, a less expensive point-and-shoot model is fine. You can even buy disposable ones! (These, however, don't have light meters, take only the most basic pictures, and can be used only in shallow water.)

LIGHT METERS Light meters are built into most good modern cameras, but professional photographers carry a separate handheld light meter for more precise measurement. Light meters tell you what combination of aperture and shutter speed you will need with the film speed you are using and the light that is available.

FILTERS Filters correct the color balance, which is distorted underwater, but they reduce the light available for the photo.
STROBE LIGHTS Strobe lights will compensate for the limited light below the surface and restore some of the natural color that is lost as sunlight is filtered through water. There are two types of strobes:

TECHNIQUE TIPS
GOOD PHOTOGRAPHY

Good photography is good photography, whether it's atop a mountain or beneath the sea. The following tips will help:

● Get close to the subject — then get closer. This not only makes for good detail, but it also reduces the scattered light from suspended particles in the water.

● Try unusual angles. Looking up so that your subject is between you and the surface often gives good light and an interesting angle.

● The shallower the dive, the more light you'll have and the truer the colors will be. Also, deep dives require you to concentrate more on diving techniques, bottom time, depth, your buddy, and air supply. On shallower dives, you still have to think about diving, of course, but you can afford to concentrate on photography, too.

● Take photographs in the middle of the day. On land, photographers avoid midday because of harsh shadows, but that's not a problem underwater. Midday light is the strongest.

● Take photographs on bright, sunny days, not on overcast ones.

● Follow a moving subject with your camera. This panning technique allows you to frame the picture even while your subject is moving. A fast shutter speed will help compensate for camera movement.

● Take pictures at night. If you like the way a well-lit jewel looks on black velvet, try underwater photography at night. With the black backdrop, good lighting, and interesting subjects like octopuses or eels, you can create stunning and dramatic pictures.

● Bracket exposures. For important shots that you really want to get right, try this professional technique: After you choose your exposure, take two more pictures of the same subject. One should be overexposed by either one-half stop or one stop; the other should be underexposed by one-half stop or one stop. One of the three should be pretty close to perfectly exposed.

through-the-lens and manual. Through-the-lens strobes work with your camera so that the exposure is calculated automatically. Take your camera to the store when you buy your strobe, because not all strobe models work with all camera types. Manual strobes are less expensive, but they require you to calculate and set the correct exposure. Although they require more effort, they give the photographer more control of the final results. Try to aim the strobe so that it illuminates your subject from the side, not head-on. You'll get more pleasing lighting. Also, a sideways angle of about 45 degrees helps reduce the spattering effect of suspended particles that catch the light and can turn photos grainy and dull.

Caring for Equipment

Delicate electronics and salt water are not a marriage made in heaven. Salt, sand, and water can all contribute to corrosion or scratching of camera parts. So maintenance has to be a regular part of your diving routine. O-RINGS O-rings create the seal that lets you take the camera underwater. Check them regularly for signs of nicks and tears, and always carry extras in your spare-parts kit. To remove an O-ring, use a blunt tool (like a butter knife), never a sharp object. Examine, clean, and lubricate the O-ring, and clean its grooves, too, because tiny specks of sand and dirt can congregate in the grooves and damage the O-ring. It's

also a good idea to periodically lubricate the O-rings, which prevents cracking and prolongs their life. BATTERIES Check batteries before every trip and bring extras, especially if you're traveling abroad. In some developing countries, batteries have a short life expectancy and a high price, and may also be hard to find. If you're using rechargeable batteries, be sure you have a way to recharge them. Don't store batteries in the camera — this leads to corrosion. SWISH AND SOAK After use, rinse your camera equipment in fresh water for a minute or so, then let it sit and soak to get all the salt off. This needs to be taken care of first thing after your dive. If you plan to clean it between the end of your dive and getting back to your home base, take along a bucket so that you can keep your equipment wet, even if all you've got is salt water. It's better to let the equipment sit in salt water than to let the salt water dry. MANUFACTURER'S DIRECTIONS Note that in some cases, not following the directions for care and maintenance can void the manufacturer's warranties.

Skills

The person who takes good underwater pictures is invariably not only a good photographer, but also a good diver.

Perhaps the most important diving skill for a photographer is close-to-perfect buoyancy control.

coral to hold yourself still, because you can destroy it. Buoyancy control is also important in good framing, especially if the fish moves and you need to move, too, to reframe the shot.

Finally, buoyancy control is important because it keeps you in place even

Deep diving, below 60 feet, holds a fascination for some divers. It also requires advanced training because the risks rapidly increase the deeper you dive.

Because divers often shoot in poor light, you may be forced to use a slower shutter speed than you might ordinarily prefer. That means you must be able to stay still enough to avoid shaking the camera when you press the shutter button. Similarly, if you use a very large aperture, you must be sure your focus is perfect, especially when taking close-ups, because of the short depth of field. Here again, if you shift position while taking the picture, the focus will be fuzzy. If you are near the bottom, you can sometimes kneel on it, but only if it's sandy, not silty. Kneeling on the bottom usually stirs up sediment, ruining not only your pictures, but also everyone else's visibility. Don't grab onto

when you are concentrating on your photography. Otherwise, you could end up banging into things, crashing to the bottom, stirring up sediment, breaking coral, damaging the reef, or even (I've seen this happen) sitting on a sea urchin. Ouch!

DEEP DIVING

It's only human nature: When we take up a new outdoor interest, we want to know everything there is to know about it. Bicyclists want to go faster, mountaineers want to go higher, back-packers want to go farther. And divers want to go deeper.

Many divers, of course, are perfectly content to stay at shallower depths. The colors are brighter on shallower dives. The air lasts longer. The chance of getting the bends is lower. But some divers are lured by the call of the deep. Perhaps it's because there's an interesting wall to dive that goes down to 80 feet. Or a wreck at 100 feet. Maybe the most interesting dives at the resort you're going to are deep dives. Perhaps there's different aquatic life down lower on a certain reef, or you're interested in search and recovery, and want the flexibility to go after something deep. Or your buddy is an advanced diver and she's constantly inviting you on dives that are deeper than 60 feet.

As an open-water diver, you should be mindful always to dive within the limits of your training and experience in conditions that are as good as or better than those you were trained in. An open-water C-card certifies that a diver is trained to go to depths of 60 feet. But with advanced training, recreational divers can go to depths of as much as 130 feet.

Why do you need advanced training?

Hazards of Deep Diving

In a word, what's different down there is risk.

● On deeper dives, your air supply runs out much faster, so you have to keep constant tabs on your gauges.

● The deeper your dive, the more vulnerable you are to depth-related problems, particularly nitrogen narcosis and the bends.

● Errors of judgment due to nitrogen narcosis can affect how you handle emergencies — or even everyday diving procedures.

● Safety stops are recommended on the ascents. They are required for dives of more than 100 feet. If something goes wrong and you go straight to the surface, you could get bent.

Equipment

You already know that diving equipment should always be well maintained. In deep diving, this is especially true. Your judgment may be impaired due to nitrogen narcosis, the dive might be more difficult because of dark or cold conditions, and the consequences of a mistake are more severe. The quality and condition of your equipment are paramount. In addition, divers should consider the following when choosing gear:

HIGH-PERFORMANCE REGULATOR A high-performance regulator is strongly recommended for any diver, but it's an absolute requirement for deep divers. High-performance regulators are specially designed to work well at deep depths so you get air without feeling like you're sucking through a straw. Another term to look for is balanced, which means that the regulator delivers a consistent air supply, regardless of tank pressure or the surrounding (ambient) water pressure.

GAUGES AND COMPUTERS Your equipment should be serviced annually. Do not put this off if you're interested in deep diving.

There's a lot less room for error. You don't want a computer telling you you're at 110 feet when you're really down at 125 feet.

TIMERS AND WATCHES Timers or watches should be rated to at least 200 feet. Be sure they are functioning and easy to read, because you don't want to risk overstaying your visit. Do not rely solely on a computer for a deep dive, because if it malfunctions, the consequences can be extremely serious. You might want to have a backup timer or watch — just in case.

FIRST AID KIT A first aid kit and oxygen should be standard equipment on all dive boats, but this goes double for deep dives. Oxygen is the primary first aid for the bends. If you're going deep, you need it on the boat, along with someone who knows how to administer it.

TANKS You use a lot more air on deeper dives, so you'll want a tank with enough capacity. Choose a tank that can hold at least 71.2 cubic feet; more if you're the type of diver who sucks air. Even if you're an efficient breather, choose a large-capacity tank. You want the assurance of having a little extra in case something goes wrong.

EXTRA TANKS You can also take down a double tank, a pony bottle, or a small container for spare air. Warning: Small air containers that can hold only a few hundred pounds per square inch may not have enough air to get you to the surface at a safe rate of ascent. These should be viewed as emergency equipment only. Never let your air supply in your main tank dwindle so low that you rely on the spare to get you to the surface.

SAFETY-STOP SUPPLIES In addition to the tank (or tanks) you carry, you can arrange to have a tank and regulator waiting for you at your safety stop. Spare tanks are often weighted, so they don't rise to the surface, and are suspended from the boat. That way, if you get as far as your safety stop and find yourself low on air, you can use the spare tank to stay underwater and complete the stop. It's a good idea to attach wrist weights to the spare tank; put these on during your safety stop, so that as the tank runs out of air (and the buoyancy increases) you don't inadvertently or uncontrollably rise to the surface. Note: For a spare tank to do you any good, you have to be able to find it. Navigation skills will help you find your way back to the boat. A reference line is a more reliable aid.

ALTERNATE AIR SOURCES Your alternate air sources should be clearly marked so that you and your buddy know where they are. Keep them in a visible place somewhere in the middle of your torso, where they'll be easy for your buddy to grab if she needs them.

EXPOSURE SUITS A warmer exposure suit might be required because it can be colder down deep. Dress for the conditions. Also, remember that your wet suit will compress more the deeper you go, and will therefore lose some of its insulating capacity. REFERENCE LINE A reference line helps you keep track of the speed of your ascent so that you rise to the surface in control. It also helps prevent disorientation by giving you something to hang onto. And it helps you stay in the same place during your safety stop. A reference line can be a separate line suspended from a float, or the anchor line of a boat. LIGHTS It gets darker as you go deeper. Not only that, but some of the colors of the spectrum are filtered out. A dive light shows the true colors of your surroundings and can help you read instruments in dim light.

WEIGHTS Because the increased pressure at depth compresses air

---

DIVE DEEP, DIVE SAFE

The following procedures will help ensure that your deep dives are safe:

● Always do your deepest dive first. If you are doing repetitive diving, limit your deep dives to one a day. Doing more than one deep dive a day requires lots of surface time between dives and increases your risk of the bends.

● If you're doing a lot of diving on a vacation, and you've been going deep, take an easy day once in a while by limiting yourself to shallow dives. Better yet, take a day off and go snorkeling instead. Or sight-seeing.

● Limit your deep dives to the depth at which you have been trained — in conditions as good as or better than those you've been trained in.

● If you and your buddy are using a computer, come up when the more conservative computer tells you to. Never share a computer, because each diver will be at a slightly different depth throughout the dive and the computer can't keep track of both of you.

● Even if you are using a computer, use tables to calculate your dives so that if the computer fails, you'll know what to do. Review your dive tables (Chapter 5) for information on safety stops and emergency decompression stops. And always take tables down with you; if you accidentally exceed the no-decompression limits (or if your computer fails), you'll be able to come up with a backup plan and ascend safely.

● Maintain buddy contact. It's important on any dive, but on deep dives you can't agree to meet

continued on page 184

continued from page 183

at the surface if you lose each other. If you lose your buddy, the dive is over. You won't have enough time or air to come up, regroup, and go back down. Plus, you and your buddy need each other down there.

● Keep track of depth, especially when diving along a wall. It's easy to get distracted and disoriented along a wall where you can't see the bottom. You could end up accidentally going beyond the recreational-dive limits.

● Pay attention to buoyancy to avoid sudden drops or out-of-control ascents. Hold onto the reference line when ascending.

● Pay attention to your ears and sinuses. There's a lot more pressure at depth, so equalize early and often to help prevent squeezes.

● Don't overexert. Overexertion can lead to "overbreathing" your regulator when you demand more air than the reg can supply. Slow down, rest, think — and if you need to, ascend.

● You use twice as much air at 99 feet, where there is 4 atms of pressure, as you do at 33 feet, where there is 2 atms of pressure. So, on deep dives, watch your SPG more often than you do on shallow dives.

● If you forget to take an emergency decompression stop or a safety stop, do not go back underwater to try to redo it. Once you're up on the surface, it's too late. Cancel the rest of your dives for the day and monitor yourself for signs of the bends. Remember, if you've put yourself at risk for the bends, and if you have symptoms of the bends, you should assume you've got the bends and get medical attention as soon as possible.

● Although some divers start their ascent just before the needle on their SPG tells them that they have 500 psi left, on deep dives, you'll want to start up earlier; a little more than 500 psi might not be enough air to get you to the surface at a safe rate of ascent, with a safety stop, especially if you have to cope with unforeseen circumstances such as buddy breathing or strong currents. So start up well before your SPG hits the red zone. You might have to start up when you've got 800, 900, or even 1,000 psi left, depending on the depth of your dive and your air consumption.

● Review the symptoms of and first aid procedures for nitrogen narcosis (pages 126–127) and the bends (pages 125–126).

spaces in a wet suit, deep divers often need fewer weights to be neutrally buoyant. Some divers use drop weights to get down the first 30 or so feet. At 30 feet, when the increased pressure makes the weights unnecessary, the diver clips them to a line of rope and descends the rest of the way using fewer weights.

NIGHT DIVING

"Is anyone afraid?"

The sun was slowly sinking into the Indian Ocean as the boat took us away from land, just off the coast of Zanzibar, where a ship had sunk on New Year's Eve 100 years earlier while laying cable. We were going to dive the wreck — at night.

As a novice diver, not to mention a novice night diver, I was excited and, yes, just the littlest bit afraid. What if I dropped my dive light? What if I lost my buddy? What if I got separated from the group? Our dive lights had brand-new batteries, but they were locally made in Tanzania, and our dive leader had a few colorful things to say about how long they didn't tend to last. We were short on backup dive lights, too. A shipment of supplies had gotten stuck somewhere in the customs office.

It seemed very quiet on the boat. The ocean was black as ink, and very, very big. On the shore, a string of lights showed the line of buildings along the seafront, but they appeared to be far away.

An open hatch on a wreck heightens a diver's curiosity. Entering a wreck must only be undertaken by divers who have received special training.

"Ready?"

One by one, we took our giant strides into the water. Dive lights bobbed and twinkled on the surface. And then, after we all gave the "okay" sign and reminded ourselves one more time to control our nerves, we descended into the dark and silent sea.

Why do it? you might quite reasonably ask.

Why dive in the dark?

It comes as a surprise to most people to learn that night diving is one of the most popular kinds of specialty diving. If you try it just once, you'll know why.

If you have ever climbed a

mountain in the dark, or sat by the side of a lake at night as its waves lapped the shore; if you have cross-country skied in a winter woods by moonlight, or lain awake under the stars in a campsite and looked up to the Milky Way; if you have ever spent a moment outside in the still of the night, you already know the answer to the question, "Why dive in the dark?"

The world looks different at night, whether on a mountain, in a desert, in a forest, or in the snow. And the same is true underwater.

Darkness somehow magnifies the intensity of the experience, the sense of being in the present moment. Daytime diving can some-times resemble a three-ring circus, with a thousand interesting things all clamoring for your attention:

SIGNING IN THE DARK

Even divers who are so fluent in American sign language that they can discuss philosophy while diving in the daytime will need a new bag of tricks for communi-cating in the dark.

● Don't flash your light in someone's eyes.

● You must adapt the signs you use in the daytime for nighttime use. Discuss how you'll do this beforehand. Communicating during the dive should be stress-free — you're not playing charades down there. An example of how you might adapt a sign: In the day-time, a diver points to his ears and wiggles his hand if he's having a problem equalizing. At night, you could shine the light on your finger when you point to your ears.

● To get your buddy's attention, focus your dive light beam into the spot his dive light beam makes on the seafloor (or whatever he's looking at). Then, move your dive light around in a circle.

● When you get your buddy's attention, hold your light so that it shines on your free hand, using that as a signal that you're going to make a sign. Or, use dive light sig-nals by shining your light on the seafloor. A big round O means "okay." An energetic wiggling back and forth means "Something's wrong."

● At the surface, use the same signals as you would in the day-time. Wave your dive light back and forth to indicate something is wrong. If you're okay, make the "okay" sign with one hand, and point your dive light at your head with the other.

● You can also use underwater slates and pencils to exchange information.

Night diving and low-light diving require a whole new sign language vocabulary. Agree on how you'll adapt standard signs to the darkness before you begin your dive.

The shark over here! The school of glass fish over there! Quick, look at the sea turtle! The ray! The barracuda! At night, it's more like watching a one-character play in a small dinner theater. The solo octopus scuttling on the sand. A single eel opening and closing its ever-pulsating jaws. The lone lobster staring back at you from under a rock. And, when you turn off your flashlight and move your hand through a sea as black as night, the sparkle of bioluminescence exploding in the darkness like microscopic fireworks.

Training

Night diving presents divers with a few new challenges: finding your way in the dark, communicating with your buddy, and managing equipment by feel rather than by sight. It's perfectly normal to feel a little stressed the first time you try it. By far the best way to learn to dive at night is to take a class. You'll learn tricks you'd never have thought of on your own, and you'll do your first night dives with the security of a trained instructor. Remember: Always dive within the limits of your training and experience.

Night-Diving Equipment

LIGHTS First on the list, of course, is a way to light the night. Obviously, you've got to have flashlights designed for SCUBA diving — not only waterproof but rugged and pressure-resistant, too. The simpler the design, the better. The fewer O-rings a light has, the less likely it is to leak. Your primary light should be one with a wide beam. Look for switches that are easy to operate (with or without gloves on) and a grip that feels comfortable in your hand. Some divers use a headlamp. If you're leaning toward a headlamp, try it on with your mask to be sure that the light doesn't interfere with the fit of the mask, and vice versa. You should also have a backup light, in case your primary light fails. Backup lights can be small enough to easily fit into a BC pocket or hang from a ring. Both your primary light and your backup should be secure. Use a wrist strap with your primary light, so that even if you drop it, it won't sink to the bottom. And be sure your secondary light is securely clipped, or, if it's in a BC pocket, that the pocket is securely closed.

To reduce the chances of light failure, be sure to use only new or newly recharged batteries for a night dive. Check the manufacturer's directions for any special care or cleaning instructions. Usually, the care of underwater lights is the same as care for underwater cameras and other sensitive equipment: Rinse and soak in fresh water, dry thoroughly, and store in a cool, dry place without the batteries. Also, note that some lights can be used both above the water and underwater; others can be used only underwater or they burn out. Finally, be sure you know how the switch on your buddy's light works and where she keeps her spare.

CHEMICAL LIGHTS Chemical lights can be used to mark everything from the buoy to the reference line to your buddy's tank. Once these lights are activated, they last for a certain amount of time. You can stick them in a variety of places. Putting one on your buddy's tank or BC is a great idea, especially if you're diving in a group. And a chemical light on the buoy or the bottom of a boat can help you orient yourself at the end of a dive.

STROBE LIGHTS Boats may use strobe lights to help divers find the boat at the end of a dive. However, if you're paying attention to where you are and you're diving a familiar site, you shouldn't need a strobe to find your way back to the boat.

WHISTLES In addition to your lights, you'll want to take along a whistle for use at the surface, just in case you lose your buddy or the boat.

COMPASS A compass is a useful tool in the daytime; at night, it can be essential. A compass with a luminous dial and a large, easily readable face is preferable for obvious reasons. Night divers use their compasses to find the dive site, to keep themselves oriented during the dive, and to find their way back to the boat or shore. This could be critically important if fog rolled in during your dive and you couldn't see the boat or the shore. Check your bearings from site to shore (or boat) before you start to dive.

CONSOLES Note that some consoles include compasses, so you can get all your information — depth, time, direction, air supply — in one place, which is handy at night when one hand is occupied with your dive light and you're paying twice as much attention to not losing your buddy. Best for night diving are consoles that have illuminated, easy-to-read faces.

REFERENCE LINE A reference line helps keep you oriented on ascents and descents. In night diving, it's especially useful because you have far fewer visual clues that can help you gauge your position and your rate of ascent or descent. Using a reference line will also help you and your buddy stay together during ascents and descents.

Night-Diving Techniques

PLANNING Night dives are best done at familiar sites where you already know what to expect and will recognize prominent features that can help you orient yourself. Many night divers prefer boat diving because they don't have to deal with the obstacles of shore entries and exits. Shore diving can be fine, however, if the entry area is obstruction-free and there is little

T R O U B L E - S H O O T I N G
PREVENTING NIGHTMARES

STRESS It's perfectly normal to feel a little stressed on your first night dive. Who wouldn't be while using life-support equipment in the dark, underwater, for the first time? But you'll soon learn that night diving can be one of the most relaxing ways to dive — it just takes a little getting used to. If you start feeling anxious, concentrate on breathing slowly and deeply. Make contact with your buddy. Frequently making physical contact, even if it's just a light tap on the elbow, or regularly exchanging the "okay" sign will reassure both of you. Always take time to stop and think before you act.

DISORIENTATION It's also normal to feel slightly disoriented during your dive because of the lack of visual reference points. By paying attention to what's around you, checking your compass, and noting natural points of reference, you can stay oriented. Remember: No matter what position you're in, your bubbles always go up to the surface. If you're so disoriented that you don't know which way is up, follow the bubbles.

continued on page 190

continued from page 189

BUMPER-CAR DIVERS Night divers in a group, especially beginners, can resemble a bunch of blindfolded kids driving bumper cars. Divers unused to diving with limited visual references often have problems controlling their buoyancy, so they pop up and down, banging into divers who happen to be above or below them. There's also the tendency to cluster near the dive master, and to move abruptly when they think they've lost their buddy. All of this can lead to divers colliding and perhaps whacking one another with arms or fins. Try to keep your distance from other divers, control your own buoyancy, and watch not only who is around you, but also who might be above or below you. Try to arrange to do your first few night dives in smaller groups. Six people is okay; 12 can be a bit chaotic.

LOST BUDDY The natural tendency in a night dive is to keep your buddy about 2 inches away from you. But in a large group, you can sometimes get separated. When that happens, it can be hard to distinguish which one of several dark wet-suited shapes is the one you're supposed to be keeping track of. Using chemical lights or wearing an identifiable piece of gear (pink fins, for instance) makes it easier to identify one another. Don't forget to look above and below you when you're searching for your buddy. If you and your buddy do get separated, look for her light. If you don't see it, try covering the bulb of your light with your hand. In the ensuing darkness, you'll probably spot the beam of your buddy's light.

LIGHT FAILURE If your light goes out, get out your spare, signal to your buddy, and surface.

or no surf. Whether boat diving or shore diving, be sure you know the entry and exit points. Use only familiar equipment (so you know automatically where the releases and controls are) and dive with a familiar buddy whose underwater habits you know. And be extra picky about the conditions: You're looking for good visibility and quiet water.

PRE-DIVE PREPARATIONS You should eat a light meal a couple of hours before the dive, ensuring you'll have plenty of energy. Prepare your gear before darkness falls, and double-check everything. Review hand and light signals (see box, page 186) with your buddy. A great way to reduce stress when you're a beginning night diver is to start your dive just after sunset. The little bit of ambient light will help you feel comfortable as you start your dive, and darkness may fall so gradually that you don't even notice it!

ENTRIES In a shore entry, turn on your lights before you start your entry. Keep in physical contact with your buddy until you are in water deep enough to swim in. From a boat, turn on your light before you jump or roll (so that if you lose your light you can easily find it), double-check the area for obstructions and other divers, then go in.

DESCENDING AND ASCENDING A feetfirst descent, face-to-face with your buddy, reduces disorientation. So does a reference line. While you're descending, point the light down to watch for the bottom so you don't crash into it, which would stir up silt and reduce visibility. When you ascend, point the light up to watch for obstructions.

NIGHT NAVIGATION Like daytime navigation, navigating at night is a matter of paying close attention. Follow any pre-established compass bearings you made during daytime dives, and look for familiar landmarks and bearings. If you're doing a shore dive, you can use shore features to help you find your exit point. If the shore area is not lit and there are no prominent features, you can place lanterns (two

in a row) on shore to help you. COMFORT Remember: It's colder at night. If you're boat diving, having warm clothes and a thermos of hot drinks on board will make for a much more comfortable ride back to shore, even in the tropics. If you're shore diving, have warm clothes waiting for you when you get out.

WRECK DIVING

From the trading ships of early maritime explorers to the warships of 20th-century navies, shipwrecks can be found in virtually all of the world's seas. From the Great Lakes to the St. Lawrence Seaway, from the North Atlantic to the South Pacific, divers can explore wrecks that sank a few years, or a few hundred years, ago. We seem to have a fascination with wrecks and their stories. Too, there is something about the measured, relaxed pace of SCUBA diving that seems especially appropriate to wandering through a place from the past. While many of us rush too quickly through museums and historic sites on land, under the sea we move more slowly and take the time to really see what we see.

Wrecks are interesting not only in and of themselves. They are magnets for sea life because they provide places for marine plants and animals to grow on and hide in. Tropical reefs actually grow on warm-water wrecks; in colder water, wrecks attract fish and lobsters. Both provide interesting sites for divers. Wrecks are such magnets for

sea life that sometimes dive operators get permission from local authorities to sink defunct ships and

WRECK-DIVING STRATEGIES

● Get local information. Local divers can tell you about the most interesting parts of the wreck, as well as other things that will help you plan your dive, including hazards and information about prevailing currents. If a wreck is very broken up, it's useful to have a description of the site, or a map showing what parts are where. It's also more interesting to dive the site if you know its history.

● It doesn't matter how interesting the inside looks, if you're not trained in wreck penetration, keep out!

● Dive the deep parts first. As with all dives, you should start at your deepest point and work your way up.

● Pay attention to where you are. Navigating your way through a wreck poses two new challenges. The first is disorientation, especially if the wreck lies on a slant. The second is your compass, which may be askew from all the metal and iron lying about. So you'll have to rely on observation. To navigate an intact wreck, you

can simply follow the line of the ship. But if the wreck is scattered and broken up, and if the visibility is poor, you might want to take notes on a slate.

● Control your buoyancy: Wrecks are silty, and if you stir things up, you'll ruin your visibility — and everyone else's.

● Leave the artifacts alone! One of the most exciting things about diving a wreck is picking up something — maybe a plate or a tool or a part of the boat — that was used on the ship perhaps many years ago. When divers take home artifacts and relics, they diminish the experience for future divers. They also disturb the site so that it is of less value to researchers and historians. It's not only inconsiderate to scavenge a wreck — it could be illegal. A diver who surfaces with a stuffed goody bag might be in for a hefty fine, especially at dive sites managed by the National Park Service. Many countries also have strict rules about scavenging artifacts, and sometimes permits are required before you can dive a wreck. Be sure you know the rules.

create an artificial reef. Finally, wrecks also provide an unusual backdrop for underwater photography.

Wreck-Diving Hazards

There are two kinds of wreck diving. The first is passive, which means that you visit the wreck but do not go inside. Many wreck dives are rewarding even if all you do is swim above or around them. But some wrecks are

Weakened structures of deteriorating ships; sharp, rusty, steel corners and protrusions; and old ropes or chains that might entrap you are some of the hazards of wreck diving.

larger, or more intact, with a lot to see inside. Entering, or penetrating, a wreck is the second advanced type of wreck diving. Because it poses serious hazards, it requires special training.

Even passive wreck diving can pose several hazards that are not commonly a problem in open-water diving.

PHYSICAL STRUCTURES The physical condition of a wreck can vary from intact to scattered in pieces, but all wrecks pose hazards as they inevitably start to deteriorate. Sharp objects and corners can protrude in every direction. Metal parts will be rusty. Old ropes can entrap you, and any number of things can stab at you or fall on you. Two good rules for wreck divers: Always keep your tetanus shots up to date, and use gloves, which can protect your hands from the venomous corals that cover many wrecks.

CURRENTS AND SURGE Unexpected surges can form as currents travel around a wreck and through its corridors. It's possible for divers to be sucked inside by a siphon or pushed by a current. Always proceed cautiously around openings that lead into the wreck.

DISORIENTATION Wrecks are often silty from years of decaying matter and organic growth. Because silt is so fine, even divers with perfect buoyancy control can stir it up merely by flapping their fins too close to a silt-covered surface. You'll want to be especially careful about stirring up silt if you're diving in waters where the visibility is limited to begin with.

The physical deterioration of a boat can also lead to disorientation. Wrecks may lie on the seafloor, but that doesn't mean that they necessarily lie flat. They may be at a steep angle. You can get dizzyingly disoriented after spending time swimming about a crooked wreck — so much so that you forget which way is up. (Remember: Look for the bubbles!)

AQUATIC LIFE What may once have been someone's first-class stateroom is now under new management as a lobster hotel. Don't put your hands where you can't see them!

OVERENTHUSIASM Like diving photography, wreck diving can be so absorbing that you forget to pay attention to your gauges. It is especially important on deep wreck dives to keep track of your bottom time so you don't risk the bends. Ditto for your air supply.

PENETRATION HAZARDS In addition to the hazards described above, penetrating a wreck poses other serious risks: overhead environments. By going into rooms and corridors, you no longer have a direct line of ascent to the surface. In an emergency, you can't simply go up; You have to find your way out first. Entrapment is another hazard. If you are pushed into a narrow corridor by surge, you might be unable to get out either because of the force of the current or because the corridor is too narrow. You could also knock something down that blocks your exit, or you might swim into a room and have a door shut behind you.

OTHER SPECIALTIES

It doesn't end here. Other diving specialties include cold-water diving (perhaps under ice in Lake Champlain? or in the North Sea?), high-altitude diving, river diving, cave and cavern diving, as well as becoming skilled in such areas as search-and-recovery, rescue, and natural interpretation.

Seventy percent of our planet is covered with water. With your C-card, your sense of curiosity, and adherence to safe diving practices, the world of inner space is yours to explore.

THE
SCIENCE
OF SCUBA

T hink for a moment about the differences between you and a fish.

As a land animal, you are adapted to life in a terrestrial environment. Your musculoskeletal system fights gravity and keeps you from collapsing into a lump on the floor. Your lungs breathe air. You walk around without noticing any particular resistance from the atmosphere around you (unless it's a really windy day, in which case you may feel a sudden and blustery reminder that air can indeed exert pressure).

For fish, however, the world is a very different place. Buoyancy counteracts the effect of gravity. Instead of worrying about standing upright, the fish needs to cope with moving about in a liquid environment that is 800 times as dense as air. He needs to breathe in this liquid environment, too, which he does by using gills to extract oxygen from the water.

There are other factors, too, that make the fish's underwater environment very different from our terrestrial home turf. These include atmospheric pressure, the partial pressure of gases, gas solubility, and a host of other things you thought you left behind in your high school science lab where (so you thought) they belonged.

We use SCUBA equipment to let us exist in an environment that does not naturally support human life. It's merely obvious that diving requires understanding what this equipment does and how it works — and that requires understanding a little bit about the science behind SCUBA. In this Appendix, we'll cover the differences between the marine and terrestrial environments (emphasizing how these differences affect divers and their experience) and the scientific laws that affect divers and their equipment.

But there's no need for science-phobes to panic. Unlike astronauts, who have to major in things like aeronautical engineering and rocket science, divers need to understand only a few simple concepts in order to comprehend how our bodies and our equipment react when we take them underwater.

LIGHT, SOUND, AND HEAT

Let's start with the obvious: What you see and feel when you go underwater is a whole lot different than what you see and feel on land.

WHAT YOU SEE Human eyes can focus only if they are surrounded by air — which is why your vision underwater is

Actual distance and size

Apparent distance and size through mask

out of focus and barely functional. It's a fairly simple thing to adapt our vision to the undersea environment. Because we need an air space in front of our eyes in order to focus them, we wear goggles (for regular swimming) or masks (for diving). But even with a mask on, there are other differences.

One of the most obvious is that, with a mask, objects appear closer and bigger than they are, by a ratio of about 4:3. (In other words, an object that looks like it's 3 feet away is probably 4 feet away; it's also about one-third smaller than it looks.) This is because of refraction. When you're wearing a mask, the light travels first through water, then through glass, then through air. It bends (refracts) because it travels through each medium at a different speed (much faster, for example, through air than through water). You're used to the way light behaves when it travels through air, but underwater, it acts differently. When you first start diving, you may find yourself reaching for something and coming away empty-handed. Or you might think you're about to run into a piece of coral, only to realize that you have plenty of room. Or you'll come to the surface with — well, let's call them fishing stories — about the size of the giant eel or the reef shark you saw. All of these distortions are due to the way light behaves underwater. Over time, you'll get used to it.

It's also darker down there. Water filters light, so the deeper you go, the less light there is. This is one of many factors that makes underwater photography so challenging. The amount of light that actually penetrates to a certain depth depends on the clarity of the water. Light sufficient to support photosynthesis can penetrate as much as 300 feet in clear water, but in murky water with lots of suspended particles such as silt and organic matter, a depth of only 10 feet can be dark and gloomy.

Water in a lake or ocean filters light according to the light's wavelength. First to go are the colors at the least-energetic end of the spectrum: the reds. Last to be filtered are the more energetic blues. The deeper you go, the more distorted the colors will be. On deep dives, the color change can be dramatic. You can check this out yourself by carrying a dive light and observing the difference in the color of your wet suit in natural and artificial light. A wet suit whose bright yellow strip virtually glows at the surface may look grayish down below. This is one reason why so many wet suits and BCs are very brightly colored. What looks garish at the surface will make you more visible to your buddy — an important safety consideration in low-light and deep-diving situations.

WHAT YOU HEAR It seems illogical, but sound travels approximately four times faster in water than it does in air. The high density of water enables sound energy to travel from one molecule to the next more easily, because water molecules are closer together than air molecules. Therefore, it's easier for sound waves to travel from one molecule to the next. The effect on divers is interesting: We actually hear better below the surface. But although we can better hear sounds coming from far away, we can't necessarily tell which direction the sound is coming from. This is because our ears are calibrated to hear sounds on land. On land, we determine the direction of a sound by minute differences in when it hits one ear and then the other. In the water, we can't do that because sound seems omnidirectional to us. This is because sound waves travel so fast through water that they arrive at both ears at almost the same instant. We can hear more — but we can interpret less.

WHAT YOU FEEL Have you ever wondered why air temperatures and water temperatures that are exactly the same feel so different? In the winter, you might turn the thermostat in your house up to 70°F and feel perfectly cozy. But if you spend a couple of hours in water that is 70°F, you'll most likely feel very chilly.

Water is a much better conductor of heat than air is — it conducts heat about 20 times as fast as air does. Also, because water is denser than air, it can absorb more heat. It takes 3,200 times as much energy to heat a given volume of water than it does to heat the same volume of air.

How do these properties of water affect you as a diver? When you are in 70°F water, your 98.6°F body is losing heat to the surrounding water. When you are in a 70°F living room, your body is similarly losing heat to the surrounding air, but at a much slower rate, because air is not as good a conductor of heat as water is. In the living room, the heat loss is slow enough that your body easily generates more heat and maintains your temperature. Not so in the water. The heat loss is too fast, and no matter how hard your body tries, it can't compensate. This is why most divers wear exposure suits (discussed in Chapter 3), even for diving in tropical waters, and always when the water temperature is less than about 75°F.

An important consequence of the heat-conducting quality of water is hypothermia, a dangerous and potentially fatal condition that occurs when your body can no longer warm itself (see Chapter 6). Hypothermia is more commonly a problem in cold-water diving. But even in tropical waters, it is common for divers to get uncomfortably chilled, especially on long boat rides after a dive, in high winds, in rain, or at night. Cool or windy air on wet skin can cause your body to lose heat faster than it can be replaced, so it's always a good idea to take a windbreaker on a boat dive.

Interestingly, many divers also find that over a period of intense and regular diving, they actually build up what is known as thermal indebtedness, which means that they chill more quickly than more casual or infrequent divers.

BOUYANCY

On land we move primarily in two dimensions: either backward and forward, or from side to side. In the water, we move in three dimensions, because we move up and down as well. Being able to control whether you are rising, sinking, or staying in the same place is called buoyancy control, and it's one of the most important skills for a diver to master (see Chapter 4).

Buoyancy control begins with understanding why some things float (a boat, an inner tube, yourself) and why some things sink (a nail, an anchor, your neighbor who runs 10 miles every morning).

ARCHIMEDES' PRINCIPLE

WHAT IT SAYS Any object wholly or partly immersed in a fluid is buoyed up by a force equal to the weight of the fluid displaced by the object. TRANSLATION Think of what happens when you get into a full-to-the-brim bathtub. When you step into the tub, the water rises because it is being displaced to make room for your body. Sometimes you displace so much water that you end up with a flood on the floor. Archimedes' principle simply (or not so simply) says that if the water you displace weighs more than you do, you float. If the water you displace weighs less than you do, you sink.

To see how this works, it might be helpful to look at a couple of different objects. An inner tube displaces a lot of water relative to its weight — and it floats. A rock displaces only a little water relative to its weight — and it sinks. An object (or a person) is said to be positively buoyant when it rises to float at the surface, negatively buoyant when it sinks to lie at the bottom, and neutrally buoyant when it simply stays in one place. WHAT IT MEANS TO DIVERS Human bodies are made up of approximately 70 percent water, which means that our body composition is similar to the water we are swimming in. That gives us a tendency to be neutrally buoyant. When you factor in body fat, which is lighter than water, most of us turn out to be positively buoyant. But not all of us: Factors affecting your buoyancy include body fat, muscle, and bone density. If your physique resembles an inner tube's (wide and soft) more than a spoon's (skinny and dense), you are more likely to float than to sink. The opposite, obviously, is also true.

Another factor that influences your buoyancy is the density of the water itself. Because it is filled with dissolved minerals, salt water is more dense than fresh water. Salt water weighs about 64 pounds per cubic foot. Fresh water weighs 62.4 pounds per cubic foot. An object (or a person) will therefore be more buoyant in salt water than in fresh water.

Some SCUBA equipment, such as a buoyancy compensator and weights, is designed specifically to help you control buoyancy (see Chapter 3). Other pieces of gear, like your tank and your wet suit, perform different functions, but they have a side effect on your buoyancy. Dressed in full SCUBA gear, most divers are positively buoyant, even if they normally sink while swimming. Below is a list of other factors that influence buoyancy.

Archimedes' principle: The rock and the inner tube weigh the same, and each displaces its own weight of water. The volume of water displaced by the rock weighs less than the rock, so it sinks. The volume of water displaced by the inner tube weighs more than the inner tube, so it floats.

GEAR THAT INFLUENCES BUOYANCY

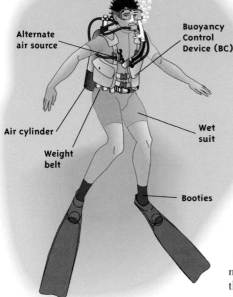

Alternate air source

Buoyancy Control Device (BC)

Air cylinder

Weight belt

Wet suit

Booties

● Lead weights. To compensate for positive buoyancy, most divers must wear lead weights in order to be able to sink to the bottom. A diver in salt water will need more weights than she will in fresh water, because she is more buoyant in salt water.
● A buoyancy compensator allows the diver to adjust buoyancy by adding or subtracting air.
● Neoprene wet suits are filled with millions of little air bubbles that help insulate the diver. These bubbles also make the wet suit extremely buoyant.
● The amount of air in your lungs can make you more or less buoyant because air is lighter than water. Take a deep breath and you'll find yourself rising. Exhale, and you start to sink.
● During the dive, your buoyancy will change because of the effect of changing air pressure as you descend, use air, and ascend. Tanks are less buoyant at the beginning of a dive, when they are full of air, than they are at the end of a dive, when they are nearly empty.

GAS LAWS

As divers, we take our air underwater with us. The problem is that air is subjected to very different conditions underwater than it is on land. To understand how it responds to these conditions, and how that behavior affects us as divers, we must understand some basic properties of the air we breathe.

First, there is the composition of air. Our atmosphere is made up of approximately 78 percent nitrogen, an inert gas. At sea level, nitrogen has no

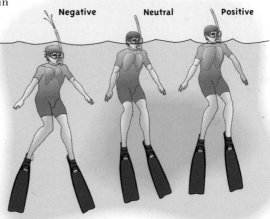

Negative **Neutral** **Positive**

Buoyancy changes with breathing: When you exhale you are negatively buoyant; when you inhale you are positively buoyant.

effect on us, even though it makes up 78 percent of every breath we take. Air also contains 21 percent oxygen, the gas that we require for our basic cellular functions to take place. The remaining 1 percent is a combination of other gases.

Like all other forms of matter, gases have mass — which means they weigh something. We aren't usually aware of the weight of air because it's constant. But observe what happens in a very strong wind: The force of fast-moving air can push you over, or make a tree fall.

The pressure (or weight) of air is measured in pounds per square inch (psi). As it turns out, a square-inch column of air measured from sea level to the edge of the atmosphere weighs 14.7 pounds. This is expressed as 14.7 psi, and it is equivalent to 1 atmosphere (atm). One atmosphere is therefore a measurement of the air pressure at sea level. This pressure decreases as you go high above sea level (which is why people are susceptible to altitude sickness at certain elevations).

Just as a column of air puts pressure on a person at sea level, so, too, will a column of water put pressure on a person beneath the sea. But because water is 800 times denser than air, a column of water puts much more pressure on an

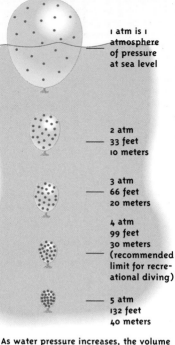

1 atm is 1 atmosphere of pressure at sea level

2 atm
33 feet
10 meters

3 atm
66 feet
20 meters

4 atm
99 feet
30 meters
(recommended limit for recreational diving)

5 atm
132 feet
40 meters

As water pressure increases, the volume of air in the balloon decreases and the density of the air in the balloon increases. In sea water, pressure increases at a rate of 1 atmosphere for each additional 33 feet.

object than does a column of air.

The deeper you go underwater, the heavier the weight of the water above you — and the more pressure it exerts on you. For each 33 feet you descend, the pressure increases by one atm. So at sea level, the pressure is 1 atm. At 33 feet below the surface, the pressure doubles to 2 atm. At 66 feet below the surface, the pressure has increased again, to 3 atm. And so on. Remember, the pressure underwater is always the sum of the atmospheric pressure (at sea level, 1 atm) and the underwater pressure (1 atm for every 33 feet).

Water is essentially not compressible, which means that a given amount of water at sea level has the same weight and density as the same amount of water 100 feet below the surface. Being 70 percent water, our bodies are also not compressible. (If this weren't true, we couldn't dive at all.) It doesn't matter whether we dive to 10 feet or 100 feet, our bodies will not be compressed. That's why we don't feel the effects of all that water weight pressing down on us.

But now we get to the problem: Gases are compressible. That includes the air in our lungs, in our sinuses and inner ears, in our tanks, and in our BCs, as well as the air trapped in the bubbles of our wet suits and between our faces and our masks. And we do feel the effect of increased water pressure in those air spaces. What happens to this air under pressure is determined by a few gas laws. These gas laws influence everything, from why your ears hurt if you descend too fast to why you can get the bends by diving too deep for too long and/or coming up too fast. Gas laws also affect buoyancy, air consumption, and a host of other issues that are important to divers. By understanding them and their effect on you, you will be able to more effectively use your equipment. And you'll understand the causes of potential problems — so you'll be able to avoid them.

BOYLE'S LAW

WHAT IT SAYS If the temperature is constant, the volume of a gas will vary inversely to the pressure. The density will vary directly to the pressure.
TRANSLATION If you put an amount of gas in a flexible container (let's say a balloon), and you then put that container under pressure (say, 30 feet below the surface of the sea), the container will shrink (the volume will decrease) and the density of the air inside it will increase. When you take the container back to the surface, the pressure will be reduced. As a result, the density of the air inside will decrease and the volume will increase.

BOYLE'S LAW AND YOUR EQUIPMENT

The following list is an introduction to some of the ways Boyle's law affects you as a diver. The techniques and equipment described below are discussed in more detail in Chapters 3 and 4.

● Wet suits and dry suits become less buoyant when you are underwater than they are at the surface. Neoprene is a material containing millions of tiny bubbles. At the surface, all those bubbles are very buoyant because they are full of air. Underwater, they become compressed and lose some of their buoyancy. Similarly, dry suits trap air inside them, making them extremely buoyant at the surface but less so underwater. If you wear a dry suit, you might actually use special hoses and vents to control the amount of air inside it. Special training is required.

● Any air in your BC will expand as you ascend. That's why the first thing you do prior to ascending is to let air out of your BC. You can always add air later if you feel you need to, but a BC that is too full of expanding air might be so buoyant that it brings you to the surface too quickly.

● As your tank empties, it becomes more buoyant.

● The amount of air in your lungs can make you more or less buoyant because air is lighter than water. Take a deep breath and you'll find yourself rising. Exhale, and you start to sink.

● Breathing air at depth uses more air from your tank than does breathing air at the surface. Demand regulators provide enough air to fill your lungs. Each time you breathe, your lungs demand the same volume of air regardless of its density. This means that you use much more air deeper down, where the pressure makes the air more dense. Breathing very dense air can also lead to two other problems: oxygen toxicity and nitrogen narcosis (see pages 126–128 and pages 203–204).

HOW BOYLE'S LAW AFFECTS DIVERS

Boyle's law affects divers in many ways. It controls the density and volume of air in our lungs, our equipment, and in so-called "dead air spaces," such as the space between our eyes and our mask. It is the cause of so-called barotraumas — injuries due to pressure. And it influences how we use our equipment to maintain and control buoyancy.

● Squeezes. The most obvious and immediate effect of Boyle's law is the pressure and pain a diver starts to feel as soon as she drops a few feet below the surface. These so-called squeezes can occur wherever there is an air space: the sinuses, ears, the space between your face and your mask. They are caused by an imbalance in pressure: Air is compressed as the diver descends and the pressure increases. To stop the squeeze, the diver must equalize the pressure by adding air. To stop mask squeeze, a diver merely breathes out through her nose into the mask, adding air and equalizing the pressure. To stop squeezes in the ears and sinuses, the diver performs the so-called Valsalva maneuver by holding her nose and blowing gently. This forces air through the nasal passages into the air spaces, and equalizes the pressure.

● Reverse blocks. Similarly, when a diver ascends, it is possible for air that is trapped in the sinuses, ears, or intestines to expand and cause pain. This occurs more rarely than a squeeze, because usually, the air simply finds a way out. However, if air is prevented from escaping, a reverse block might occur. For example, if a diver has been using medication for a cold and it wears off, the sinuses could become blocked and prevent air from escaping. (For this reason, do not dive with a cold or when using cold medication. Also avoid anything that could create a block, such as ear plugs or a too-tight hood.) Reverse blocks can also occur in the intestines, especially if you've been eating gassy foods before a dive. Reverse blocks are more easily prevented than cured: About the only thing you can do is descend a little, wait a moment for the air to find its way out, and then ascend slowly.

● Lung overexpansion injuries. These are among the most serious of all potential diving injuries. They occur when a diver holds her breath and ascends. As the diver ascends, the pressure decreases and the air in the diver's lungs, following Boyle's law, expands. If the lungs expand too much, they can be seriously and permanently damaged. Fortunately, lung overexpansion injuries are easy to prevent if you follow one of diving's fundamental laws: Breathe slowly and continuously and never hold your breath. By breathing continuously, your lungs are constantly equalizing to the changing pressure.

● Teeth. Rarely, an air space between a filling and a tooth will be subject to a squeeze. There's nothing you can do about this underwater. Prevention via regular dental care is the only solution.

CHARLES'S LAW

WHAT IT SAYS If pressure is kept constant, the volume of a gas will vary directly with the temperature.
TRANSLATION As temperature increases, molecules of gas become energized by the heat and move around more. This means that the volume of a given amount of air expands when it is heated, and contracts when it is cooled. You can see this in cold weather, when a balloon seems to suddenly shrink. But an inflexible container (like a SCUBA tank) can't expand, so pressure inside it builds up when it is heated (Guy-Lussac's Law). If it builds too much, it will burst. (Note: It's extremely rare for a tank to actually

explode unless it is defective or damaged. Tank valves have a specially designed safety feature called a burst disk that will rupture if the air pressure in the tank becomes dangerously high.)

HOW IT AFFECTS DIVERS For divers, the most important consequence of Charles's law involves air in a tank. As the temperature changes, the air pressure in the tank will change, about 5 psi for each degree Fahrenheit. It's important to keep tanks out of situations where they could overheat, like the trunk of a car on a hot day, or in a place exposed to reflected heat from rocks and sand. If a tank overheats, it could actually burst its safety disk and let out all the air.

DALTON'S LAW

WHAT IT SAYS Dalton's law explains how each component in a mixture of gases behaves. It says that each gas acts as though it were the only gas present. It also says that the total pressure exerted by a mixture of gases is equal to the sum of the pressures of each of the component gases in the mixture.

TRANSLATION Air is a mixture of gases, primarily oxygen and nitrogen. Nitrogen and oxygen affect divers differently under pressure than they do at the surface. Dalton's law helps divers calculate what the effect of each gas will be under

A skin diver's lungs are full size at the surface, but only half their normal size at a depth of 33 feet.

pressure. To calculate how a gas will affect a diver, we need to know the depth of the dive and the partial pressure of the gas. The partial pressure is simply a particular gas's percentage in the mixture. In normal air, nitrogen has a partial pressure of 78 percent, and oxygen has a partial pressure of 21 percent. In enriched air, there is less nitrogen and more oxygen than in regular air. Therefore, the nitrogen has a lower partial pressure than it does in ordinary air (making divers less susceptible to nitrogen-related problems like the bends), and the oxygen has a higher partial pressure than it does in ordinary air (making divers more susceptible to oxygen-related problems like oxygen toxicity).

HOW IT AFFECTS DIVERS This law helps divers calculate the effects of nitrogen and oxygen at different depths (under different pressures), and it pertains to the use of different mixtures of gases such as Nitrox. This law also explains some depth-related problems such as nitrogen narcosis and oxygen toxicity.

Although it's not essential for open-water divers to be capable of solving detailed physics problems, it is important that they understand the concept. Let's look at oxygen toxicity. We have adapted to breathing the air in our atmosphere, which is only 21 percent oxygen. At sea level, when we breathe the compressed air in a tank (assuming that the tank is filled with normal air), we are getting exactly the same amount of oxygen as we are when we are breathing normally. However, as we descend, the pressure increases, so (following Boyle's law) the density of the air we are breathing increases. This means that each time we take a breath, we are breathing more molecules of air. It also means that we are taking in more molecules of whatever gases there are that make up air — in this case, oxygen and nitrogen. At a certain point, the air becomes so dense that we will end up breathing in an amount of oxygen that is toxic.

Typically, oxygen toxicity is not a problem when diving with normal air (78 percent nitrogen, 21 percent oxygen). Just how much oxygen is toxic varies from diver to diver, but for most people the threshold occurs at about 220 feet. Of course, 220 feet is well beyond recreational diving limits, and this is why oxygen toxicity is not a frequent problem for divers using regular compressed air. Oxygen toxicity does become a problem, however, when divers use enriched air, such as Nitrox, which is composed of less nitrogen and more oxygen. Because it contains less nitrogen, Nitrox reduces the risk of the bends while permitting divers to stay down longer. When using Nitrox, it is possible to be affected by oxygen toxicity at depths of only about 100 feet — well within the limits for recreational divers. For this reason, divers should be specially trained in the use of Nitrox and its specially formulated tables. It's especially important to understand that Nitrox is not used to prolong deep dives; it is used to increase your bottom time on shallower dives. There are, additionally, other gas mixtures used in diving that also require special training and tables.

Nitrogen narcosis is another problem that occurs because of the effect of nitrogen's high partial pressure at depth. At sea level, nitrogen doesn't have an effect on us, but under pressure, usually at depths of 100 or more feet, it can produce the intoxicating effects of nitrogen narcosis. As with oxygen toxicity, nitrogen narcosis is the result of increased pressure making us take in more of a gas than our bodies can cope with.

HENRY'S LAW

WHAT IT SAYS The amount of a gas that will dissolve in a liquid at a given temperature is almost directly proportional to the partial pressure of that gas.
TRANSLATION Think about a can of soda: Carbon dioxide is dissolved in the liquid. This law says that the more pressure there is, the more gas can be dissolved into a liquid.
HOW IT AFFECTS DIVERS As we dive and the pressure increases, it is possible for gases to dissolve in our body tissues because the human body is about 70 percent water. Just as carbon dioxide dissolves in a soda can, nitrogen under pressure dissolves in our tissues. The deeper the dive, the higher the pressure, and the more nitrogen can dissolve.

Initially, the nitrogen doesn't cause trouble. It dissolves in teeny little microscopic bubbles that easily pass through blood and tissues. But when it's time to ascend, the picture changes. The pressure decreases, so (following Boyle's law) the bubbles get bigger. (You can see how dramatically bubbles get bigger by watching a stream of bubbles exhaled by a diver. At first they are very small, but as they rise to the surface they expand until they are the size of big balloons.) When the bubbles in our tissues get so big that they interfere with circulation or lodge in the tissues, they cause a condition known as decompression sickness, or the bends. These bubbles can be tiny, blocking only small capillaries, or they can be large, expanding in joints, nerves, skin, and fat, or blocking the blood supply to critical organs.

The bends is a serious, potentially fatal condition. Knowing how to prevent it is one of the key skills of diving. Ascending slowly enough to allow the nitrogen to off-gas — that is, exit the tissues before they cause problems — is a basic tenet of safe diving. Another is to follow the dive tables, which tell you how long you can dive, how deep, and how much time you should spend on the surface between dives to let the nitrogen exit your system. Dive tables are designed solely to help you avoid decompression sickness. Dive tables are discussed in Chapter 5; symptoms and treatment of decompression sickness are discussed in Chapter 6.

FOLLOWING THE RULES

The motivation for understanding the science behind diving isn't to impress our non-diving friends — it's to help us understand the nature of the at-times inhospitable environment we propose to enter so our time there will be safe and enjoyable.

In the world of inner space, we are visitors. Water distorts everything — from how we move to how we breathe, from how we see to what we hear. Poorly adapted and unable to survive without life support, we are vulnerable to scientific laws that affect us whether we understand them or not. Sometimes disoriented, sometimes under stress, we may sometimes find simple tasks difficult to perform.

As we must any time we travel to a foreign land, we should remember that we are subject to new rules. If we understand them, we are better able to fit in, to function, and, finally, to enjoy ourselves.

APPENDIX II

RESPONSIBLE DIVER'S CODE

The following code is promoted by the Divers Alert Network to help divers plan and execute responsible, safe — and therefore enjoyable — dives.

ARE YOU A RESPONSIBLE DIVER?

As a responsible diver, I understand and assume all the risks I may encounter while diving.

MY RESPONSIBLE DIVING DUTIES INCLUDE:

I Diving within the limits of my ability and training

II Evaluating the conditions before every dive and making sure they fit my personal capabilities

III Being familiar with and checking my equipment before and during every dive

IV Respecting the buddy system and its advantages

V Accepting the responsibility for my own safety on every dive

VI Being environmentally conscious on every dive

I Diving within the limits of my ability and training

AS A RESPONSIBLE DIVER, I UNDERSTAND...

● My certification card qualifies me to engage in diving activities consistent with my training and experience.

● The importance of continuing my diving education in the form of supervised activities and training such as night diving and deep diving specialties.

● The need to keep proficient in my diving skills and to refresh them under supervision if I have not been diving recently.

● There are no limits to what I can learn about diving. The more I know, the safer I'll be.

● My maximum depth should be limited to my level of training and experience.

● I must have training in the proper use of equipment.

● The value of getting specific training in the proper use and application of specialized equipment such as dry suits and computers.

II Evaluating the conditions before every dive and making sure they fit my personal capabilities

AS A RESPONSIBLE DIVER, I RECOGNIZE...

● The need for being familiar with my dive sites and the importance of getting a formal orientation to unfamiliar dive sites from a knowledgeable local source.

● The dangers of overhead environments (caves, wrecks, etc.) and the need to seek specialized training before doing such diving.

● I should postpone my dive, or choose an alternate site, if I evaluate the dive-site conditions as being more difficult than my experience and training level.

● I should use a surface support station, such as a boat or a float, whenever feasible.

III Being familiar with and checking my equipment before and during every dive

AS A RESPONSIBLE DIVER, I UNDERSTAND...

● That simply owning my equipment does not give me the knowledge and ability to dive safely.

● I must have training in the use of my equipment.

● I should maintain comfort in the use of my equipment through practice.

● My equipment must be equal to the type of diving I will be doing.

● I need to check that my equipment is operating properly before each dive.

● My equipment must be treated with respect and properly maintained and serviced.

● My equipment must be serviced according to manufacturers' specifications by a qualified service technician.

● I must follow manufacturers' recommendations on the use of my equipment and must not modify it to perform in a way not intended by its maker.

● I need to be properly trained before using EANx (Nitrox) and must use proper EANx-designated equipment displaying the appropriate markings.

● The importance of being able to easily release my weights if in distress.

● The value of an alternate air source and low-pressure buoyancy-control inflation system.

● How to adjust my weights for neutral buoyancy at the surface with no air in my buoyancy control device.

IV Respecting the buddy system and its advantages

AS A RESPONSIBLE DIVER, I RECOGNIZE...

- The need to keep my diving emergency response skills sharp through practice and mental role playing.
- The importance of planning my dives with my buddy, including communications procedures for reuniting if separated and emergency procedures.
- Diving the plan which my buddy and I agreed to follow helps provide a safe dive.
- I should always deny the use of my equipment to uncertified divers.

V Accepting the responsibility for my own safety on every dive

AS A RESPONSIBLE DIVER I KNOW...

- The importance of maintaining good mental and physical fitness for diving.
- I must not dive while under the influence of alcohol or drugs.
- Postponing the dive is the correct action if I am suffering from a cold, hangover, flu, or other health deficiency that may cause complications.
- To be watchful for and avoid overexertion.
- Diving will be safer if I listen carefully to dive briefings and respect the advice of those overseeing my diving activities.
- The operators I dive with are not responsible for my decisions and actions.
- I should be proficient in dive-table use and make all dives no-required-decompression dives, allowing for a margin of safety, ascending no faster than 60 feet (18 meters) per minute (Note: The YMCA

recommends an ascent rate of not more than 30 feet per minute), and making a safety stop at the end of every dive.
- To always breathe continuously while diving and never skip-breathe or hold my breath.
- Proper buoyancy should be maintained at all times — buoyant for surface swimming, neutral while swimming underwater.

VI Being environmentally conscious on every dive

AS A RESPONSIBLE DIVER, I...

- Am careful about what I touch underwater.
- Do not break plants or coral or collect souvenirs.
- Respect laws on size and limits for game.
- Collect and dispose of trash I find while diving.
- Let dive buddies, resorts, and dive operators know how I feel about environmental irresponsibility.
- Never dive in a manner that would hurt the environment.

THE RESORTS AND OPERATORS I DIVE WITH...

- Use mooring buoys whenever available or anchor in areas free of live bottoms.
- Give thorough environmental briefings to divers before they enter the water.
- Contain photoprocessing chemicals for proper disposal.
- Dispose of trash responsibly.
- Uphold environmental regulations and game limits.

GLOSSARY

ATMOSPHERE (OR ATM) A unit of measurement used to denote air pressure. (Europeans use a measurement called *bars*; it's almost exactly the same as atm.) The pressure at sea level is 1 atm. As you descend on a dive, the pressure increases by 1 atm every 33 feet.

THE BENDS Otherwise known as *decompression sickness*, or DCS, the bends (or "getting bent") is a dangerous condition caused by spending too much time too deep, and/or coming up too fast. Decompression sickness is discussed in detail in Chapters 5 and 6, and in Appendix I.

BUOYANCY A diver's ability to control whether he sinks (negative buoyancy), rises (positive buoyancy), or hangs in one place (neutral buoyancy). When someone asks, "How's your buoyancy?", they're referring to your ability to control whether you float, sink, or lie perfectly still in the water.

BC (OR BCD) *Buoyancy compensator or buoyancy control device* (see Chapter 3). A BC is a vest that you inflate and deflate to help control whether you go up, go down, or stay still. Experienced divers prefer to control buoyancy with breathing techniques, whereas novices rely more on their BC controls.

BOTTOM TIME The amount of time spent on a dive. Some agencies teach divers to calculate bottom time from when the diver starts to descend to when the diver starts to ascend. A more conservative approach is to calculate bottom time from the time you leave the surface to the time you return to it.

BURST LUNG Lung overexpansion injury caused by ascending too fast while holding your breath (see Chapter 6 and Appendix I).

C-CARD Stands for *Certification card*, which is your license to dive. Don't leave home without it.

COMPRESSED AIR The air in your tank. It's made up of the same stuff — mostly nitrogen and oxygen — you breathe on land, but it has been filtered, dried, and compressed.

DECOMPRESSION SICKNESS See *the bends*.

DECOMPRESSION STOP A required pause for a certain amount of time at a certain depth, taken during the ascent from a dive, to give the body a chance to safely release dissolved nitrogen. Recreational dives should be calculated so that decompression stops are not mandatory.

FIRST STAGE The part of the regulator that attaches to the tank valve.

LIVE-ABOARDS These boats are for divers who want to get wet and stay wet. For a week, or two, or three, you live aboard, diving as much as the tables and your computer allow. Live-aboards can be expensive, but they are sometimes the only way to get to a prize dive site.

LOGBOOK A book in which you record your diving experiences. A *C-card* will get you on a dive boat, but some operators will want to look at your logbook before signing you up for advanced dives.

MASK SQUEEZE A feeling of pressure that occurs around your face when you descend because the air in the space between your mask and your face is being compressed. To relieve mask squeeze, breathe out through your nose.

NARKED *Nitrogen narcosis* is a feeling of intoxication that tends to occur below 100 feet. A *narked diver* may have impaired judgment or feel panicky and anxious. Ascending usually solves the problem (see Chapter 6 and Appendix I).

NEOPRENE The rubbery material used in SCUBA gear, especially wet suits, booties, hoods, and gloves.

NEWBIE A new diver.

NITROGEN NARCOSIS See *narked*.

NITROX A special combination of nitrogen and oxygen formulated to allow divers more bottom time on shallow dives (see Appendix I).

OCTOPUS The spare mouthpiece that attaches to the regulator to provide a secondary air source. (The whole contraption, with regulator and hoses put together, looks like an octopus. Hence the name.)

RECOMPRESSION CHAMBER Also called a *hyperbaric chamber*. A facility for treating *decompression sickness*.

REFERENCE LINE A weighted length of rope suspended from a boat or buoy that divers use to help control their rate of ascent and descent.

REGULATOR (OR REG) The contraption that lets you breathe. It consists of a first stage, which reduces air pressure coming from the tank; a hose; and a second stage, which further reduces the air pressure so you can breathe it.

SAFETY STOP A short stop taken during the ascent, usually for three minutes at about 15 feet below the surface, to let excess nitrogen leave the body. Unlike a decompression stop, a safety stop may not be required by the dive profile — but it's a good idea anytime, and should be performed on all deep dives.

SCUBA Stands for self-contained underwater breathing apparatus.

SECOND STAGE The part of the regulator that contains the mouthpiece.

VIS Visibility. If you're beginning to think that some divers groove on one-syllable abbreviations and acronyms, you're right. Maybe they're just anxious to spend less time talking and more time diving.

SOURCES & RESOURCES

ORGANIZATIONS

Besides certifying agencies, there are a number of organizations devoted to areas of particular interest to divers, including assistance to individuals with disabilities, cave diving, environmental and conservation groups, marketing, safety, underwater sports, and training standards.

ALPHA ONE
Open Waters
c/o Alpha One
127 Main Street
South Portland, ME 04106
1-800-640-7200
email: owscuba@aol.com
Alpha One has developed an Open Waters program to assist individuals with disabilities in learning to SCUBA dive. Supported by PADI, Alpha One-Open Waters is an information referral service.

CEDAM INTERNATIONAL
Conservation, Education, Diving, Awareness and Marine-Research
One Fox Road
Croton-on-Hudson, NY 10520
914-271-5365
www.cedam.org
email: cedamint@aol.com
A non-profit organization dedicated to marine conservation, diving, and archaeology. Members on CEDAM diving expeditions participate in scientific research and conservation-oriented education projects, contributing to the fields of marine biology and marine/terrestrial archaeology.

CORAL REEF ALLIANCE
64 Shattuck Square, Suite 220
Berkeley, CA 94704
510-848-0110
www.coral.org
email: info@coral.org
A conservation group that works

with the diving community and others to promote coral reef conservation around the world.

COUSTEAU SOCIETY
870 Greenbrier Circle,
Suite 402
Chesapeake, VA 23320
800-441-4395
www.cousteausociety.org
email: cousteau@infi.net
An environmental organization documenting natural systems to increase knowledge and awareness of marine and environmental subjects while also advocating for protection of the marine environment.

DAN
Divers Alert Network
The Peter B. Bennett Center
6 West Colony Place
Durham, NC 27705
1-800-446-2671
www.dan.ycg.org

email: dan@diversalert–
network.org
A non-profit dive safety organization. Members become part of
a worldwide network committed
to dive safety and accident
prevention. Membership includes
medical air evacuation assistance, a subscription to Alert
Diver magazine, eligibility for
dive accident insurance program, a 24-hour diving emergency hotline, a medical information line, and safety seminars
and educational materials.

DEMA

Diving Equipment and
Marketing Association
2050 South Santa Cruz Street,
Suite 1000
Anaheim, CA 92805-6816
1-714-939-6399
www.dema.org
A global professional organization which represents the entire
diving industry including manufacturers, retailers, publications,
travel, resorts, educational and
certification agencies, and
government and non-government
tourism organizations. Produces
the industry's largest annual
national trade show.

MORAY WHEELS

Moray Wheels — Adaptive
Scuba Association
P.O. Box 1660 GMF
Boston, MA 02205
603-598-4292
email: info@MorayWheels.org
www.moraywheels.org
A non-profit SCUBA club made
up of able-bodied and physically
disabled divers. The Moray
Wheels offers certification
classes, local activities, and
accessible tropical diving
vacations.

NACD

National Association
for Cave Diving
P.O. Box 14492
Gainsville, FL 32604
www.afn.org/"nacd
A non-profit organization whose

purpose is safer cave diving
through training and education.
NACD has established standards
for safe cave diving, organizes
seminars and workshops concerning equipment, techniques,
safety, education, training, conservation, and exploration, and
publishes information regarding
cavern and cave diving. NACD
also maintains records of certified cavern and cave divers and
instructors.

REEF

Reef Environmental
Education Foundation
P.O. Box 246
Key Largo, FL 33037
305-451-0312
www.reef.org
A non-profit organization
striving to educate, enlist, and
enable both divers and non-
divers to become active stewards
in the conservation of coral reefs
and other marine habitats.
REEF volunteers conduct
marine life surveys which are
used to develop strategies for
habitat conservation and
resource management.

REEF KEEPER INTERNATIONAL

2809 Bird Avenue, Suite 162
Miami, FL 33133
305-358-4600
www.reeefkeeper.org
email: ReefKeeper@
ReefKeeper.org
A non-profit organization exclusively dedicated to the worldwide
protection of coral reefs and
their marine life. Reef Keeper
conducts an integrated program
of field inventory, policy
analysis, grassroots organization, agency monitoring, advo-
cacy, technical assistance, and
public awareness.

RSTC

Recreational Scuba
Training Council
3047 Joan Court
Land O'Lakes, FL 34639
813-996-6582
The Recreational SCUBA

Training Council (RSTC) is
the secretariat for the American
National Standards Institute
(ANSI) committee for diving
instructional standards and
safety in all levels of certification. RSTC creates minimum
training standards for the diving
industry and addresses many
diverse issues in the diving
industry involved with leadership
training, along with establishing
industry-wide quality control
procedures.

USOA

Underwater Society of America
P.O. Box 628
Daly City, CA 94017
650-583-8492
www.underwater-society.org
email: croseusoa@ aol.com
The USOA is the public diving
organization of the United States
with over thirty councils/ clubs.
It is the sanctioning body of
CMAS for underwater sports in
the U.S., authorizing yearly
local, regional, and national
underwater championships in
SCUBA, Free Diving, U/W
Hockey, U/W Rugby, Fin
Swimming, and U/W Photog-
raphy. The USOA is also eligible
and sends teams to all World
Underwater Sports Champi-
onships.

DIVE CLUBS

Dive clubs can be found virtually anywhere there is diving.
Information on local and
regional clubs can be found
at local dive centers where
informal groups and buddy
systems are also formed.

Other sources of information on
dive clubs/councils are:

USOA

Underwater Society of America
P.O. Box 628
Daly City, CA 94017
650-583-8492
www.underwater-society.org
email: croseusoa@aol.com

RODALE'S SCUBA DIVING
Rodale Press, Inc.
33 East Minor Street
Emmaus, PA 18098
610-967-7929
www.scubadiving.com
email: fziegle1@rodalepress.com

CERTIFYING AGENCIES

ANDI
American Nitrox Divers
International, Ltd.
74 Woodcleft Avenue
Freeport, NY 115209-3342
1-800-229-2634
www.andihq.com
email: andihq@aol.com
*An educational agency for
advanced diving technologies,
providing diver education
through an international network of professional training
facilities and instructors.*

BSAC
British Sub-Aqua Club
Telford's Quay
Cheshire L65 4FY
United Kingdom
www.bsac.com
email: postmaster@bsac.com
*World's largest diving club,
BSAC is based in the United
Kingdom with branches in other
countries.*

CMAS (WORLD UNDERWATER FEDERATION)
Confederation Mondiale Des
Activities Subaquatiques
Viale Tiziano, 74
00196 Rome, Italy
(39)6.3685 8480
www.cmas.org
email: cmasmond@tin.it
*The only world diving organiza-
tion, CMAS is composed of some
14,000 diving clubs, 82 national
federations, and 4.5 million
divers. CMAS international certifications cards are issued at all
levels for both divers and
instructors. YMCA SCUBA is the
only SCUBA certification organization in the United States to
offer the CMAS international
certification card.*

DRI
Dive Rescue International
201 North Link Lane
Fort Collins, CO 80524-2712
1-970-482-0887
www.diverescueintl.com
email:training@
diverescueintl.com
*A certifying agency whose
training programs are designed
specifically for water rescue,
recovery, and investigative
teams.*

HSA INTERNATIONAL
Handicapped Scuba Association
1104 El Prado
San Clemente, CA 92672
1-714-498-6128
http://ourworld.compuserve.com/
homepages/hsahdq/
email: 103424.3535@com-
puserve.com
*An independent diver training
and certifying agency which
develops programs and training
standards to advance and
promote SCUBA diving among
people with disabilities. Offers
training and certification for
instructors, Open Water certification, a Dive Buddy program,
and accessible dive vacation
opportunities.*

IANTD
International Association of
Nitrox and Technical Divers
World Headquarters
9628 N.E. 2nd Avenue, Suite D
Miami Shores, FL 33138-2767
305-751-4873
email: iantdhq@ix.netcom.com
www.iantd.com
*Training programs for all levels
of advanced recreational and
technical diving. Was the first
program to offer certification in
EAN. (Enriched Air Nitrox).*

IDEA
International Diving
Educators Association
IDEA North America
P.O. Box 8427
Jacksonville, FL 32239-8427
904-744-5554

www.idea-scubadiving.com
email: ideahq@idea-
scubadiving.com
*An international certification
agency represented in the
continental United States and
over 30 other countries. Offers
complete continuing education
program from Skin Diver
through Instructor Trainer, along
with a variety of specialty
courses for both students and
instructors. IDEA course
standards are based on ANSI
(American National Standards
Institute) guidelines.*

NASDS
National Association of
Scuba Diving Schools
*This agency has merged with
SSI (Scuba Schools International). NASDS cardholders can
contact SSI which has become
the education arm of the new
organization.*

NASE
National Academy of
Scuba Educators
1728 Kingsley Avenue, Suite 105
Orange Park, FL 32073
904-264-4104
www.nasescuba.com
email: nasescuba@classic.
msn.com
*Programs for all levels of diving.
Instructors and students have the
option of home study.*

NAUI WORLDWIDE
National Association of
Underwater Instructors
9942 Currie Davis Drive, Suite H
Tampa, FL 33619-2667
800-553-6284
www.naui.org
email: nauihq@nauiww.org
*Nonprofit organization with
instruction ranging from
beginner level to instructor
certification provided through
worldwide affiliated dive centers. Also offers certification in
over twenty specialties including
wreck diving, cave diving,
deep diving, ice diving, and*

photography. Flexible teaching programs allow academic freedom for qualified professional educators to teach diving in any reasonable manner as long as NAUI standards and policies are met.

PADI
Professional Association of Diving Instructors
30151 Tomas Street
Rancho Santa Margarita, CA 92688-2125
800-729-7234 (U.S.)
949-858-7234
www.padi.com
Professional Association of Diving Instructors offers instruction ranging from entry level to instructor level through worldwide PADI dive centers. Specialty diver courses include altitude diving, boat diving, cavern diving, deep diving, drift diving, dry suit diving, ice diving, underwater navigation, search and recovery diving, underwater naturalism, and regional courses developed by local PADI instructors. Also offers a first aid course, a travel network, and underwater preservation education.

PDIC INTERNATIONAL
Professional Diving Instructors Corporation
P.O. Box 3633
Scranton, PA 18505
570-342-1480
www.pdic-intl.com
email: info@pdic-intl.com
An international SCUBA training and certification agency with instructors and training facilities worldwide. Provides all levels of certification from Open Water through Instructor. All instructors teach each course identically following the PDIC system.

SDI/TDI
Scuba Diving International/Technical Diving International
9 Coastal Plaza
Bath, ME 04530

1-207-729-4201
www.tdisdi.com
email: worldhq@tdisdi.com
A certifying organization with two branches: SDI focuses on sport diving and recreational diving standards, while TDI focuses on technical diving.

SSI
Scuba Schools International
2619 Canton Court
Fort Collins, CO 80525
970-482-0883
www.ssiusa.com
email: admin@ssiusa.com
A certification agency that requires instructors to be associated with a Retail Dive Store Facility. SSI Affiliated Dive Training Facilities provide all levels of training from Snorkeling through Master Instructor. Instructors use SSI's Total Training System which includes manuals, study guides, videos, teaching outlines, and other support material. SSI is the education arm of the organization formed from the merger of SSI and NASDS (National Association of Scuba Diving Schools).

USAUF
U.S.A. Underwater Federation
P.O. Box 13754
Gainsville, FL 32604
904-372-0805
An international diving association offering certification and instructor trainer courses. Also sponsors research and educational programs.

WASI
World Association of Scuba Instructors
134 South Main, Suite M140
Salt Lake City, UT 84101
801-363-9274
www.divewasi.com
email: wasi@divewasi.com
A full range of training programs from Open Water to Instructor are offered through affiliated dive shops and independent instructors.

YMCA SCUBA
Young Men's Christian Association
5825-2A Live Oak Parkway
Norcross, GA 30093-1728
888-464-9622
www.ymcascuba.org
email: scubaymca@aol.com
Largest not-for-profit organization to provide community-oriented education for divers and instructors. Certification for snorkeling, entry level open water, and specialty courses through instructor trainer.

CONVENTIONS EXHIBITIONS TRADE SHOWS

BENEATH THE SEA
495 New Rochelle Road
Bronxville, NY 10608
email: info@BeneaththeSea.org
The largest consumer SCUBA and dive travel show in America. BTS is a non-profit corporation dedicated to increasing awareness of the earth's oceans and the sport of SCUBA diving. Beneath the Sea expositions are held annually and feature dozens of seminars and workshops, an underwater film festival, and exhibits and demonstrations by hundreds of manufacturers, dive clubs, dive shops, and resorts.

DEMA TRADE SHOW
Diving, Equipment and Marketing Association
PGI Exhibitions
8989 Rio San Diego Drive, Suite 160
San Diego, CA 92108-1647
1-619-294-2999
www.dema.org
email: demashow@pgi.com
The SCUBA and diving industry's largest national professional trade show. This annual show highlights the newest products for SCUBA diving, snorkeling, ocean sports, and adventure travel and is designed for professionals in the diving industry including manufacturers, retailers,

publications, the travel and tourism industry, and educational and certification agencies.

OCEAN FEST
c/o Neal Watson's
Undersea Adventures
1043 Southeast 17th Street
Fort Lauderdale, FL 33316
800-327-8150
email: nealwatson@aol.com
www.oceanfest.com
Billed as an ocean festival, this consumer trade show features over 200 dive related exhibits under giant tents at the edge of the Atlantic Ocean in Fort Lauderdale. Offered are introductory SCUBA and snorkeling courses, technical diving programs, and equipment repair clinics. Experienced divers and snorkelers can participate in a reef clean-up. A portion of the proceeds will benefit the Ocean Watch Foundation and other environmental organizations.

OUR WORLD-UNDERWATER
P.O. Box 803
Tinley Park, IL 60477
708-403-5447
email: info@ourworldunderwater.com
www.owu.ycg.org
A large three-day conference/dive show devoted to SCUBA diving, underwater exploration, and preservation of the marine environment held annually in Chicago, Illinois. The show features educational seminars on environmental issues, photography, archaeology, wreck diving, and many other topics, along with specialized training and workshops, and over 185 exhibitors of products and services. The conference financially supports the Our World-Underwater Scholarship Society which provides internship opportunities and local outreach programs to promote education related to the underwater world.

SEASPACE
SEASPACE-Scuba Diving & Adventure Travel Expo
P.O. Box 3753
Houston, TX 77253-3753
713-467-6675
www.seaspace.org
The largest consumer SCUBA diving and dive travel show in the Southwest. SEASPACE is a not-for-profit organization which has been dedicated for over 30 years to education and protection of the marine environment. Proceeds from the expo benefit a Marine Scholarship Fund.

MAGAZINES
DISCOVER DIVING
Petersen Publishing Company
6420 Wilshire Boulevard
Los Angeles, CA 90048
323-782-2960
www.petersenco.com
Focuses on the lifestyle associated with the sport of SCUBA diving with information on gear, travel, technical and safety issues, and personalities in the industry. Affiliated magazines are SKIN DIVER and DIVE REPORT.

DIVE GIRL
64 Essex Road, Islington
London N1 8LR, UK
+44-171-226-9925
web: www.divegirl.com
email: girls@divegirl.com
A U.K. based magazine about women who dive, with an aim to amuse and inspire divers everywhere. "Dive Girl is about anything that promotes women, encourages women, and demystifies the stuff the boys get up to."

DIVE REPORT
Petersen Publishing Company
6420 Wilshire Boulevard
Los Angeles, CA 90048
332-782-2960
www.petersenco.com
A business magazine for those involved in the SCUBA diving field including retailers, instructors, travel professionals,

resort managers, dive boat operators, manufacturers, and media. Affiliated magazines are Discover Diving *and* Skin Diver.

DIVER: THE MAGAZINE OF SUB-AQUA DIVING, UNDERSEA EXPLORATION AND RESEARCH
Eaton Publications
55 High Street
Teddington, Mddx. TW11 8HA
England
44-181-943-4288
www.divernet.com
email: 100737.2226@compuserve.com
Covers topics in sport sub-aqua diving, including introduction to the sport, training, underwater recreation, travel, technology, equipment, wrecks and salvage, conservation, exploration, marine archaeology, marine biology, and underwater photography.

DIVER MAGAZINE
P.O. Box 1312, Stn. A
Delta, B.C. Y4M 3Y8
Canada
604-274-4333
www.divermag.com
email: divermag@axion.net
Canadian publication covering Canadian and North American dive destinations, travel features, and equipment reviews. Has web edition with searchable database including information on photo equipment and training.

DIVE TRAINING
Dive Training LLC
201 Main Street
Parkville, MO 64152
Subscriptions: 816-741-5151
or email: divetraining@spc-mag.com
A monthly magazine for new divers and their instructors, filled with back-to-basics information to help divers become safer and more knowledgeable. Dive Training is specifically aimed at providing information to people in SCUBA courses.

IMMERSED: THE INTERNATIONAL TECHNICAL DIVING MAGAZINE
IMMERSED, LLC
P.O. Box 638
Chester, NY 10918-0638
818-760-8983
web: www.immersed.com
email: rosie@starkservices.com
An international quarterly featuring new faces and places, personalities, and destinations previously known only to local networks of divers. Features articles about projects, ideas, developments, and practices in technical diving.

PACIFIC DIVER
Western Outdoors Publications
3197-E Airport Loop Drive
Costa Mesa, CA 92626
714-546-4370
Bimonthly magazine for Pacific Coast sports divers. Features dive boat schedules and other information.

SCUBA DIVER
Yaffa Publishing Group
17-21 Bellevue Street
Surry Hills, N.S.W. 2010
Australia
61-2-9281-2333
email: yaffa@yaffa.com.au
Bimonthly magazine providing comprehensive coverage of the recreational diving field.

RODALE'S SCUBA DIVING
Rodale Press, Inc.
33 East Minor Street
Emmaus, PA 18098
Subscriptions: 800-666-0016
www.scubadiving.com
email: scubadivdm@aol.com
Founded in 1992, Rodale's Scuba Diving magazine has been called the Consumer Reports for divers, providing objective evaluations of SCUBA equipment, dive operators, and dive resorts. RSD also features tips and techniques for safe diving at a variety of levels, novice to advanced. RSD's online magazine claims the net's largest SCUBA travel database,

along with feature articles, equipment evaluations, underwater photo instruction, and a SCUBA message board.

SEARCHLINES
International Association of Dive Rescue Specialists
Box 5259
San Clemente, CA 92674-1690
714-369-1660
email: iadrs@fia.net
Trade publication which covers techniques, equipment, and experiences pertinent to the job of public safety diver. For professional dive rescue specialists.

SKIN DIVER
Petersen Publishing Company
6420 Wilshire Boulevard
Los Angeles, CA 90048
323-782-2960
www.skin-diver.com
email: skindiver@petersenpub.com
A monthly publication of recreational diving covering SCUBA technology, wreck exploration, travel, underwater photography, snorkeling, and diving education. Publisher also produces affiliated magazines Dive Report and Discover Diving

SPORT DIVER
World Publications
330 West Canton Avenue
Winter Park, FL 32789-3195
Subscriptions: 800-879-0478
www.sportdivermag.com
email: sportdiver@worldzine.com
A bimonthly focusing on adventure in both exotic locales and little-known sites in well-known places. It features stories on people and places around the world, new and innovative dive equipment, and news and events important to the diving community. Regular columns offer tips on improving dive skills and photography.

SPORTDIVING MAGAZINE
Mountain, Ocean & Travel Publications

P.O. Box 167
Narre Warren, Vic. 3805
Australia
61-3-59443774
www.home.aone.net.au/sport-diving
email: motpub@r150.aone.net.au
Bimonthly which covers dive travel, wrecks, marine natural history, equipment overviews, technical information, and diver safety.

UNDERCURRENT
Elephant Socks Publishing, Inc.
125 E. Sir Francis Drake Blvd.
Larkspur, CA 94939
800-326-1896
www.undercurrent.org
email: webmaster@undercurrent.org
A monthly consumer magazine for the sport diver with no advertising. It features resort and equipment reviews, safety tips, and ways to have more fun underwater. Available through mail or on-line subscription.

ON-LINE MAGAZINES
Many diving print publications also have on-line versions of their magazines. There are also a number of magazines available exclusively on-line.

AQUANAUT
www.aquanaut.com
The internet's first and largest on-line magazine dedicated to the recreational and technical SCUBA diving community. Maintains Aquacrawler, a database of links to thousands of other Web sites containing SCUBA information. Also provides dive gear and equipment reviews, links to SCUBA newsgroups, medical information, temperature & weather, site reviews, and an image gallery.

ASIAN DIVER ON-LINE
www.asiandiver.com
Information on diving in the Asia-Pacific region. Also markets merchandise — apparel,

books, and CD-Rom titles. Is a major support of the annual Asia Dive Expo trade show in Singapore. Print issues of Asian Diver magazine are available through on-line subscription.

DESTINATIONS
www.divetravel.net
On-line dive travel articles on the best ways to submerge oneself around the world.

DIVE TRAVEL ON-LINE
www.divetravel.net
Extensive information on destinations.

FREEDIVING INTERNET MAGAZINE
www.freediving-mag.com
Reviews, profiles, techniques, training, destinations, products, manufacturers, and other resources.

BOOKS
DESTINATION GUIDES
Adventuring in Belize: The Sierra Club Travel Guide to the Islands, Waters, and Inland Parks of Central America's Tropical Paradise (Sierra Club Adventures), Eric Hoffman. 1994. $16.00. Sierra Club Books.

Aqua Quest Diving Series. $18.95 each. Aqua Quest Publications.
  Baja California
  Belize
  Bonaire
  British Virgin Islands
  Cayman Islands

Best Dives of the Caribbean (Serial), Joyce Huber, Jon Huber (Contributor). 1997. $18.95. Hunter Publications.

Best Dives Snorkeling Adventures: A Guide to the Bahamas, Bermuda, Carribbean, Hawaii & Florida Keys, Joyce Huber, Jon Huber. 1998. $15.95. Photo-Graphics Publishing.

Diver's Guide to Florida and the Florida Keys, Jim Stachowicz. 1990. $5.95. Windward Publication Company.
'Dive Sites Of...' Series. $24.95 each. Passport Books.
  Red Sea
  Cayman Islands
  Philippines
  Great Barrier Reef and the Coral Sea
  Thailand
  Malaysia and Singapore
  Papua New Guinea
  Kenya and Tanzania: Including Pemba, Zanzibar, and Mafia
  Cozumel and the Yucatan

'Diving and Snorkeling Guide to...' Series. $14.95 each. Pisces Books
  Australia: Coral Sea and Great Barrier Reef
  Bali and the Komodo Region
  Bonaire
  British Virgin Islands
  Cayman Islands: Grand Cayman, Little Cayman, and Cayman Brac
  Cocos Island
  Cuba
  Curacao
  Fiji
  Florida Keys
  Hawaiian Islands
  Jamaica
  Northern California and the Monterey Peninsula
  Pacific Northwest: Includes Puget Sound, San Juan Islands, and Vancouver Island
  Palau
  Puerto Rico
  Roatan & Honduras' Bay Islands
  Seychelles
  Southern California
  St. Maarten, Saba, and St. Eustatius
  Texas: Includes Inland, Coastal, and Offshore Sites
  Truk Lagoon
  U.S. Virgin Islands: St. Croix, St. Thomas, and St. John

Diving in the Caribbean, Lawson Wood. 1998. $50.00. Rizzoli International Publications.

Diving: The World's Best Sites, Jack Jackson (Editor). 1997. $50.00. Rizzoli Bookstore.

Fielding's Guides. $19.95. Fielding Worldwide.
  Asia's Top Dive Sites: The Best Diving in Indonesia, Malaysia, the Philippines and Thailand
  Diving Australia: Fielding's In-Depth Guide to Diving Down Under
  Diving Indonesia: A Guide to the World's Greatest Diving

Lonely Planet Diving & Snorkeling Belize (2nd Ed), Franz O. Meyer. 1998. $15.95. Pisces Books.

Ned Deloach's Diving Guide to Underwater Florida, Ned Deloach. 1996. $18.95. New World Publications.

Snorkel Hawaii: Maui and Lanai and The Big Island, Judy Malinowski, Mel Malinowski. 1996. $14.95 each. Indigo Publications.

Snorkeling Guide to Marine Life: Florida Caribbean Bahamas, Paul Humann, Ned Deloach. 1995. $12.95. New World Publications.

The Caribbean (Abbeville's Dive Guides to the World's Best Sites), Kurt Amsler. 1998. $24.95. Abbeville Press, Inc.

The Dive Sites of the Maldives, Sam Harwood, Robert Bryning. 1998. $24.95. NTC Publishing Group.

The Florida Keys Dive Guide (Abbeville Dive Guide), Stephen Frink, William Harrigan (Photographer). 1998. $24.95.

Abbeville Press, Inc. *Underwater Wonders of the National Parks: A Diving and Snorkeling Guide (1st Ed)*, Daniel J. Lenihan, John D. Brooks. 1998. $19.95. Compass American Guides.

DIVING ADVENTURE BOOKS
Down Time: Great Writers on Diving, Casey Kittrell, Ed Kittrell (Editor), Jim Kittrell (Editor). 1998. $15.00. Look Away Books.

The Fireside Diver: An Anthology of Underwater Adventure, Bonnie J. Cardone (Editor). 1996. $14.95. Aqua Quest Publications.

DIVING & SNORKELING TECHNIQUES (HOW-TO GUIDES)
An Introduction to Technical Diving, Ann Kristovich, et al. 1999. $29.95. Grale Company.

Diving on the Edge: A Guide for New Divers, Michael Bane. 1998. $14.95. The Lyons Press.

Free Dive!, Terry Maas and David Sipperly. 1997. $39.95. Blue Water Freedivers Publishing.

Jeppesen's Open Water Sport Diver Manual, Richard A. Clinchy, et al. 1992. $19.95. Mosby-Year Book.

Scuba Diving Explained: Questions and Answers on Physiology and Medical Aspects of Scuba Diving, Lawrence Martin. 1997. $19.95. Best Publishing Company.

Scuba Equipment Care and Maintenance, Michael B. Farley. 1980. $13.95. West Coast Divers Supplies.

Scuba Talk: A Guide to Underwater Communication: Florida, Bahamas, and Caribbean Edition, Keith A. Ellenbogen.

1997. $14.95. Blue Reef Publications Inc.

The Essentials of Deeper Sport Diving: An Overview of the Theory and Requirements of Deeper Diving, John Lippmann. 1992. $21.95. Aqua Quest Publications.

Underwater Navigation, C. Royer. $7.95. International Marine Publications Systems.

FIELD GUIDES
Indo-Pacific Coral Reef Field Guide, Dr. Gerald R. Allen, Roger Steene. 1996. $39.95. Odyssey Publishing.

Reef Creature Identification: Florida, Caribbean, Bahamas, Paul Humann. $37.95. New World Publications.

The Snorkeler's Guide to the Coral Reef: From the Red Sea to the Pacific Ocean, Paddy Ryan (Photographer), Peter Atkinson (Photographer). 1994. $19.95. University of Hawaii Press.

SAFETY & FIRST AID
DAN Pocket Guide to First Aid for Scuba Diving, Dan Orr, et al. 1998. $12.95. Greycliff Publishing Company.

Oxygen First Aid for Divers, John Lippman. 1992. $14.95. J.L. Publications.

The DAN Emergency Handbook, John Lippman, Stan Bugg. 1995. $14.95. J.L. Publications.

UNDERWATER PHOTOGRAPHY
Jim Church's Essential Guide to Composition, Jim Church. $19.95. Aqua Quest Publications.

Jim Church's Essential Guide to Nikonos Systems, Jim Church. 1998. $22.95. Aqua Quest Publications.

The Art and Technique of Underwater Photography, Mark Webster, Grant Bradford (Illustrator). 1999. $29.95. Fountain Press Limited.

The Underwater Photography Handbook, Annemarie Kohler, Danja Kohler. 1999. $21.95. Stackpole Books.

Underwater Paradise: A Guide to the World's Best Diving Sites Through the Lenses of the Foremost Underwater Photographers, Robert Boye, et al. 1989. $39.95. Harry N. Abrams.

Wonders of the Reef: Diving With a Camera, Stephen Frink (Photographer). 1996. $39.95. Harry N. Abrams.

WRECK DIVING
Advanced Wreck Diving Guide, Gary Gentile. 1988. $12.95. Cornell Maritime Press.

Pisces Guide to Shipwreck Diving: New York & New Jersey, Henry C. Keatts. 1992. $16.95. Pisces Books.

Shipwrecks: Diving the Graveyard of the Atlantic. 1991. $14.95. Menasha Ridge Printing.

ON-LINE DIVING BOOK SOURCES

www.adventuroustraveler.com
A comprehensive selection of diving books.

www.amazon.com
A good selection of top-selling diving books.

www.barnesandnoble.com
A good selection of top-selling diving books.

www.bluewaterweb.com
The on-line location of Blue-water Books and Charts. Primarily cruising books, but also some diving and destination books.

www.marineguides.com
Several dive-related books along with other marine books.

www.seabooks.com
The on-line location of the Armchair Sailor bookstores. Has a comprehensive selection of diving books along with some diving videos.

VIDEOS

A comprehensive collection of videos on dive instruction, dive destinations, and underwater exploration are available through local dive shops and certifying organizations. Another source for dive-related videos is:

Bennett Marine Video Inc.
8436 West 3rd Street
Los Angeles, CA 90048-4100
800-733-8862 for a catalog

EQUIPMENT MANUFACTURERS

In an attempt to save money, some divers may consider purchasing equipment through mail order. This has been controversial for reasons of diver safety. There are serious concerns that diver life-support products might be sold to unqualified buyers. Serious problems have also been found with the quality of some private-label equipment sold through mail order. In addition, gear obtained through mail order can be sold without regard to proper fit and function, can be operated incorrectly, and support is limited or non-existent.

Local retail dive stores are a focus for dive support, instruction, dive travel, local dives, inspection and repair services, compressed air, rental equipment, and equipment advice. They also offer the opportunity to look at, feel, compare, and test equipment before purchase, and they back up these products if necessary.

Some experienced divers feel comfortable buying mail order gear, especially if it's a brand of equipment they've used before or which has been recommended by other experienced divers. Most beginning and intermediate divers, however, will benefit from the support and expertise of professional dive shops.

MANUFACTURERS OF EQUIPMENT, APPAREL, ACCESSORIES

AERIS
14212 Doolittle Drive
San Leandro, CA 94577
510-346-0010 for an authorized dealer
www.diveaeris.com
email: info@diveaeris.com
Computers

APOLLO SPORTS USA
12322 Highway 99S, Unit 102
Everett, WA 98204
800-231-0909
www.apollosportsusa.com
email: apollous@aol.com
Fins

AQUA LUNG
2340 Cousteau Court
Vista, CA 92083
760-597-5000
www.usdivers.com
Regulators, BC jackets, tanks, computers, depth gauges, dive instruments, lights, wet suits, fins, snorkels, masks, knives, spearguns

ATOMIC AQUATICS, INC.
714-375-1433
www.atomicaquatics.com
Regulators

BEUCHAT
677 S.W. First Street
Miami, Florida 33130
800-248-0005 for an authorized dealer
Regulators, BC jackets, tanks, computers, depth gauges, dive instruments, lights, wet suits, fins, snorkels, masks, knives, spearguns

CRESSI-SUB
10 Reuten Drive
Closter, NJ 07624
800-338-9143
www.cressi-sub.it
email: info@cressi-sub.it
All levels of equipment including lightweight fins, masks, snorkels, regulators, free-diving gear, BCs, goggles, and torches

DACOR CORPORATION
Shore Pointe,
One Selleck Street
Norwalk, CT 06855
800-323-0463
www.divedacor.com
A division of Mares. Regulators, instruments, BCs, DPV's, masks, fins, snorkels, wet suits, dry suits, hoods, gloves, boots, and accessories

DIVE RITE
117 West Washington Street
Lake City, FL 32055
904-752-1087
www.Dive-Rite.com
Buoyancy compensators, depth/time gauges available through authorized dealers

DIVESKINS
Oztex, Inc.
7717 SW Nimbus Avenue
Beaverton, OR 97008
800-827-3483 for an authorized dealer
email: diveskin@teleport.com
Thermal protection suits

HALCYON
954-462-5570
(networked dealerships)
www.halcyon.net
Winged BC and "stable harness" system

HENDERSON
301 Orange Street
Millville, NJ 08332
609-825-4771
www.hendersonusa.com
Comprehensive line of wet suits and diveskins

MARES AMERICA CORPORATION
Shore Pointe, One Selleck Street
Norwalk, CT 06855
203-855-0631
www.htmsport.com
email: tech@maresscuba.com
Comprehensive line of diving equipment — regulators, jackets, dive instruments, wet suits, fins, masks, snorkels, and accessories

NITE RIDER TECHNICAL LIGHTING SYSTEMS
619-268-9316
www.niterider.com
email: dive@niterider.com
Underwater lighting

OCEANIC U.S.A.
2002 Davis Street
San Leandro, CA 94577
510-562-0500
www.oceanicusa.com
Full line of diving gear — computers, regulators, gauges, BCs, DPVs, masks, fins, snorkels, thermal wear, and accessories

OCEAN MASTER
800-841-7007 for an
authorized dealer
www.oceanmaster.com
Dive equipment — equalizers, snorkels, fins, titanium knives

OCEAN TECHNOLOGY SYSTEMS
2950 Airway Avenue Suite D-3
Costa Mesa, CA 92626
714-754-7848 for an
authorized dealer
www.oceantechnolgysystems.com
email: ots4com@aol.com
A complete line of underwater communication systems and related accessories

PRINCETON TEC SPORTS LIGHTS
P.O. Box 8057
Trenton, NJ 08650
609-298-9331 for an
authorized dealer
www.ptsportlights.com
Dive lights

SCUBAPRO
1166-A fesler Street
El Cajon, CA 92020

www.scubapro.com
A full line of high-perfomance dive equipment available through authorized SCUBAPRO retailers

SEAQUEST
2340 Cousteau Court
Vista, CA 92083
www.sea-quest.com
Manufacturer of buoyancy compensators and regulators. Distributor of Technisub fins and masks and Suunto computers. Also wet suits, boots, and accessories

SEA VISION
800-732-6275 for a
participating dealer
www.seavisionusa.com
Prescription dive lenses

ZEAGLE
813-782-5568
www.zeagle.com
Dive gear — buoyancy compensators, fins, wet suits, masks

CAMERAS & ACCESSORIES — UNDERWATER PHOTOGRAPHY

AQUATIX INTERNATIONAL
7202 Arlington
St. Louis, MO 63117
877-581-5660
www.aquatix.com
Underwater videography

IKELITE UNDERWATER SYSTEMS
50 West 33rd Street
Indianapolis, IN 46208
317-923-4523
www.ikelite.com
Underwater photography

GATES UNDERWATER PRODUCTS
5111 Santa Fe Street #H
San Diego, CA 92109
800-875-1052
www.gateshousings.com
email: info@gateshousings.com
Underwater videocamera housings

LIGHT & MOTION INDUSTRIES

300 Cannery Row
Monterey, CA 99940
832-645-1525
www.lmindustries.com
Sting Ray and Alpha underwater video housings

PIONEER RESEARCH
97 Foster Road
Moorestown, NJ 08057
800-257-7742
www.pioneer-research.com
SeaLife camera

R.T.S. INC.
40-11 Burt Drive
Deer Park, NY 11729
516-242-6801
email: rtsinc@erols.com
Ewa-marine & Epoque cameras

SEA & SEA UNDERWATER PHOTOGRAPHY USA
1938 Kellogg Avenue
Carlsbad, CA 92008
760-929-1909
www.seaandsea.com
Available only through authorized dealers

SEKONIC
8 Westchester Plaza
Elmsford, NY 10523
914-347-3300
www.sekonic.com
email: infor@sekonic.com
Marine light meters available only through authorized dealers

ULTRALIGHT CONTROL SYSTEMS
3304 Ketch Avenue
Oxnard, CA 93035
805-984-9104
www.ulcs.com
email: infor@ulcs.com
Aluminum arms

SEAVIEW UNDERWATER RESEARCH, INC.
4229 Gulf Boulevard
St. Pete Beach, FL 33706
727-866-3660
www.seaviewresearch.com
Underwater television systems

PHOTO
CREDITS

INDEX